INTERNATIONAL AND TRANSNATIONAL POLITICAL ACTORS

Centre de Sciences Humaines (Centre for Human Sciences): Created in 1990, the CSH is part of the network of 27 research centres of the French Ministry of Foreign Affairs. In 2007 it became UMIFRE 20 CNRS-MAEE, that is, a financially autonomous research institution under the dual tutelage of the French Ministry of Foreign and European Affairs (MAEE) and the French National Centre for Scientific Research (CNRS). The Centre's research work is primarily oriented towards the study of contemporary issues in the development of India and South Asia. The activities of the Centre are focused on four main areas, namely: Economic reforms and sustainable development; Politics and social change; Regional dynamics in South Asia and international relations; and Urban dynamics.

Centre de Sciences Humaines,
2 Aurangzeb Road,
New Delhi 110011, India
Tel: (91 11) 3041 0070
Fax: (91 11) 3041 0079
Email: infos@csh-delhi.com
Website: http://www.csh-delhi.com

Institut Français de Pondichéry (French Institute of Pondicherry): Created in 1955 under the terms agreed to in the Treaty of Cession between the Indian and French governments, the IFP (UMIFRE 21 CNRS-MAEE) is a financially autonomous research institution under the dual tutelage of the French Ministry of Foreign and European Affairs (MAEE) and the French National Centre for Scientific Research (CNRS).

It fulfills its mission of research, expertise and training in human and social sciences, and ecology, in South and South-East Asia. Major research works focus on Indian cultural knowledge and heritage (Sanskrit language and literature, history of religions, Tamil studies etc.), contemporary social dynamics (in the areas of health, economics and environment) and the natural ecosystems of South India (sustainable management of biodiversity).

Institut Français de Pondichéry
11 Saint Louis Street, PB 33,
Pondicherry 605 001, India
Tel: (91) 413 2334168
Fax: (91) 413 2339534
Website: http://www.ifpindia.org

INTERNATIONAL AND TRANSNATIONAL POLITICAL ACTORS

Case Studies from the Indian Diaspora

Edited by
ERIC LECLERC

MANOHAR

CSH
UMIFRE 20
CNRS-MAEE

CENTRE DE SCIENCES HUMAINES
2011

First published 2011

ISBN 978-81-7304-925-5

Published by
Ajay Kumar Jain *for*
Manohar Publishers & Distributors
4753/23 Ansari Road, Daryaganj,
New Delhi 110 002

Printed at
Salasar Imaging Systems
Delhi 110 035

Contents

Foreword

The present volume touches upon, and then elaborates, in a series of persuasive articles, something that is counter-intuitive as regards the 'diaspora' phenomenon. While it is by definition true that the diasporic experience refers to relations between two or more states or, in terms of *actors*, the interactions among migrants—with their respective 'referent origin(s)' (Dufoix, 2008)—that are spread over a vast geo-political global arena, there has been a tendency in the social sciences and international studies literature to downplay precisely this international and transnational dimension. Let me explain this paradox. Among the diaspora scholars Sheffer (1986; 2003) has undertaken comparative studies of international politics though it would not be unfair to say that these pioneering efforts have been mainly descriptive and classificatory. To take one among many examples of a view similar to ours, Axel (2001) has remarked that studies of diaspora tell us a good deal about the sending and receiving nation states of migrants but more often than not the characteristics of the diaspora phenomenon *sui generis* escape their analytical net. And this is because, as Dufoix explains and Axel argues in detail, the political processes imbricated in defining international and transnational relations of nation states and their actors are not only volatile and constantly changing but often remain hidden because of their extremely sensitive and contentious character. Thus if we look at some of the burning global examples of transnational migrants—typically refugees and asylum-seekers—the Tamils, Sikhs, Fijian Indians, Mohajirs, Kurds, Afghans, Burmese and Tibetan, to name only a few, their status as diasporics defy a cut-and-dried categorization in 'types' or even 'ideal-types' so caught up they are in the vicissitudes of their existential dilemmas. There is an immense need among diaspora scholars to begin to formulate a preliminary framework for theoretically grappling with this complexity by focusing on governmentality, diplomacy, visible and invisible survival technologies, 'comprador' attitudes, even subversive tactics or silences that may be deafening. The case studies reported in this volume constitute a most welcome step in that direction.

'The worst thing one can do with words', wrote George Orwell more than half a century ago, 'is to surrender to them'. If language is to be 'an instrument for expressing and not for concealing or preventing thought', he continued, one must 'let the meaning choose the word, and not the other way about' (Orwell, 1953: 169-70). Diaspora, as practice and concept, is nothing if not a construction. The Hindu Sindhis who do the work of traders are known as 'sindhworkis' the world over (Falzon, in this volume). The concept diaspora is also know by the 'work' it does. And that work, as Therwath (also in this volume) aptly discusses about diaspora in the South Asian context, is to provide a convenient handle to the government of the day, the Bharatiya Janata Party (BJP), ruling party in India from 1999 to 2004, for example, to propagate its ideology of *Hindutva* (aggressive Hinduism) nationalism among overseas Indian migrants. This was done through constituting a high-level government committee on 'Indian Diaspora' and instituting an annual *Pravasi Bharatiya Divas* (Rememberance Day for the Indian Diaspora) with an eye on attracting their economic and political involvements in the Indian nation state and its overseas allies/partners in global capitalism and geopolity. Several of the papers in this volume (e.g. Kanungo, Rao, Leclerc) examine the detailed working out of this political economy especially in relation to the Indian diaspora in the US, UK and Malaysia. Interestingly enough, as pointed out earlier, the play of practices and interactions of Indian diasporics are sketched out either in bilateral relations between the sending nation state (India) and the receiving nation state when the actors are based in the latter countries or, to take a reverse example, India as 'receiving' diaspora of

Tibetan, Afghan and Burmese refugees (Baujard, in this volume). There is a subtle interplay here between the status of these migrants as 'refugees' or as 'a diaspora'. The factors at play are the definitions imposed by international agencies and non-governmental organizations on the one hand, and the Indian government of the day, on the other hand. The statuses 'refugee' and 'diaspora' also keep vacillating over a period of time.

Besides the fact of 'construction', the other common denominator of the working out of the South Asian diaspora in concrete terms is the process of mobilization. Dufoix (2008: 80-105) gives lucid expression to the spring-board of the process of mobilization in diaspora in terms of contrary pulls between spatio-temporal rupture and resistance to that rupture not only among the diasporics but also between the sending and receiving states. Further, for the diasporic, the sending country, region or ascribed ethnicity may not remain a nation state as such but what Dufoix intriguingly calls a 'referent origin'. Thus for example, Fiji Indians though descendants of original migrants from India, do not, as settlers in Australia, New Zealand or US and Canada, look upon India as the 'sending state' or may not even regard Fiji as such (especially as national citizens) but India and Fiji remain their 'referent origin'. The same applies to the Gujarati population of twice-thrice migrants from India to Uganda, to Britain, to US or Canada. And yet, though severed or cut loose from any single nation state or other 'referent origin' the diasporic immigrant may become an active agent in ethnic, linguistic, regional or any other political movement of a transnational character (see, for example, Sokefeld, 2006: 265-84). This is precisely the nexus of international and transnational political actors that our authors talk about, and whose contributions have been summarized in the editor's Introduction.

I sincerely hope that the lively conversation between international relations specialists and social scientists of multi-disciplinary persuasion generated by this volume will lead to further conceptual refinements and, in turn, result in fresh empirical explorations in the dynamic field of diaspora studies.

RAVINDRA K. JAIN

REFERENCES

Axel, B.K., *The Nation's Tortured Body: Violence, Representation and the Formation of a Sikh 'Diaspora'*. Durham: Duke University Press, 2001.

Dufoix, Stephane, *Diasporas* (tr. William Rodarmor), Berkeley: University of California Press, 2008.

Orwell, George, 'Politics and the English Language', in *A Collection of Essays,* New York: Harcourt Brace, 1953.

Sheffer, Gabriel (ed.), *Modern Diasporas in International Politics*, London: Croom Helm, 1986.

Sheffer, Gabriel, *Diaspora Politics: At Home Abroad*, New York: Cambridge University Press, 2003.

Sokefeld, Martin, 'Mobilizing in Transnational Space: A Social Movement Approach to the Formation of Diaspora', *Global Networks*, 6(3), July 2006, pp. 265-84.

Acknowledgements

This book is the result of a collective research project on the Indian diaspora in international relations, started at the Centre de Sciences Humaines (Center of Social Sciences) in New Delhi by a multidisciplinary team of researchers in social sciences between 2004 and 2005. Five meetings were organized at the Centre de Sciences Humaines (CSH, New Delhi) with specialists from different universities of Delhi (Jawaharlal Nehru University, University of Delhi and Jamia Millia Islamia University). We had also the pleasure to discuss actual trends of Indian diaspora research with scholars from the Maulana Abul Kalam Azad Institute of Asian Studies in Kolkata, the Centre for the Study of Indian Diaspora in Hyderabad, and the University of the Witwatersrand, Johannesburg in South Africa. These seminars were succeeded by an international conference 'Actors and Models of the Indian Diaspora in International Relations', held from 26 to 27 September 2005 at the India International Centre (New Delhi). Even if this book includes only a selection of papers presented at this conference, every contributor should know how much we appreciate their contribution.

The conference received financial and organizational support from CSH and IIC, which jointly organized it, we would like to express our gratitude to their respective directors Véronique Dupont (CSH) and P.C. Sen (IIC) at the time of the conference. They mobilized their entire team to make this event a success. Our sincere thanks are also due to those who took an active part in the debates during the conference, panelists and participants with a special mention to the chairpersons: Chandrashekhar Bhat, Ajay Dubey, Man Mohini Kaul, Shri Prakash, P.V. Rao and Swaran Singh. The publication of this book may have not been possible without the valuable comments that helped the authors for the revision of their papers. We are deeply grateful to them: Aparajita Biswas, Sanjay Chaturvedi, N. Jayaram, M.A. Kalam and Patricia Uberoi. We will not forget the students (Narender Thakur, Geeta Verma, Priya Srivastava, Sridhar Bhagavtaula, Durgesh K. Rai) from the Zakir Husain Centre for Educational Studies, Jawaharlal Nehru University, who transcripted the debates and shared their enthusiasm. The logistical task of the conference was made easier with the efficiency of our assistant Sharad Baviskar.

Many thanks to Arpita Mitra for the preparation of the manuscript and for being a sustainable link from a distant place, and to the present director of the CSH, Basudeb Chaudhuri for the renewal of the financial support and his keen interest in this publication.

ERIC LECLERC

1

Introduction

ERIC LECLERC

The present book is the culmination of a project started at the Centre de Sciences Humaines (Centre of Social Sciences) in New Delhi by a multidisciplinary team of researchers in social sciences between 2004 and 2005. Through regular meetings during one year, the objective was the review of the political actors of the Indian diaspora and the identification of political models followed either by importing models developed by other diasporas, or by creating a new model to fit the Indian diaspora. The seminars helped to prepare a call for contributions to an international conference held from 26 to 27 September 2005 at the India International Centre (New Delhi) in order to share the results of the team with international experts. This book includes only a selection of papers presented at this conference due to editorial constraints, but every contributor should know how much we appreciate their contribution.

By limiting our investigations to the field of politics in international relations, the project intended to clear a new field of diasporic studies. At the time when there is a widespread usage of the word 'diaspora,' and even certain specialists observe a diasporization of the concept (Brubaker, 2005), it's surprising that several theoretical issues remain unanswered. Some of them raised by Gabriel Sheffer about two decades ago in his book *Modern Diasporas in International Politics* (1986), and even in his recent publication *Diaspora Politics: At Home Abroad* (2003), which examines 'the triadic relations between ethnic diasporas, their host countries and homelands', have not yet even echoed in India's debates on diaspora. As a result, except for a few recent political studies (Lall, 2001), the bulk of the other publications[1] about the Indian diaspora have dealt with issues of identity in the host country, both in terms of religion, caste or gender (van der Veer, 1995; Vertovec, 2000; Rukmani, 2001; Shukla, 2003; Varma, 2003), and integration and assimilation in the economies of the host countries (Helwegg, 1990; Parekh, 2003). The relations between the Indian diaspora and its homeland have dealt with remittances (Nayyar, 1994) or the consequences of the migration (the brain drain problem) (Sukhatme, 1994; Khadria, 2004). The trans-State political activities involving the Indian diaspora have hardly been addressed so far, and which as a matter of fact was the main criterion to select the papers for this publication.

Many studies on the political dimension of diasporas have for a point of departure the ethnic issue in the host countries in which they explore the international dimensions, for instance G. Sheffer studying 'the international dimension of the ethnic question.' Instead we raised the question of the place of the Indian diaspora in international relations from the perspective of the country of origin (Sheffer, 1986: 2). Firstly, this reverse point of view changes the approach of the diasporas from a negative one, as a problem for the host countries, to a more positive one, they may become solutions for the country of origin. Secondly, this paradigm shift fits well with the new perception of its diaspora by the Indian government at the turn of this century.

The involvement of diasporas in international relations should be assessed on two criteria—their global expansion, and how they define new areas of legitimacy. The globalization of diaspora increases the number of interaction between States. The Indian diaspora is no exception and its development in the long run offers both a wide variety of situations and complex dynamics. It follows the cycles of expansion and concentration of human history in a dialogic relation with the State. British colonization resulted in increased movement of Indian merchants and the export of manpower from India to the rest of the plantation economy of the Empire. The collapse of colonial empires a century later was followed by a phase of concentration of people, the descendants of Europeans (about 6 million) who had to return to their metropolis, while the numbers of States increased. For the Indian diaspora, this phase of expansion of the State, saw a greater dispersion. In the wake of independence of East Africa (Kenya, Uganda), the Caribbean or Surinam, people of Indian origin went through a phase of re-diasporization toward the colonial metropolis rather than to their homeland.

From this historical sequence was derived the opposition between the diaspora and the nation state. The process of homogenization that is central to the construction of the State and the sole allegiance to its political authority, experienced in India with the Partition, does not provide space for the diaspora. This approach defined an issue around the only legitimate space, the nation state. Thus the definition of a diaspora refers only to it. You can read this change in G. Sheffer between his denomination of 'modern diasporas' in 1986 (Sheffer, 2003: 3), which in 2002 became the 'ethno-national diasporas' (Sheffer, 2003: 9). This restriction of the definition of diaspora is a reaction against the post-modern paradigm which dropped the reference to the state of origin. The works of Clifford (1994), Hall (1990) and Gilroy (1993), rather than defining the identity of a diaspora in relation to the preservation of the inherited culture of the country of origin, use the concept of hybridity, the antithesis of national ideologies. These post-modern analyses put forward the transnational character of diasporas, and from a political point of view, considered that these social entities put 'into question the principle of modern political organization' (Schnapper, 1999: 227).

It is true that some diasporas challenge the authority of a State either to enforce the recognition of rights, as the practice of a language or a religion, or to demand the independence of a part of the territory of this State. South Asia provides many such examples of these situations. The diaspora can pre-exist before the territorial claims and mobilize in favour of independence when the crisis inside the State comes into view. Sikhs emigrated from the beginning of the twentieth century to Canada and the United States and then in the 1960s to the United Kingdom before the separatist demand for Khalistan was taken up in India. The uprising in the Punjab from 1980 onwards had the support of the diaspora and was relayed by local political movements (see Gayer). Financially and logistically, the Sikh diaspora supported the insurgency movement and provided a platform for it on the international arena. The situation is very similar to Tibetans who escaped from China with the Dalai Lama in 1959, and struggle for the recognition of their territory, independent between 1911 and 1950. The globalization of the Tibetan diaspora was a strategy to legitimize their political demand (see Baujard). The exiled government closely supervises the Tibetan diaspora spreading Buddhist practice of non-violence to achieve this end. In both examples the objective remains the same—territory—even if the means of action use a range of solutions extending from soft power for the Tibetans, to hard power for the Sikhs. These diasporas do not weaken the nation state. Although they are fighting against one nation state and are involved in trans-state terrorist's networks, they aim at creating a territory on this model.

We cannot thus set in an antagonistic way diaspora and nation state, as done by post-modernist which see in the emergence of the diaspora, the disappearance of the nation state, because both terms tend to define themselves one to another. We can see this in the way nationalism can cross the project of a diaspora and conversely the way diasporas can serve a national project.

Nowadays, States try to mobilize their diaspora by recognizing them as actors in the international relations arena (see Lall-Thandi). They use the principle of the soft power[2] that can be applied in both directions: if the host State converted to its values the diasporas present on its territory, they would have an impact on their State of origin; for the State of origin it use its diaspora to lobby on its behalf. As we adopted in this work the point of view of the State of origin, we shall focus on this second perspective. The State can be in the heart of the strategy of a diaspora, in a relation of mutual strengthening. The action of the diasporic lobbies in the United States is best known with the example of the Greeks who managed in 1974 to make vote for an embargo on the deliveries of weapons to Turkey following the occupation of Cyprus (see Rao).

The successive Indian governments had refused until recently that their diaspora engage itself politically in their host country. Even when they acquired democratically the power, the Indian government did not want to support them as when they faced a takeover in Fiji in 1987 and 2000. However, India under the rule of the nationalist party of the BJP, elaborated a new policy to its diaspora (see Thewart). The successes of the last wave of Indian emigrants in the developed countries inverted the value of the diaspora which became a driving element of the economic liberalization of the country. A Ministry for Overseas Indians Affairs was created and the Indian State organizes since 2003 national festivities intended to honour eminent members of the diaspora. New rights were granted to Non-Resident Indians to facilitate their investments in the country. These measures have widened since 2005 to all the members of the diaspora with the creation of an overseas citizenship which gives them access to the Indian system of higher education and eliminates visas to facilitate their visits to India.

It is in this backdrop that the first objective of the project was to identify the political models that have been mobilized—both within and outside the Indian diaspora—as also effectively used as new referents in international relations. But beyond some general statement about the models of diaspora organization and their influence, the Jewish model on various diaspora in the US, and the Chinese model of organization on 'Asian incipient diasporas' (Sheffer, 2003), no political model has been identified so far. So the first step was to identify the trans-State actors in the Indian diaspora and their influence on international relations. We have already some recent examples of Indian diaspora's active role in international relations. Especially on issues between the host States and the homeland, the Kargil conflict of May-June 1999 had witnessed the Indian diaspora in the US trying to promote the interest of its homeland to US policy makers (Ghosal, 2003). This influence has been even greater in the case of the nuclear deal between India and the USA (2005). We had another type of involvement of the Indian diaspora during the earthquake in Gujarat (2001) or the communal riots (2002) which had resulted in a outpouring of aid from all directions.

The papers collected in this volume look at the role of the Indian diaspora in international relations within and beyond the traditional triangular framework diaspora, State of origin and host State. Two texts (Leclerc, Rao) focus on the diplomatic relationships between India and foreign countries challenged by the Indian diaspora. Its situation in the host country is the subject of a single text (Kanungo), and secondarily in that of M.A. Falzon, to conclude that the Sindhi diaspora develops an invisibility policy, where it remains. The reversal of perspective, that of host countries to the country of origin, dominates this selection with four texts. One takes as its starting point India (Therwath), the three others (Falzon, Gayer, Lall-Thandi) the Indian diaspora in its relations with it. The two dimensions of the relationship, Indian State/Diaspora should be considered equally. Changes in government policy towards the Indian diaspora have so far received priority (Lall, 2001; Singh, 2005), the three selected texts show the autonomy of the Indian diaspora in its relations with its country of origin. They highlight the influence of the situation of the Indian diaspora in their host countries on its external attitude. We can conclude that it is impossible to completely take into account the triangular relationship without one of its poles.

Two texts suggest new approaches that can exceed the triangular framework and should stimulate more researches in the field of international relations. To analyse the relationship between a State and the diaspora, you have also to take into account its relations with the diasporas settled on its territory. Baujard proposes to us this reverse perspective based on the cases of Tibetan, Burmese and Afghan refugees in New Delhi. This approach helps to highlight the contradictions between the policy of the Indian State as a country of origin and as a host country. The Indian government modifies also its attitude to the various diasporas according to its relationship with their State of origin. The second new approach was proposed by the text of Moliner, interested in trans-State relations not covered by diplomacy. It is also a relatively neglected area of international relations despite the growing role given to diasporas (Shain, 2007). She studies the mobilization of the Sikh diaspora in Europe against a French law, showing how a very small group in one country can receive the support of many other nearby communities. In an inter-connected world, the relation between a host State and a diaspora can no longer be limited to a single territory.

Relations between the different poles formed by the Indian diaspora, host States and India are explored in all their dimensions, with particular importance for the view from the diaspora. This trend is reflected in the actors identified and studied in these texts. It is mainly collective actors among whom the recent Indian governments. I use the plural as the attitudes of the Indian State toward the Indian diaspora have varied, depending on the leaders and political parties in power (Therwath, Leclerc, Rao). The other actors are State governments of the host countries with a focus on a few spaces: the United States (Kanungo, Rao, Gayer, Lall-Thandi) and the United Kingdom (Moliner, Gayer, Lall-Thandi). This approach relates more particularly to the most recent diaspora, many of those that the Indian government still considers as nationals—the non resident Indians. The position of the oldest Indian diaspora, the People of Indian Origin, more discreet on the international scene for a long time should not be overlooked. At least, it enjoys the recognition brought by the Indian government to the NRI and tries to exist politically both in host countries and in international relations (Leclerc). The case studies compiled in this book make little reference to international bodies, except when they are committed on the territory of India (Baujard).

The main actors analysed are organizations from the Indian diaspora itself in their political activities. Particular attention is given to what Anderson (1992, 1998) named the 'long-distance nationalism.' The picture depicted for other diasporas (Jewish, Kurdish, Palestinian, Tamil) is completed and enriched here by the case of India. Indeed, there is not one single form of long-distance nationalism in this case. If the Sikh example is explored intensively in this book (Moliner, Gayer, Lall-Thandi), the Sindhi case presented by Falzon is very original. The Sindhi community is a stateless diaspora but contrary to the Sikhs, they don't claim for one. This may explain why some of them have joined the ranks of the most virulent Hindu nationalism (L.K. Advani). The Indian case also offers an example of reverse long-distance nationalism. Indeed, the Hindu nationalist organizations have been very active outside India to mobilize the newest members of the Indian diaspora to their mutual benefit (Kanungo, Lall-Thandi). Compared with other political parties in India, Hindu nationalist organizations have so far been more effective. They managed to raise funds in the Indian diaspora, sometimes under cover of humanitarian action, to carry out their projects in India. By the way, they give rise to political awareness among other members of the Indian diaspora, to defend the Nehruvian values of India. The diversity of situations for the Indian diaspora shows the difficulty for it to define a legitimate political representation. Even in its most favourable dispensation to its diaspora, the Indian State refuses to grant political rights on its soil, except if the expatriate resumes his nationality. The same is true for host States that give more or less rapidly these rights in different countries. Trapped by the imperative of loyalty imposed by States, the Indian diaspora has not been able to define the contours of a political trans-State actor. But the book affords us to analyse the construction of these new actors in international relations, in their many forms that rely on the host countries: lobbying, political parties, and cultural associations.

The second major contribution of these texts is the comparative perspective followed by many authors. Many have accepted this challenge posed in the call for papers of the conference to cross the limits of its speciality and take the risk of comparatism. Indeed, in this volume, the comparative approach is not limited to the juxtaposition of case studies. The reader's effort will be still useful to compare situations taken in the different countries that we have mentioned above. The reader will also have to compare identical communities in different texts along various angles: for Sikhs (Moliner, Gayer, Lall-Thandi), for Hindu nationalism (Kanungo, Lall-Thandi). But the comparison is at the heart of four of the nine texts. Baujard shows the changing attitudes of the Indian government for different refugee populations on its territory. In the same way, on the international scene, the stakes in the Indian diplomacy influence the attitude of its government in the countries which use its workforce (Leclerc). Lall and Thandi share their knowledge to compare two forms of long-distance nationalism in the Indian diaspora. Finally, Gayer opens a window outside the Indian diaspora field study by comparing the Sikh long-distance nationalism in India and the Mohajir's long-distance nationalism in Pakistan.

In his study of the Sindhi diaspora, Falzon raises a major issue that which is the definition of the Indian diaspora. The only author who proposes a definition of a transnational political actor (Therwath) that 'it has to be unified or at least have some degree of cohesion, have an awareness of its own identity, have umbrella representative bodies and be recognized as legitimate by the transnational community' applies it to the case of India considering that 'the Indian State has been central to the creation of the Indian diaspora as a political project'. The Indian diaspora is defined through the limits given by the Indian State as an official category, the census of the High Level Commission under the leadership of L.M. Singhvi in 2001. As this text came after the conference, the authors of this volume were not required to adhere to this definition. Nevertheless, we have to check how each author defines its community as a part of the Indian diaspora. The criteria are very diverse, religion is a significant marker for four texts (Falzon, Moliner, Gayer and Lall-Thandi). The communities analysed are explicitly restricted to Hindus (Lall-Thandi, Falzon) or Sikhs (Gayer, Moliner, Lall-Thandi), even if the authors never claim that they represent the whole Indian diaspora. For the United States and the United Kingdom, these two communities are particularly interesting because the mobilization of the Sikh community against the actions of the Indian government in Punjab, is partly responsible for the awareness of the other Indian emigrants (Rao). Muslims are the major missing community of this book. Mohammad-Arif (2001), Leonard (2007) and Ghosh's (2007) works must be used to have a complete picture of the Indian diaspora and to expand cross-analysis with other South Asian diasporas, modelled on the text of Gayer. Leclerc's essay looks at the Indian diaspora in its sociological changes from an economic definition (expatriate workers). It was an important factor in the formation of a transnational political actor before Independence as shown by Tinker (1977). Further analysis should check if the category of proletarian diaspora (Armstong, 1976) is still valid in the current age of globalization.

The diversity of communities analysed in this book is not an obstacle to the understanding of Indian diaspora as a political actor in international relations. Except to adhere to the idea that the Indian diaspora is defined by a list of cultural traits, the variability of the borders of the group is heuristic. In the current state of research on the Indian diaspora, a very recent scientific category, this seems the most fruitful. This book is also a reflection of the state of research in international relations on the issue. The developed countries in host countries is dominant. A consideration of Indian communities in other parts of the globe will complete the picture, while the latest waves of the diaspora have returned to pre-Independence locations.

The texts of this book have been re-organized into two parts. The first is a perspective from the State actor after a synthesis by Khadria who raises the stakes of this research on the role of the Indian diaspora in international relations. The Indian State is at the first place in the texts of Therwath and Baujard in its relations to diasporas, its own diaspora, but also those settled on its territory. Leclerc's text continues to analyse the behaviour of the Indian government by expanding the scope to its diplomatic relations when they are influenced by the presence of the Indian diaspora. The paper, which is focused on the Asian situation, is completed by Rao and Kanungo with the case of the United States. These two texts provide additional insights: the first on the changing role of the Indian diaspora in American diplomacy, from the host country to the country of origin, the second text, on the influence of Hindu nationalism on the Indian diaspora in the United States, from the country of origin to the host country.

The second part of the book puts at the centre of the stage the diaspora actor. Studying specific communities, the authors explore the processes of building transnational political actors in the Indian diaspora. Falzon inaugurates this series by the figure of the absent, with the case of the Sindhi diaspora where cosmopolitanism replaces international political action. In contrast, the protagonists of the other texts are recurring actors of long-distance nationalism studies but each time put into perspective in different ways. Moliner focuses on the trans-State interactions between European Sikhs through the example of the law on the Islamic headscarf in France. Through their brilliant comparative analyses, Gayer, Lall and Thandi build the first political models of these transnational political actors in the UK and the US.

NOTES

1. A complete list of the themes is given by N. Jayaram (2004) in the introduction of his book, *The Indian Diaspora: Dynamics of Migration*, pp. 22-31.
2. *Soft power:* The concept developed by the economist Joseph S. Nye to determine the ability of a State to impose its will on others by influence and conviction.

REFERENCES

Anderson, B.R.O.G., *The Spectre of Comparisons: Nationalism, South-East Asia, and the World*, London/New York: Verso, 1998.

Anderson, B.R.O.G. and G. Kligman, *Long-Distance Nationalism: World Capitalism and the Rise of Identity Politics*, Berkeley,

CA: Center for German and European Studies, University of California, 1992.

Armstrong, J.A., 'Mobilized and Proletarian Diasporas', *American Political Science Review*, vol. 70, no. 2, 1976, pp. 393-408.

Brubaker, R., 'The "Diaspora" Diaspora', *Ethnic and Racial Studies*, vol. 28, no. 1, 2005, pp. 1-19.

Clifford, J., 'Diasporas', *Cultural Anthropology*, vol. 9, no. 3, 1994, pp. 302-38.

Ghosal, B., 'Indian Diaspora in South-East Asia and the Emerging Relations between India and Asean', in *Beyond the Rhetoric 2: The Economics of India's Look East Policy*, ed. F. Grare and A. Mattoo, New Delhi: Manohar, 2003, pp. 115-28.

Ghosh, P., *Partition and South Asian Diaspora: Extending the Subcontinent*, New Delhi: Routledge, 2007.

Gilroy, P., *The black Atlantic: Modernity and Double Consciousness*, Cambridge, Mass.: Harvard University Press, 1993.

Hall, S., 'Cultural Identity and Diaspora', in *Identity: Community, Culture, Difference*, ed. J. Rutherford, London: Lawrence & Wishart, 1990, pp. 222-37.

Helweg, A.W. and U.M. Helweg, *An Immigrant Success Story: East Indians in America*, New Delhi: Oxford University Press, 1990.

Jayaram, N., *The Indian Diaspora: Dynamics of Migration, Themes in Indian Sociology*, New Delhi; Thousand Oaks, California: Sage, 2004.

Khadria, B., 'Migration of Highly Skilled Indians: Case Studies of It and Health', *STI Working Paper 2004/6*, Paris: Directorate for Science Technology and Industry, Organisation for Economic Cooperation and Development, 2004.

Lall, M.-C., *India's Missed Opportunity*, London: Ashgate, 2001.

Leonard, K.I., *Locating Home: India's Hyderabadis Abroad*, Stanford: Stanford University Press, 2007.

Mohammad-Arif, A., *Salam America: L'islam indien en diaspora*, Monde indien. Sciences Sociales, 15e-20e siècle, Paris: CNRS, 2001.

Nayyar, D., *Migration, Remittances and Capital Flows, the Indian Experience*, New Delhi: Oxford University Press, 1994.

Parekh, B., G. Singh and S. Vertovec, *Culture and Economy in the Indian Diaspora*, London: Routledge, 2003.

Rukmani, T.S., ed., *Hindu Diaspora Global Perspectives*, New Delhi: Munshiram Manoharlal, 2001.

Schnapper, D., 'From the Nation-State to the Transnational World: On the Meaning and Usefulness of Diaspora as Concept', *Diaspora*, vol. 8, no. 3, 1999, pp. 225-54.

Shain, Y., *Kinship and Diasporas in International Affairs*, Ann Arbor: University of Michigan Press, 2007.

Sheffer, G., 'A New Field of Study: Modern Diasporas in International Politics', in *Modern Diasporas in International Politics*, ed. G. Sheffer, London: Croom Helm, 1986, pp. 1-15.

——, *Diaspora Politics: At Home Abroad*, Cambridge: Cambridge University Press, 2003.

Shukla, S.R., *India Abroad: Diasporic Cultures of Postwar America and England*, Princeton, N.J.: Princeton University Press, 2003.

Singh, S., *Overseas Indians: The Global Family*, New Delhi: Shipra, 2005.

Sukhatme, S.P., *The Real Brain Drain*, Hyderabad: Orient Longman, 1994.

Tinker, H., *The Banyan Tree : Overseas Emigrants from India, Pakistan, and Bangladesh*, London/New York: Oxford University Press, 1977.

Varma, S., R. Seshan, and University of Poona, *Fractured Identity: The Indian Diaspora in Canada*, Jaipur: Rawat, 2003.

Veer, P. v.d., *Nation and Migration: The Politics of Space in the South Asian Diaspora, South Asian Seminar Series*, Philadelphia: University of Philadelphia Press, 1995.

Vertovec, S., *The Hindu Diaspora: Comparative Patterns*, New York: Routledge, 2000.

PART I

Diaspora and Indian Foreign Policy

2

Indian Diaspora in International Relations

'Tinker, Tailor, Soldier, Spy', or a 'Great Off-White Hope' of the New Century?[1]

BINOD KHADRIA

Talking of the actors and models of the Indian diaspora, I have not so far come across any definite existing discourse that has dealt with a clearly defined category called 'models' of Indian diaspora. On the other hand, 'actors' would perhaps be a more obvious category in the Indian diaspora as a holistic entity. The two alternative sets of adjectives in the sub-title that I have chosen for this article to describe the Indian diaspora reflect my impression that the models could be based on how the actors in the Indian diaspora are going to be viewed in the arena of international relations in the twenty-first century—whether with suspicion, or with awe. Secondly, they also reflect a transition from the first to the second that might have taken place over time or that is in progress. For obvious reasons, I have left it as an open question.

I have tried to begin with constructing a framework of an underlying matrix, comprising a limited number of typologies of models and a few typologies of actors. The first I have called Model I, Model II, etc.—a set on the side of the rows, and the second, Actors A, B, etc.—another set on the side of the columns. Such an underlying matrix, I suppose, would pave the way for addressing each of the binaries of models and actors that one could allocate to the cells created in the sub-matrices, still keeping the issues together under a holistic umbrella. The next step would be to name the models and actors in each typology of the matrix for the purpose of placing the issues in one cell or the other.

In the prototype matrix (Figure 2.1), for example, I have named the models as the Persons of Indian Origin (PIO), and the Non-Resident Indians (NRI) in Models Typology I. Similarly, in Actors Typology A, I have named them as i, ii, iii, iv, v, vi—representing, respectively—the unskilled labourer, the semi-skilled workers, the traders, the entrepreneurs, the professionals, and the students under a typology of actors.

Though not spelt out in the prototype matrix, as an extension of these typologies, in Models Typology II, the 'twice banished', and the returnees may form another typology of models; in Models Typology III, the temporary migrants, the circulatory migrants, and the sojourners could appear as a third typology; in Models Typology IV, the indentured workers and their earlier variants—the slaves, soldiers, policemen, the lascars, the maids, etc., the present-day refugees/asylees, the voluntary migrants could make still another typology where the degree of coercion could be the index. One can also have a typology of models based on plain geographical location, or complex geopolitical occupation of space by the Indian diaspora. There could still be one more typology comprising the 'brawn drain', brain drain, brain bank, brain gain, etc., as categories of models.

Similarly, in the extended typology of Actors, we could have Actors Typology B with the principal 'seed migrants', the dependent spouses, the pre-generation parents, the second-

			Typology of Actors								
			A						B	C	D
			i	ii	iii	iv	v	vi			
Typology of Models	I	PIO		√	√	√	√	?			
		NRI	√	√	√	√	√	√			
	II										
	III										
	IV										

FIG. 2.1: THE MATRIX OF TYPOLOGIES OF ACTORS AND MODELS IN INDIAN DIASPORA

generation progeny, other relatives, and even sponsored friends as a second typology. Actors Typology C could be the diasporic associations based on provincial, linguistic, art and culture, religious, and professional groupings. Another important one, Actors Typology D, could comprise men and women as separate actors. And then, we could also have *occupational actors* like doctors, nurses, engineers, information technologists, architects, lawyers, masons, drivers and so on in one more typology, and the *generic actors* like the writers, teachers, scientists, inventors, innovators, managers, white-collar workers, blue-collar workers and so on in various fields, as yet another Actors Typology.

Irrespective of how one finds slots in the matrix—whether *implicitly* in a fuzzy manner, or *explicitly* by creating well-defined typologies—as a next step, we would still need to probe further in terms of *contextualizing* a myriad of models and actors with international relations *per se*. International relation in itself is a mystical category as it covers a whole lot of space with distinctly different, although not disjointed, aspects of civil society: the political, the economic, the cultural (which includes the religious), and the security-related—to name some of the most important ones only.

One way or the other, i.e. implicitly or explicitly, it seems the field of diaspora studies is poised for the challenge of addressing a new perspective. Its novelty would lie in the *deconstruction* of the interface between the two variables, the Indian diaspora and international relations, and playing with the interpretation of phrasing that interface—in terms of identifying each of them as the dependent variable under one construct and independent variable under a different construct. In other words, we have a choice to say that ID (short for Indian Diaspora) is the dependent (or determined) variable, and IR (short for International Relations) is the independent (or determining) variable; or vice versa. For example, we may wish to know how international relations—through the immigration policies—have been instrumental in determining *the actors* and *the models* of the Indian diaspora, and the roles they had assumed or been assigned to play in the host societies so far: Often actors are determined by the quantitative and qualitative immigration quotas for importing 'seed migrants' in the labour market, by the family-reunification clause in the family preferences, and so on. Similarly, models are determined by temporary entry and stay rights of Indians as exchange visitors or intra-company transferees, transition categories like the H-1B visa holders, or permanent residents with green cards and the like, and as citizens by naturalization or birth.

Alternatively, we may say that we want to learn how the actors and models of the Indian diaspora, as pressure groups in host societies, and now increasingly in India too as their country of origin, affect international relations: Whether (1) bilaterally between India and each of the destination countries, or (2) multilaterally amongst the nations globally. This might be examined (1) historically through the past, (2) contemporarily through the state of affairs that are current, or (3) futuristically in the times to come.

One may choose to address it in either of the two ways. However, it is my impression that if we were to assess it in a 'more or less' sense, the policy concerns in the host countries have dealt more with the first perspective in terms of looking at questions of assimilation (or integration) of Indians as well as all other foreigners into the local society and community, whereas the policy concerns in India have lately been more with the second perspective of how the Indian diaspora could be mobilized to influence, to the advantage of India, the bilateral and multilateral relations from across the borders. While I suppose both the perspectives of the interface between the Indian diaspora and international relations—one of the receiving country and the other of the sending country—would be important, the novel part would be the outcome of a fusion between the two approaches, with focused attention on the actors either as 'traitors' in home countries and 'spies' in host countries, or as 'prodigal children' in the former and 'rays of hope' in the latter.

There would perhaps be enough literature on how international relations have shaped the actors and the models or vice versa in the past. What I have attempted in this paper is to contemplate the links between the actors and models of Indian diaspora with international relations in a contemporary as well as a futuristic way. The boundaries between disciplinary approaches in diaspora studies are getting blurred, and the diaspora experts are increasingly adopting multidisciplinary outlook, which I think is a welcome sign for the field. Keeping this in mind, I have tried to address some of the issues with a holistic perspective of international development in mind, whether local or global. In doing so, however, I have mainly used a limited example of the Non-Resident Indian (NRI) diaspora in the United States.

Figure 2.2 presents the regional distribution of an approximate 20 million-strong *stock* of the Indian diaspora at the close of the twentieth century, about half of them PIOs and half NRIs (ICWA, 2001). It is common knowledge that the earlier migrants who formed the basis of an Indian diaspora mainly involved 'cheap' manual labourers leaving India in large numbers to meet

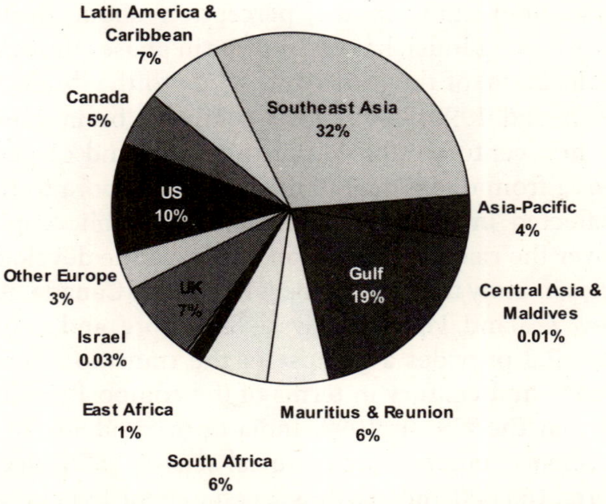

Source: ICWA, *Report of the High Level Committee on the Indian Diaspora*, New Delhi: Indian Council of World Affairs, 2001.

FIG. 2.2: PERCENTAGE DISTRIBUTION OF NRIS AND PIOS BY REGION

the enormous quantitative demand for indentured workers that arose in the plantations, mainly in South-East Asia and the Pacific, but also in the Caribbean and the African countries immediately after the British had abolished slavery in 1834—leading to what is sometimes also called the 'brawn drain'. The 'brain drain'—a quality exodus of India's cream of highly skilled professionals—comprising doctors, engineers, scientists, teachers, architects, entrepreneurs, and more recently the IT workers, and nurses on the other hand, appeared a century-and-a-quarter later. From the post-mid-1960s, it has continued in the twenty-first century, flowing westward and contributing, *inter alia*, to the concentration of Indian diaspora's 10 per cent share in the USA.

From the perception of a highly-educated or skilled knowledge workers supposedly 'draining' India of its knowledge wealth and human resources, professional Indian immigrants have come to be seen as 'angels' with a perfected image of transnational 'global citizen' of the twenty-first century within the short span of the closing decade of the twentieth century. This paradigm shift, in the perception about professional migrants leaving India, has taken place in phases though—from the 'brain drain' of the 1960s and 1970s to the 'brain bank' of the 1980s and 1990s, and subsequently to 'brain gain' in the twenty-first century. This complete turnaround of perception in moving from one model of the Indian diaspora to the other gets reflected in the current official and public euphoria in India over the rising immigration quotas in the developed host countries, mainly the US and the UK, the EU, Canada, Australia and New Zealand, Japan, Malaysia, Singapore, and so on.

Figure 2.3 provides a glimpse of the transition period into the twenty-first century in terms of the composition of Indian diaspora in the US. In 1999, India-born residents in the US with a science, engineering or social science (SES) degree had numbered 165,000. Indians thus accounted for 13 per cent of the total number of all foreign-born US residents with SES degrees, which was more than the proportion for any other foreign-born diasporic residents including the Chinese.

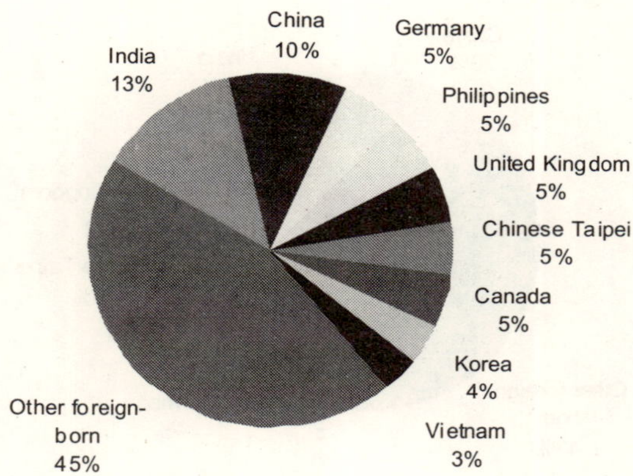

Source: Author, using National Science Foundation, Division of Science Resources Statistics (NSF/SRS), Scientists and Engineers Statistical Data System (SESTAT), 1999.

FIG. 2.3: SIZE OF FOREIGN-BORN DIASPORIC RESIDENTS IN THE US WITH SES DEGREES, BY COUNTRY OF BIRTH, 1999

Figure 2.4 is a subset of Figure 2.3, showing county-wise origin of all foreign-born residents with a doctorate degree in SES, residing in the US in 1999, and India accounting for a high share of 16 per cent or 30,000 people, second only to the Chinese.

This is about the stock profile of the NRI human capital in the US. Table 2.1 presents another picture of the transition period—the *flow* profile of the occupational shift of the NRI human capital entering the US between 1999 and 2001. It shows a substantial increase in the proportion of those holding the highest-rung 'professional and technical' occupations over the three transition years into the new century (from 12 to 21 to 28 per cent respectively), conveying that the position of the highly skilled and knowledgeable amongst the Indian diaspora workforce in the US labour market has undergone significant enhancement. In addition, their share amongst immigrants of all foreign nationalities entering and settling in the US has also been increasing over this period (from 9 to 15 to 24 per

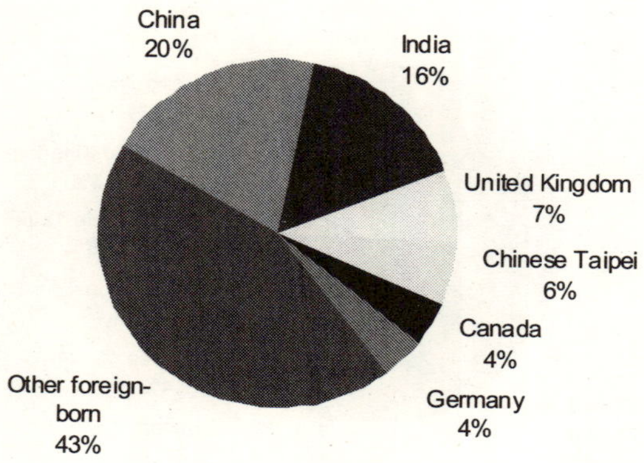

Source: Same as Figure 2.3.

FIG. 2.4: SIZE OF FOREIGN-BORN DIASPORIC RESIDENTS IN THE US WITH SES DOCTORATE DEGREES, BY COUNTRY OF BIRTH, 1999

cent). This is true for the second tier of occupations too, viz., the 'executive, administrative and managerial' occupations, on both counts, though at a smaller scale.

At a generic level in the knowledge sector, Table 2.2 presents a very comprehensive overview of the presence of Indian diaspora in the SES faculties of the US higher education system, by teaching field and gender, in a comparative perspective with the total faculty, as well as all diasporas, and all Asian diasporas. It shows that amongst the American faculties in 1997, almost 7,000 teaching staff were of Indian origin, constituting 3 per cent of the total faculty strength, 15 per cent of all foreigners, and 23 per cent of all Asians, with the share of Indian women being more than a quarter of all female faculty, and over one-eighth amongst the Asian female diaspora. The picture leaves enough scope for one to contemplate on the potential for bilateral as well as multilateral advocacy and linkages the Indian academic diaspora would command in the US and the rest of the world.

Initially, beginning in the early 1960s, the brain drain from India was associated with the public recognition that the Nobel Prize had brought to the gifted PIO scientists like Har Gobind

TABLE 2.1: OCCUPATIONAL PROFILE OF THE NRIs ENTERING THE US, 1999-2001

	1999			2000			2001		
	Number	Share of all Indian immigrants (%)	Share of all immigrants (%)	Number	Share of all Indian immigrants (%)	Share of all immigrants (%)	Number	Share of all Indian immigrants (%)	Share of all immigrants (%)
Professional and technical	3,492	11.6	9.4	8,632	20.6	14.7	19,935	28.4	23.8
Executive, admnstrative and managerial	1,112	3.7	7.1	1,644	3.9	7.9	3,062	4.3	11.1
Clerical and administrative support	576	1.9	4.2	573	1.4	3.9	643	0.9	3.9
Sales	648	2.1	6.1	689	1.6	5.3	842	1.2	5.4
Service	559	1.9	3.2	798	1.9	2.6	1,041	1.4	2.7
Farming, forestry and fishing	1,328	4.4	11.7	1,080	2.6	9.5	1,161	1.7	12.8
Skilled workers	301	0.9	0.9	308	0.7	0.8	389	0.6	0.8
Total with occupation	8,016	26.5	5.7	13,724	32.7	7.2	27,073	38.5	11.3
Occupation not specified	22,221	73.5	4.4	28,322	67.3	4.3	43,217	61.5	5.2
Total immigrants	30,237	100	4.7	42,046	100	4.9	70,290	100	6.6

Source: Author, using data from the US Immigration and Naturalization Service Yearbooks, the latest being from the Yearbook 2001, published in 2003.

TABLE 2.2: INDIAN DIASPORA AMONGST THE US FACULTIES, BY TEACHING FIELD AND GENDER, 1997

	Total SES faculties	Indian Diaspora (ID) as SES faculties	ID as % of Total SES faculties	ID as % of All diasporas	ID as % of all Asian diasporas	Female % in Indian diaspora	Indian Female Diasora (IFD) as % of Total female	IFD as % of Asian female diaspora
Total SES	224,707	6,876	3.1	15.3	23.2	12.1	26.8	12.9
Physical sciences	37,020	688	1.9	9.3	19.4	16.7	18.8	9.9
Life sciences	53,055	1,014	1.9	13.4	31.2	31.6	38.7	15.7
Math. & computer	44,375	2,086	4.7	18.3	33.0	13.9	39.6	24.5
Social sciences	65,509	1,491	2.3	15.5	32.2	6.3	10.7	5.1
Engineering	24,748	1,597	6.5	17.8	27.4	0.9	23.3	6.3

Note: Data include first jobs of post-secondary teaching at four-year colleges and universities in the US, but exclude faculties in two-year or community colleges, or those who teach as a secondary job.

Source: Author, computed and compiled from National Science Foundation, United States, *Science and Engineering Indicators 2000.*

Khorana (Medicine 1968) who had a naturalized American citizenship at that time, or Subramanyan Chandrasekhar (Physics 1983), who having naturalized in 1953, had made the US his home. Gradually, following the landmark 1965 Amendments to the US Immigration and Nationality Act, the migration of professionals became a mass phenomenon through the 1970s and onwards, with the Indian professionals enjoying the distinction of being one of the best-educated, highly employable, and high-income earning ethnic groups in the US census data, yet in their own country disdained as 'deserters' of the 'motherland India,' either openly or subtly.[2] It was only towards the end of 1990s that the success and achievements of the Indian diaspora in the US drew real attention of the developed countries in the West and the East alike, subsequently or simultaneously followed by a change of attitude in India too towards its diaspora.[3]

Apart from the US, within the European Union (EU) in the West—the largest economic entity in the world today—two-thirds of the entire Indian diasporic community still resides in the UK. Here too, the Indian community is one of the highest-earning and best-educated groups, achieving eminence in a variety of fields comprising business, information technology, the health sector, the media, and entertainment industries. In Canada, with just 3 per cent share in a population of 30 million, Indo–Canadians have recorded high achievements in the fields of medicine, academia, management, and engineering. The Indian immigrants' average annual income in Canada is nearly 20 per cent higher than the national average, and their educational levels too are higher. In the East, there are 30,000 Indian citizens in Australia; and New Zealand has also witnessed a rise in the entry of Indian professional immigrants, those engaged in domestic retail trade, medical, hospitality, engineering, and Information Technology (IT) sectors; and countries like Japan, Korea, and Singapore are trying to attract Indian talent in large numbers, testifying the importance of the Indian diaspora in international development.

Another important point to be noted is that the highly skilled Indians have joined the diaspora not only through the 'employment gate' but also through the 'academic gate' as a revolving diaspora of students that forms a distinct set of actors in the Indian diaspora—the 'semi-finished' Indian professionals abroad.[4] Data collated by the US Institute of International Education's *Open Doors 2009* survey reveal that in 2008-9 India retained its No. 1 position in the US university enrolments (followed by China, Korea, Japan, Canada, and Taiwan) for the eighth year in a row (Khedria 2009). Indians now account for 15 per cent of all foreign students in the US. To serve the dual purpose of sustaining an expensive higher education system, and meeting *short-term* labour shortages, both the UK and the US, with other countries following suit, have adopted a policy of allowing foreign students in their universities respectively, to stay on and work, rather than return to their countries of origin on completion of their degrees (*The Hindustan Times*, 25 March 2005). In addition, the destination countries gain political mileage in the form of a bonus: The foreign students become their long-term ambassadors in the international political arena.[5] India has thus become a 'must destination for internationally renowned educational institutions shopping for 'knowledge capital', i.e. to woo the Indian student (*The Hindu* 26 November 2000). In October 2000, four countries had mounted education 'fairs' in Delhi and other Indian cities, and since then it has become a regular feature of international relations in India. Most diplomatic missions project these as ways 'to facilitate the search of a foreign education to Indian citizens', but the countries also compete against each other for the generic Indian 'semi-finished human capital', the student. Figure 2.5 shows that Indian students accounted for 4 per cent of all foreign students enrolled in tertiary education in OECD countries in 2001. A far larger share was registered for the US, where 10 per cent of enrolled foreign students were Indian. By 2009-10, this share of Indian students amongst all foreign students in the US went up to 15 per cent.

The growing competition among countries like the US, UK, Canada, Australia, New Zealand, and Ireland, and also non-English-speaking countries like France, Germany, and the

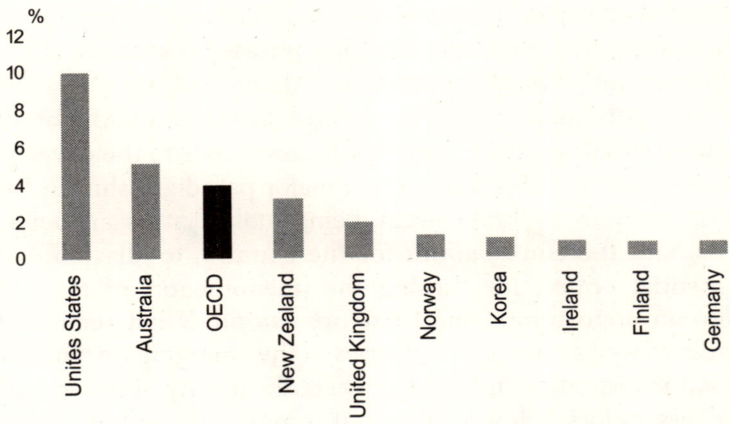

Note: Excluding data for Canada, Greece, Luxembourg, and Portugal.
Source: OECD Education database.

FIG. 2.5: INDIAN STUDENT DIASPORA AMONGST ALL STUDENT DIASPORAS IN RECEIVING COUNTRIES, 2001 (%)

Netherlands have been bringing even the Ivy League institutions to India, and to other South Asian countries too, to look for the cream of students (*The Economic Times*, 24 November 2004).

CONCLUSION

To conclude, the perception of the destination countries in which the Indian professional migrants have settled to form a diaspora has undergone a significant reversal. Britain has come a long way since the days of Enoch Powell and his prophecy of 'rivers of blood' flowing if economic immigrants were allowed to settle in Britain. The change in values since 1971 could be primarily attributed to the Indian diaspora itself that has defied the anticipated doom by rising to unforeseeable economic success.[6] The reason why the paradigm shift in the societies and regions where Indians have settled is important for the hosts lies in their realization that, given the appropriate support, one type of diasporic actors—the abhorred and suspect 'tinkers, tailors, soldiers, and spies,' if not outright 'social parasite'—can become the social boon, or as someone has phrased it sarcastically, the white man's 'great *off-white* hope'! (Albinia, 2000).

Presently thus, India has emerged as the most sought after source country for the supply of professionals to the developed host countries. This has led to a major paradigm shift in India too—away from 'brain drain' being looked at as an outright loss, and therefore *painful* for the country, to 'diaspora' as a potential option for turning the phenomenon of migration into an opportunity, and therefore *gainful.* What remains for India as well as the host countries in the emerging international relations paradigm is to judge where the loyalty of the so-called tinkers, tailors, soldiers, spies that comprise the Indian diaspora would lie? Whether they would prove to be a real great 'off-white hope'—not only for Europe or Australia or America, but also for the world as whole? Or, whether it will depend on which way the wind of international relations would first blow in the new century, rather than be blown by the diaspora?

NOTES

1. This is a revised version of the Keynote Address delivered at the seminar. The first description is an allegory of doubtful loyalties adapted from the title of Le Carre's bestseller of the 1970s—itself borrowed from a well-known nursery rhyme; the second is an expression used by Albinia (2001) for the brown-skinned Asian Indians.
2. Even socially, crossing the seas was at one time considered a taboo in high-caste communities in India, e.g. as depicted in Munshi Premchand's novels and stories. Perhaps it was the cumulative effect of the nexus between the diaspora and the aspiring migrants that led to the crumbling of such taboos over time, resulting in swelling streams of migrants joining the Indian diaspora wherever it grew.
3. There is enough evidence of diaspora-India interaction that has been documented in the media lately.
4. The term 'semi-finished human capital' was first used by Tapas Majumdar (1994).

5. They play important role in world politics as they have done in the past as, for example, some of the well-known NRI students, belonging to a few iconic families in India, did play in mobilizing public opinion in the US during India's independence struggle! (Jensen, 1988, as cited in Khadria, 1999).
6. Today, Britain is an endless repository of success stories of the Indian professional diaspora, ranging from Lord Swraj Paul, to steel magnate Laxmi Mittal, and icons like Nobel Laureate Amartya Sen, who subsequently remigrated to the US a second time.

REFERENCES

Albinia, A., 'The Great Off-White Hope', *The Hindustan Times*, New Delhi, 26 September 2000.

BBC, Viewpoints on Migration, Online News Series, views of eight commentators, 22 March 2004 http://news.bbc.co.uk/1/hi/in_depth/3512992.stm.

ICWA, *Report of the High Level Committee on the Indian Diaspora*, New Delhi: Indian Council of World Affairs, 2001.

IMD, *The World Competitiveness Yearbook 2000*, Lausanne: Institute of Management Development, 2000.

IOM, *Return Migration: Policies and Practices in Europe*, Geneva: International Organization for Migration, 2004.

IMF, *World Economic Outlook, April 2005: Globalization and External Imbalances*, International Monetary Fund, Washington, D.C., 2005.

Jensen, J.M., *Passage from India: Asian Indian Immigrants in North America*, New Haven, Yale University Press, 1988.

Khadria, B., *The Migration of Knowledge Workers: Second-Generation Effects of India's Brain Drain*, New Delhi: Sage, 1999a.

———, 'Of Dreams, Drain, and Dams: Metaphors in the Indian Emigration of Talent', *India International Centre Quarterly*, vol. 26, no. 3, Monsoon, 1999b, pp. 79-90.

———, 'Skilled Labour Migration from India', in Hisaya Oda (ed.), *International Labor Migration from South Asia*, ASEDP 70, Chiba, Japan: IDE-JETRO, 2004, pp. 7-55.

———, *Migration in South and South-West Asia*, Regional Study No. RS 6, Policy Analysis and Research Programme of the GCIM, September 2005, supporting evidence of the Commission's main report, *Migration in an Interconnected World: New Directions for Action*, GCIM, Geneva, October 2005.

———, 'Tracing the Genesis of Brain Drain in India through its State Policy and Civil Society', in Nancy Green and François Weil (eds.), *Citizenship and Those Who Leave: The Politics of Emigration and Expatriation*, Urbana: University of Illinois Press, 2007.

Khadria, B. ed., *India Migration Report 2009: Past, Present, and the Future Outlook*, International Migration and Diaspora Studies (IMDS) Project, Jawaharlal Nehru University, distributed by Cambridge University Press India, New Delhi, 2009.

Le Carre, J., *Tinker, Tailor, Soldier, Spy*, Westminister, Maryland: Random House, 1974.

Majumdar, T., 'Old World is the New World', *The Telegraph*, Calcutta, 8 August 1994.

Martin, P., 'Economic Trends and Professional Labour Migration: US Experience and Implications for Asia', Report presented at the Workshop on International Migration and Labour Markets in Asia, 1-2 February 2001, Tokyo: *mimeo*.

OECD, *Trends in International Migration: Annual Report 2003 Edition*, Paris: Organisation for Economic Cooperation and Development, 2004.

3

The Indian State and the Diaspora

Towards a New Political Model

INGRID THERWATH

INTRODUCTION

Since the end of the Cold War, nation states have been commonly presented as old if not inadequate political entities, while globalization and diasporas have been heralded as new symbols of our post-modern age. Although some researchers have tried to balance this view, this systematic confrontation still prevails in political science and international relations. This paper wishes to transcend this binary opposition and suggest a new political model where transnational groups and the State do not work against each other but interact in a mutually beneficial manner. This model, by definition not territorially-bound, restores the nation state as an important and still potent political actor, while providing an integrated vision of political and economic life. The relationship between the Indian State and the 20 million strong Indian diaspora offers a particularly striking example of collaboration between structurally different groups, and between the public and the private sector. I shall therefore suggest a new model of international relations in the light of this case-study and of fieldwork conducted in India from 2002 to 2011. In order to do so, I shall first assess the state of research in diaspora studies and political sciences more generally and analyse the traditional opposition of State and diaspora, before discussing the role of the Indian State in the shaping of the Indian diaspora as a political entity. Eventually, I shall focus on a yearly forum, the Pravasi Bharatiya Divas (PBD, Overseas Indians Day), started in 2003 and which provides a unique interface between the State and the diaspora.

THE STATE AND THE DIASPORA: OLD ACTORS IN A NEW MODEL OF INTERNATIONAL RELATIONS

STATE *VS* DIASPORA

Contemporary security issues linked to transnational terrorism and difficulties encountered by governments to control human and financial flows have given a new currency and acuity to the opposition between State and diaspora (or between the nation state and the diaspora, but certainly not between the concepts of nation and diaspora, which are often considered complementary). This dichotomy is actually deeply rooted in the history and the concept of the word 'diaspora' itself. While the Greek etymology of 'diaspora' (literally, to sow across) is a well-known fact, many people tend to ignore that the term was first used by the Greeks to mention their populations settled abroad in order to widen the empire after victorious conquests. This stems from the fact that the understanding of diaspora prevailing in Western thinking over the years has not been the Greek but the Jewish one. The triumphalist Hellenic concept has been superseded by the catastrophist Jewish version, which now informs any discussion about the diaspora in relation with the nation state. Historically, the Jewish 'diaspora' results from the dispersion of the Jews after their exile and deportation from Babylon in 586 BC and since then, as the 'Jewish diaspora' imposed itself as the reference and the matrix of all subsequent diasporas, 'diaspora' has been associated with victim communities traumatized by forced exile at the hand of a persecuting power.

The advent of Zionism further contributed to the schism between the concept of a territorial power and diaspora. The theory of *shelilat ha-galut*, literally negation of exile, goes even further in opposing the State and the diaspora. According to this Zionist concept, the creation of Israel marks the *de facto* disappearance of the Jewish diaspora. Of course, the Jewish diaspora's self-assertion as powerful transnational group seems to prove this theoretical vision wrong. However, the opposition between the nation state and the diaspora is propagated by most specialists of diasporas, by and large. George Prevelakis, a French specialist of the Greek diaspora, for instance, wrote about the 'fundamental dilemma' between the State and the diaspora, which he deems structurally incompatible. So, whether diasporas are seen as a liability or on the contrary as a chance for development, they seem to be intrinsically linked and opposed to the concept of nation state. The realization that we live in the era of globalization and the new emphasis laid on flows and transnational entities like NGOs, multinational companies, supra-national governments and, of course, diasporas, have reinforced and seemed to confirm this traditional dichotomy.

The Advent of Cosmopolitanism

Modern and then post-modern thought has heavily fed upon the notion of cosmopolitanism since the very beginning of the twentieth century. In recent years, the coming of age of several ethnic lobbies in the United States, like the Indian–American lobby for instance in the 1990s, on the model of the Jewish lobby, has been systematically highlighted by the international and national media around the world, giving various diasporas unprecedented attention as political and financial actors. At the same time, 'diaspora' became 'one of the buzzwords of the post-modern age' and even the mere presence of this term on a book-cover was enough to increase the sales, as Phil Cohen, an author who criticized the 'diaspora industry' aptly remarked.[1] In this context, many sociologists, political scientists, anthropologists and artists deemed the nation state moribund and dreamt about the advent of a cosmopolitan, borderless world where global citizens would be the norm. This post-modernist vision is based on the possibility of homogeneous, continuous and deterritorialized communities and has been heralded by Stuart Hall for instance.

The rise of the internet from the mid-1990s onwards, the increasing migration and financial flows, the rise of transnational terrorism and long-distance nationalism seemed to confirm the post-modern hypothesis. From this moment, globalization, understood as a paragon of post-modernity, would entail the ultimate death or at least weakening of the nation state. Expressions like 'borderless nations', 'transnations' and 'translocalities' were summoned to explain this new order. After almost ten years of intense discussion on this subject, many scholars have refined their thoughts. Besides, their post-modern views have now come under the criticism of a new generation of diaspora theorists like Stéphane Dufoix. While the previous state-centred approach may be obsolete, a new model integrating nation states and diasporas has to be worked out.

Collaboration in a Global System

Nation states and diasporas are certainly not new concepts but never before have they availed of such importance in the political and economic life of the globe. Diasporas are increasingly being instrumentalized as lobbies or as financial assets, while there has never been as many sovereign nation states in the world as today with a staggering number of 197 according to the United Nations as compared to 72 in 1900. The interactions between the Indian State and the Indian diaspora show that, while the State and the diaspora function as actors in an extrasocietal, 'global system',[2] they also work together at the intrasocietal level, so much so that the Indian diaspora is now factored in the Union budget and has the power to influence the political decision-making process for example. This raises the question of the links between a territorialized political system and a larger and partly transnational society.

The economic, public political and social spheres depend on each other for either legitimity, funding, growth, regulation, or economic access. The Indian example reveals two fundamental facts: the nation state can and does function in collaboration with a diaspora, and elites, whether domestic administrative and entrepreneurial elites or transnational ones (or both), are the building-blocks of this threefold public-private-transnational collaboration system as they often belong to more than one sphere. And, in order to understand how far a State and a diaspora can be linked, the role of the Indian State in the creation of the Indian diaspora has to be highlighted.

MARCHING TOWARDS A NEW DIALECTIC

Whether at the international extrasocietal level or at the domestic intrasocietal level, the State and the diaspora work together in an integrated political system based on mutual benefits. This, of course, has hardly been the case after India's Independence and until the late 1990s. In this period of about forty years, the Nehruvian territorially-bound vision of the polity prevailed and the State distanced itself from the diaspora.[3] However, the Indian State and the diaspora have since the late 1990s become partners engaged in a dialogue based on economic benefits under the dual compulsion of economic liberalization and the rise of a Hindu and ethnic form of nationalism.[4] They have in the process become interdependent actors. Now, a causal and chronological dimension can even be read into their relationship: indeed, the diaspora, far from being a *sui generis* phenomenon, actually proceeds from the State. They then work together, while the State eventually provides the means for the diaspora to function on its own in a dialectic process.

THE INDIAN DIASPORA: A CREATION OF THE STATE?

The idea that the Indian State created the Indian diaspora is deliberately provocative. Many will object that the diaspora preceded the birth of an independent Indian State or even the notion of nation state itself and that it has been existing for centuries. It did not therefore need State patronage to thrive.

Needless to say, these objections are legitimate in as far as they assume the Indian diaspora to be a historical entity existing in the larger chronological framework of world migrations. Scholars have debated on the actual age of the Indian diaspora and some date it back to the fifth century BC, while most tend to view the beginning of the indentured system as its birth-date.[5] Besides, overseas Indians have managed to maintain links, whether matrimonial, linguistic or religious, with India despite not being able to get dual citizenship before this policy was reversed in 2003 and not being viewed positively by the State.

I wish, however, to consider here the Indian diaspora not as a sociological and historical aggregate of populations scattered in 110 countries around the world but as a political actor. For a transnational political actor to exist as such, it has to be unified or at least have some degree of cohesion, have an awareness of its own identity, have umbrella representative bodies and be recognized as legitimate by the transnational community members. The Indian diaspora satisfied none of these criteria until the late 1980s-early 1990s, when the Global Organization of Persons of Indian Origin (GOPIO) was created and mostly when the Indian State started looking at Non-Resident Indians (NRI) and Persons of Indian Origin (PIO) as a diaspora. Bearing these facts in mind, I wish to argue that the Indian State has been central to the creation of the Indian diaspora as a political project.

As Frederic Barth, Nathan Glazer and Daniel Patrick Moynihan have pointed out in their seminal works, public policies are crucial for the constitution of social groups, who name and organize themselves in the most profitable way to gain from particular incentives.[6] The US census has for example led some communities to lobby for a new categorization or a new entry line in order to benefit from positive discrimination. Before 1980, NRIs and PIO living in the United States appeared in the section 'other whites' and had to compete with other ethnicities for reserved seats. The introduction of the category 'South Asian Americans' and then 'Indian Americans' not only gave them increased visibility but also made access to education or jobs easier than previously. A similar phenomenon has been widely observed in Great Britain, Malaysia or even Fiji to quote only a few examples. But this trend inevitably leads to the segmentation of social groups in the country of residence and to the fragmentation of a larger transnational group as a consequence. By contrast, the country of origin, often heralded by nationalists as the common denominator binding scattered and heterogeneous communities, can be used as a unifying factor. But its influence in the homogenization and the fostering of a horizontal transnational population has been surprisingly understated or overlooked.

This stance is understandable since the Indian government ceased to consider the overseas Indians as nationals and somehow as a constituency after Independence, although their well-being had been an important issue before 1947 and their support had fuelled the nationalist movement in India. This can be inferred from the Nehruvian conception of the national identity as territory-based and not ethnic.[7] Not surprisingly the word 'diaspora' became commonly used only in the 1990s while it started to appear in academic publications in the mid-1980s. The advent of the BJP, the rise of Hindu nationalism and the economic reforms changed the State's perception of these peripheral populations, which were incorporated in the national ethnic imagination mostly for their financial strength. The NDA government, with its nationalist and ethno-religious ideology, has thus been central in the conceptualization of what has often been marketed as 'The Great Indian Diaspora', the transnational counterpart of 'The Great Indian Middle Class'. The BJP, at the head of the NDA coalition and of the Indian State from 1998 to 2004, had always showed great interest for the word 'diaspora'. For example, Murli Manohar Joshi commissioned a report entitled *Indian Diaspora: In Search for Identity* from the Central Institute of Indian Languages, a public institute, in 2003 when he was the Minister of Human Resources, following a request from the BJP.[8] But it is L.M. Singhvi, member of the Rajya Sabha and former High Commissioner of India in the

United Kingdom, who best personifies the new constructions of national identity as an ethnic Hindu exclusivist identity. In his book *Towards Global Togetherness*, he ponders over the natural links uniting India and its 'diaspora' and writes about inherent Indian values. The Indian State commissioned a report by a High Level Committee in 2001. The committee, headed by L.M. Singhvi, released its report entitled 'The Indian Diaspora' in December 2002.[9] Before this date, State actors and the media talked only of NRIs, PIO (acronyms created for fiscal purposes), 'overseas Indians' (an expression hailing back from the Raj), 'migrants' or 'expatriates'.

From the Singhvi report onwards, the Indian diaspora became a much-used official denomination and category (along with the more recent 'Overseas Indian Community'). From then on and thanks to the publicity given to this report and to subsequent political measures in India, NRIs and PIO knew they came under a wider category than those linked to their place of residence and could relate to each other irrespective of where they lived. The process of transnationalization started by GOPIO in 1989 found a strong governmental backing and a legitimate and publically recognized existence through the report. Besides, the report contained a supposedly exhaustive list of NRIs and PIO around the world and constituted the first State-sponsored public transnational census in the country. Most Indian missions abroad had for several decades held precise accounts of the number of Indian citizens and people of Indian origin, but this work had not been systematic and certainly not in the public domain.[10] Although the 2002 census excludes some countries like Sri Lanka and Nepal and only takes into account people whose Indian ancestry can be traced up to the fourth generation, barring thus many descendants from indentured workers in East Africa and the Caribbean, the report lists the countries of residence by alphabetical order regardless of the size of their Indian population and does not underline the preferred countries whose citizens are eligible for dual citizenship. This presentation tends to put all the receiving countries on the same level and hence create the illusion of a united and undifferentiated worldwide Indian diaspora.

This levelling blurs the disparity between what has often been termed the old and the new diaspora, mainly the descendants of indentured and pre-Independence migrants on the one hand and the generally more affluent and educated post-1947 migrants on the other hand. However, the transnational census and the subsequent introduction of a seemingly homogeneous population labelled as 'the diaspora' should not detract from the fact that the NDA regime clearly vowed the new diaspora, for economic as well as political purposes. The introduction of the PIO card in 1999 and the first decisions taken on the eligibility for dual citizenship before the Overseas Citizenship of India (OCI) was implemented in 2005 clearly favoured the most recent migrants. Indeed, the government restricted the eligibility for these schemes to migrants originally from India up to the third generation and within the limits provided by the 1955 Citizenship Act, excluding thus many descendants of the 'coolies' and Muslim migrants to Pakistan between 1947 and 1955. Moreover, the price of the PIO card at its inception was US $1,000. In the following years, this fee was lowered to Rs 15,000 (about $330) for an adult but this set-up still indicated that the scheme was aimed at the richer sections of the emigrant populations and that the government was practising a 'dollar apartheid'. The creation of a uniform diasporic category is therefore wholly artificial as it neither corresponds to a sociological reality nor to the actual Indian policies that seek to target specific populations like potential investors or unskilled labourers from the Gulf. It has, however, become a prominent trope in the official rhetoric and a potent concept in rethinking the position of India on the international arena.

This diasporization of 'overseas Indians' was induced by a nationalist, BJP government wishing to reincorporate these non-nationals and expatriates in the national fold while tapping their financial resources and their expertise. In this context, the banalization of the word 'diaspora' in the High Level Committee report is a carefully chosen way to reject the discussion about the validity of the term and its connotations. In the preface, L.M.

Singhvi uses 'diaspora' as a generic term and does not further discuss the scientific ideology of such a claim or allude to the heterogeneity of Indians abroad.[11] This lexical strategy enables the authorities to create and spread what Stéphane Dufoix identified as the three properties of 'diaspora': 'the illusion of essence', 'the illusion of community', 'the illusion of continuity'.[12] By broadcasting these three fictions, the Indian State, in the race for the superpower status and a seat in the UN Security Council, consciously sought to place India on the same level as Israel and China and assert its status as a meaningful country on the international scene, a major civilizational centre and a great economic power. Indeed, the Jewish diaspora is often cited as a diasporic paragon in the report and provides a model the Indian State wishes to inculcate the diaspora especially in the United States where Indian associations are encouraged to lobby and learn from the well-organized Jewish community. This urge to affirm India's power through the introduction of a new lexical trope confirms the hypothesis that 'diaspora' as a concept in India is a governmental construction and a particularly potent instrument of the nation state.[13] Indeed, the authorities use it as a tool to position India on the map of world leading powers and hence consider the fact of having a diaspora as a symbol of international status. It participates hence in the self-projection of India as a great power and initially resonated well with concerns of the ethno-religious nationalists who governed India from 1998 to 2004 as well as with the subsequent governments' quest for building the 'Brand India'.

Having a diaspora and not merely expatriate workers became thus a matter of prestige and signalled a coming of age of India as a country that mattered. This renaming partook of the communication drive induced by the NDA government with private PR firms and slogans like 'India Shining'. Later, the creation of Ministry of Overseas Indian Affairs and the presence in the Lok Sabha of several MPs who have retained their NRI status and wish to treat the diaspora as their constituency point out to this ongoing political interest under the Congress rule.

The Work of Elites

Neither the Indian diaspora nor the Indian State could work together in a domestic system of political economy without their respective elites. Of course, the domestic State elite, foreign State elites and the transnational, diaspora elites are not totally separated entities and often overlap. For Leslie Sklair, the transnational elite plays a crucial role in integrating the public and the private spheres, as well as local States and transnational organization in a single global system whose mission is capitalist gains and the imposition of consumerism. She points out the contacts and even familiarity of this diasporic bourgeoisie with other State-based elites:

> virtually all senior members of the TCC [Transnational Capitalist Class] will occupy a variety of interlocking positions, not only the interlocking directorates that have been the subject of detailed studies for some time in a variety of countries, but also connections outside the direct ambit of the corporate sector, the civil society as it were servicing the state-like structures of the corporations (. . .) globalizing bureaucrats, politicians and professionals, and consumerist elites bring state apparatuses and agencies and institutions of civil society in a variety of localities on board for the great global capitalist project.

This understanding of powerful and interlocking elites also illustrates Paul Brass's instrumentalist vision of elites as the force driving political life. Indeed, in *Ethnic Group and the State*, Paul Brass argues that cultural identity symbols are being selected by a State elite so that it can obtain concrete material profits. In any case, as Jean-François Bayart put it, 'les stratégies identitaires trahissent l'appetit d'élites nouvelles en mal d'intégration, de pouvoir, de richesse'[14] (identity stratégies betray the new appetite for integration, power and money). Much of the dialogue between the Indian State and the Indian diaspora can be understood in the light of these analyses.

One of the most potent examples of the role of various elites is certainly Madhu Goud Yaskhi, a Congress MP from Andhra Pradesh, who managed to obtain both power in his country of origin and money in his country of residence. Yaskhi was born in India but left for the United States for undergraduate studies in law. He went on to have a very successful legal practice in New Jersey. His two children are American citizens, while he has retained his Indian citizenship. A member of the Lok Sabha since May 2004, he still retained his NRI status for more than a year after his election, being thus one of the exceptional cases of an elected national representative not officially residing and paying taxes in his country. After his victory in the polls, he kept his business in America and devoted much time to it whether on the phone or through frequent visits. He views himself as 'an interface' between the government and the diaspora as 'nobody can understand better than me' and 'they (officials) give "weightage" to what I say since I am an NRI'.[15] During his first term he belongs to the Standing Committee on External & Indian Overseas Affairs, the Indian Council for World Affairs, the Indo–US Parliamentarian Forum, the Indo–Singapore Parliamentary Forum, and the American Indian Chamber of Commerce. He even personally contacted the Finance Minister about lowering taxation on NRI deposits. When invited to speak in corporate conferences or meetings, he introduces himself as an MP but his hosts prefer referring to him as an NRI, as they can probably relate easier to an expatriate capitalist than to an Indian official.[16] Madhu Goud Yaskhi personifies therefore the importance of interlinking elites in the State-diaspora relationship and in the domestic system uniting the State, the national and transnational civil society and the national private sector. This example is striking because Yaskhi belongs to several spheres simultaneously. But it is quite frequent that top Indian bureaucrats or MPs have close family members residing abroad as NRIs or foreign citizens. State actors and transnational actors can thus benefit from close contacts in a formal as well as informal manner within their own families. With a highly competitive private sector and a less prestigious civil service, sending a relative overseas can be construed as a rational strategy to maintain or even increase the social and financial status of the family. Since the 1970s, *pardes* had been constituting a new *debouché* for the national bourgeoisie. The current India-diaspora relationship heavily draws upon this continuing trend.

Moreover, the existing elite links are also fostered by frequent official meetings such as the three successive PBD. In 2003, at the first PBD, 1,330 out of 1,890 delegates, i.e. more than 70 per cent of the total number of participants, enlisted as members of an organization, be it a civil society association, a governmental body or a private company.[17] In 2004, this figure fell to 67 per cent and in 2005 to about 55.5 per cent. However, the private sector represented 82.2 per cent of the organization mentioned in the directory in 2005, compared to 68.3 and 68.9 per cent in 2003 and 2004 respectively. This can be explained by the overtly non ideological character of the last PBD, organized for the first time without the support network of the Sangh Parivar, previously mobilized for the first conference by the BJP government. Besides, after each PBD a decreasing number of members of many small civil society associations attend as they probably fail to see how they can benefit from such events. By contrast, more powerful and elitist groups, like the Indian–American lobby, Jewish American pressure groups, major multinationals and foreign governments, send a growing number of members to meet prominent Indian officials, in posts at the Union or at the State level, and even the top-brass of the Indian military. It is therefore not surprising that the Marathi newspaper *Sakal* labelled this conference as a 'VIP cha mela', a VIP fair.[18] The fact that the State and the private sector, namely Federation of Indian Chambers of Commerce and Industry (FICCI) and from 2006 onwards the Confederation of Indian Industries (CII) co-organized the PBD brings some additional light to the elite interactions at work in the system uniting the economic, state-based and transnational spheres.

The Emancipation of the Diaspora

It seems that the diaspora would now be irremediably linked to the Indian State after eight years of PBD, almost seven years after the creation of the Diaspora Division at FICCI and almost six years after the creation of the Ministry of Overseas Indian Affairs. However, although the Indian State was central in the advent of the diaspora, diasporic Indians seem to dispense themselves of the State structures. After its initial impulse the State is now viewed more as a hindrance and Yaskhi, in spite of being an Indian MP, went as far as saying in 2005 that 'the state is not doing anything. This PBD that started two years ago was asked by the NRIs'.[19] Similarly, Amita Sarkar, the head of the Diaspora Division at FICCI, minimizes the role of the State in organizing and especially funding the PBD. According to her,

> over the years the government will spend less because they have to justify it in public perception. And ultimately the event has to fend for itself, from delegates fees. Maybe not now but in a few years. Maybe through a special fee for businessmen who take many things from networking from the PBD. We do that in other programs. Paying for facilitation is possible.[20]

In addition to these impressions of State withdrawal, the last PBD witnessed another phenomenon on a large scale: delegates spent more time meeting each other than attending the talks, including the one given by the Finance Minister, for which they had paid up to US $200. The *Times of India*, picking on this new behaviour, published an article entitled 'Don't Mind, *Beta*, but Are You Married?' about the marriage market flourishing amongst NRIs and PIOs at the PBD. According to the newspaper, 'the marriage market is only one of the parallel businesses flourishing at the PBD. In some ways it's almost like being at the World Social Forum of NRIs. According to some it's a great place for networking and scouting for possible business collaborations'.[21] Finally, the reappropriation of this State-sponsored forum by the NRIs is confirmed by the simultaneous organization of independent conferences at the margin of the PBD. GOPIO had started this trend in 2003 by holding its annual convention the day before the PBD in Delhi. The fact that GOPIO has been organizing its annual conferences in major capitals all over the world for more than ten years should not detract from the fact that the PBD exerts a real attraction power for diasporic associations. For instance, in 2010 and since 2005, GOPIO and the NRI Welfare Society of India held their annual events a few days away from the PBD, while other organizations like the India International Friendship Society has sent all the PBD 2005 delegates invitations to attend its 'Global Friendship Day' the day before the inauguration of the next PBD in Hyderabad in January 2006.[22] Even though the MOIA's *Annual Report 2008-2009* further mentions that the actual PBD expenditure from the ministry (after deduction of the generated revenue) has decreased from Rs. 45,000,000 in 2005 to about Rs. 70,00,000 in 2009,[23] nine years after the creation of the High Level Committee on the Indian Diaspora, the diaspora finally seems to have come into its own.

CONCLUSION

India offers a striking example of a State building horizontal contacts among expatriates and 'ethnics' and fostering a new diasporic community. In order to tap the financial resources of their overseas populations, other countries as well have carved a space for these deterritorialized people in their own national political sphere. In India itself, Mexico, China and Israel are often quoted as models of State-diaspora collaborations. It seems therefore that the trend visible in India goes beyond the particular policy of a nationalist party and beyond the geographical and cultural specificity. The change of government in New Delhi in May 2004 and the return of the Congress party at the helm of affairs have not for instance derailed the pro-diaspora measures decided by the previous Hindu nationalist BJP party. And, dual citizenship has been defended by the Congress, in spite of being at odds with its Nehruvian territorially-bound notion of nationality. Actually, the Indian case-study points out to a wider cross-party and international tendency to redefine the nation ethnically and to revert to a *jus sanguini* vision of citizenship. In this context, the State and the diaspora are bound to become important actors at the national as well as the international level.

NOTES

1. P. Cohen, 'Rethinking the Diasporama', *Patterns of Prejudice*, vol. 33, no. 1, 1999, pp. 3-22, especially pp. 3 and 6.
2. L. Sklair, 'Transnational Practices and the Analysis of the Global System', Seminar delivered for the Transnational Communities Programme Seminar Series, 22 May 1998; Working Paper 98-04, www.transcomm.ox.ac.uk/working%20papers/sklair.pdf, pp. 1-14.
3. S. Khilnani, *The Idea of India*, New York: Farrar, Straus & Giroux, 1998 (1997), p. 263.
4. M.C. Lall, *India's Missed Opportunity: India's Relationship with Non-Resident Indians*, Aldershot: Ashgate, 2001.
5. See for example: G. Sheffer, *Diaspora Politics: At Home Abroad*, Cambridge: Cambridge University Press, 2003, p. 62. A.W. Helweg, 'The Indian Diaspora: Influence on International Relations', in Gabriel Sheffer (ed.), *Modern Diasporas in International Politics*, London: Croom Helm, 1986, pp. 103-29.
6. See N. Glazer and D.P. Moynihan, *Ethnicity*, Cambridge (Mass.): Harvard University Press, 1975. F. Barth, *Ethnic Groups and Boundaries: The Social Organization of Cultural Difference*, London: Allen & Unwin, 1969.
7. K. Adeney and M.C. Lall, 'Institutional Attemps to Build a "National" Identity in India: Internal and External Dimensions', *India Review*, vol. 4, no. 3, July 2005, pp. 1-29.
8. R. Sharam and E. Annamalai (eds.), *Indian Diaspora: In Search for Identity*, Mysore: Central Institute of Indian Languages, 2003.
9. L.M. Singhvi et al., *High Level Committee Report on the Indian Diaspora*, New Delhi, 8 January 2002, http://indiandiaspora.nic.in/contents.htm.
10. Arthur Helweg for instance quoted figures obtained from Indian consulates for the year 1970. Helweg, op. cit., p. 103.
11. Singhvi et al., op. cit., p. viii.
12. S. Dufoix, 'Notion, concept ou slogan: qu'y a-t-il sous le terme "diaspora" ?', Paper presented at the conference '2000 ans de diasporas', Poitiers, février 2002, p. 4.

13. T. Blom Hansen, 'Diasporic Dispositions', *Himal: South Asia*, Special issue on Indian diasporas, December 2002, vol. 15, no. 12, pp. 12-20 especially, p. 13.
14. J-F. Bayart, *L'illusion identitaire*, Paris: Fayard, 1996, p. 95.
15. Madhu Goud Yaskhi, interview with the author, New Delhi, 1 March 2005.
16. Ibid., 3 March 2005.
17. All the figures pertaining to the three PBD have been obtained thanks to a statistical study of the three delegates directories. A complete version of these directories, partially published and handed to the participants, has been obtained thanks to the Diaspora Division at FICCI.
18. 'VIP cha mela', *Sakal*, 8 January 2005, Mumbai, p. 1.
19. Madhu Goud Yaskhi, interview with the author, New Delhi, 1 March 2005.
20. Amita Sarkar, interview with the author, New Delhi, 2 February 2005.
21. 'Don't Mind, *Beta*, but Are You Married?', *Times of India*, 8 January 2005, Mumbai, p. 3.
22. Letter sent by Gurmeet Singh, Secretary General of India International Friendship Society, to the author, 11 August 2005.
23. Ministry of Overseas Indian Affairs, *Annual Report 2008-2009*, p. 69. http://moia.gov.in/services.aspx?mainid=17

REFERENCES

Adeney, K. and M.C. Lall, 'Institutional Attemps to Build a "National" Identity in India: Internal and External Dimensions', *India Review*, vol. 4, no. 3, July 2005, pp. 1-29.

Barth, F., *Ethnic Groups and Boundaries: The Social Organization of Cultural Difference*, London: Allen & Unwin, 1969.

Bayart, J.-F., *L'illusion identitaire*, Paris: Fayard, 1996.

Blom Hansen, T., 'Diasporic Dispositions', *Himal: South Asia*, Special issue on Indian diasporas, December 2002, vol. 15, no. 12, pp. 12-20.

Brass, P., *Ethnic Group and the State*, Londres: Croom Helm, 1985.

Cohen, P., 'Rethinking the Diasporama', *Patterns of Prejudice*, vol. 33, no. 1, 1999, pp. 3-22.

Cohen, R., 'Diasporas and the Nation-State: From Victims to Challengers', *International Affairs*, vol. 72, no. 3, July 1996, pp. 507-20.

Dufoix, S., 'Notion, concept ou slogan: qu'y a-t-il sous le terme "diaspora" ?', Paper presented at the Conference '2000 ans de diasporas', Poitiers, February 2002.

———, 'Genealogie d'un lieu commun, "Diaspora" et sciences sociales', *Actes de l'histore de l'immigration*, Paris, 2002, vol. 2. Disponible sur: http://barthes.ens.fr/clio/revues/AHI/articles/preprints/d-uf.html.

———, 'L'objet diaspora en question', Cultures et conflits, Paris, printemps-été, 1999, nos. 33-4, pp. 147-63.

———, 'Notion, concept ou slogan: qu'y a-t-il sous le terme "diaspora"?', in Lisa Anteby-Yemeni, William Berthomiere, Gabriel Scheffer (dir.), *Les diasporas. 2000 ans d'histoire*, Rennes: Presses Universitaires de Rennes, 2005, pp. 53-78.

———, *Les diasporas*, Paris: Presses Universitaires de France, 2003, collection 'Que sais-je?'.

Easton, David, *A Framework for Political Analysis*, Englewood Cliffs: Prentice Hall, 1965.

———, 'Categories for the System Analysis of Politics', in Bernard Susser (ed.), *Approaches to the Study of Politics*, New York: Macmillan, 1992, pp. 188-200.

Glazer, N., D.P. Moynihan, *Ethnicity: Theory and Experience*, Cambridge (Massachussetts): Harvard University Press, 1975.

Hall, S., 'Subjects in History: Making Diasporic Identities', in Wahneema Lubiano (dir), *The House that Race Built*, New York and Londres: Pantheon Books, 1997, pp. 289-99.

———, 'Introduction: who needs "identity"?', in Stuart Hall, Paul Gay (du) (dir.), *Questions of Cultural Identity*, Londres: Sage, 1996, pp. 1-17.

Hall, S., Paul Gay (du) (dir.), *Questions of Cultural Identity*, Londres: Sage, 1996.

Helweg, A.W., 'The Indian Diaspora: Influence on International Relations', in Gabriel Sheffer (ed.), *Modern Diasporas in International Politics*, London: Croom Helm, 1986, pp. 103-29.

Khilnani, S., *The Idea of India*, New York: Farrar, Straus & Giroux, 1998 (1997).

Lall, M.C., *India's Missed Opportunity: India's Relationship with Non-Resident Indians*, Aldershot: Ashgate, 2001.

Nye Jr., J.S. and R.O. Keohane, 'Transnational Relations and World Politics: An Introduction', *International Organization*, vol. 25, no. 3, 1971, pp. 329-49.

Prevelakis, G., 'Finis Greciae or the Return of the Greeks? State and Diaspora in the Context of Globalisation', Working Paper Transnational Communities Program 98-14, Centre for Migration, Policy and Society (COMPAS), Economic and Social Research Centre, University of Oxford, 12 November 1998, pp. 1-10.

Sharam, R. and E. Annamalai (eds.), *Indian Diaspora: In Search for Identity*, Mysore: Central Institute of Indian Languages, 2003.

Sheffer, G., *Diaspora Politics: At Home Abroad*, Cambridge: Cambridge University Press, 2003.

Singhvi, L.M. et al., High Level Committee Report on the Indian Diaspora, New Delhi: 8 January 2002, http://indiandiaspora.nic.in/contents.htm.

Sklair, L., 'Transnational Practices and the Analysis of the Global System', Seminar delivered for the Transnational Communities Programme Seminar Series, 22 May 1998, Working Paper 98-04, www.transcomm.ox.ac.uk/working%20papers/sklair.pdf, pp. 1-14.

4

Refugees or Diasporas?

The Indian Policy on Refugees: The Case of Delhi

JULIE BAUJARD

INTRODUCTION

The present paper[1] analyses the situation of three groups of refugees—Tibetans, Afghans and Burmese—living in Delhi, in the light of the Government of India's policies towards them. As a starting point, refugees will be considered as the 'diaspora' of their country of origin, with the term to be understood as defined by Sheffer:[2] 'Modern diasporas are minority ethnic groups that stem from migration and who live and act in their host countries while maintaining strong affective and material links with their countries of origin, their homelands.'

There are three parts to this definition. If we examine the first one, whilst considering refugees from a juridical perspective they are migrants who cross borders and approach a foreign State in search of a legal status. They constitute minority groups in the host society. Depending on the reason that have motivated their migration and on their situation in the host country, they will define themselves in terms of nationality, ethnicity, or religion, putting forward one of these dimensions. The third part of Sheffer's definition deals with ties to the country of origin. Refugees are deprived of their homeland and of the protection of the State they belong to (a situation that enables them to obtain a refugee status), but most of them are nevertheless still driven by strong links with their homeland.

In this context, affective bonds are particularly strong, and are often accompanied by material bonds as well.

However, this paper intends to explore the second point of Sheffer's definition (the matter of living in India) focusing on two key aspects—resident status, and access to the labour market—of the integration into the host country for it is a characteristic of a diaspora.[3]

After a brief overview of India's position regarding the international refugee system and the refugees living on its territory (section 1), this paper will look at the different policies the Indian government has implemented for Tibetans on one side (section 2), and Afghans and Burmese on the other side (section 3) for two different approaches that were defined. Lastly, the analysis will focus on the response given by the refugees themselves to their living conditions in New Delhi, more specifically through the various networks they have created (section 4). It will then allow us to determine the relevance of the term 'diaspora' with regard to the Tibetan, Afghan and Burmese refugees living in Delhi.

1. INDIA AND THE INTERNATIONAL REFUGEE REGIME

India and the Refugee Status

India did not sign the 1951 Geneva Convention nor the 1967 New York Protocol on the status of refugees. Two main reasons can explain this choice. The first stems from the very origin of the refugee status. Two questions were central to the preliminary discussions of the international community to define this status: the first one was linked to the spatial and temporal limitations that northern countries wanted to introduce in the definition of 'refugee'. The other concerned the need to differentiate (or not) between the legal protection and the material assistance.

Debates took place while India and Pakistan were facing tremendous population displacements: a total of 14 million people crossed the border created by Partition which gave birth to the two countries. Given the scale of the crisis and pretending that refugees from both side could benefit from the protection of a State, the international community, personified by the International Refugee Organization (IRO) which preceded United Nations High Commissioner for Refugees (UNHCR), refused to provide assistance. The financial burden the two countries had to deal with made their contribution to IRO impossible. Moreover, they both felt it very unfair as they would not get anything in return. In 1949, India abstained from voting at the General Assembly's resolution, which gave birth to UNHCR.

The second reason for India for not signing the international texts on the status of refugees stems from its involvement in the Non-aligned movement, of which it was one of the instigators. In 1951, India declared it did not want to jeopardize its non-aligned stand by associating with the international refugee regime.

India and UNHCR

Being very critical towards the UNHCR, protesting against the absence of international recognition of its efforts following the Partition and facing the arrival of Tibetans, India decided to boycott the first World Refugee Year in 1959. Initially opposed to international assistance in the Tibetan case, the Government of India (GoI) eventually allowed the UN implication and an office of the UNHCR was officially opened in Delhi in 1969.

In 1971, when the civil war broke out in what would become Bangladesh, the UNHCR was in the foreground assisting India to host the flow of refugees. After 1972, the UNHCR especially focused on resettlement programmes for Tibetans. Yet China's entry at the UN in 1971 will question the agency's involvement: in 1972, China asked the UNHCR to stop 'the illegal activities on the question of so-called "Tibetan refugees"'.[4] In 1975, the UNHCR unilaterally withdrew its operations from India, justifying its departure by a need to redeploy its resources to Africa while the urgency of the Tibetan situation in India had lessened. The GoI saw a political motivation in this decision while UNHCR's mandate was supposed to be non-political.

Unsurprisingly, when, in 1979, UNHCR asked India to reopen its office in Delhi to assist Afghan asylum-seekers, India didn't allow it. Yet, it agreed that UNHCR representative worked as the UNHCR component of the United Nations Development Programme (UNDP) in Delhi. In 1981, the UNHCR was allowed to reopen its office in the capital city after a significant number of Iranian and Afghan refugees had arrived, but still under the supervision of UNDP. Since then it has had no direct or indirect access to the Tibetans.

Thus, since 1981, the UNHCR's activities are allowed by the GoI who refuses to formalize the agency status in the country. The Indian stand can be qualified as ambiguous as it considers the UNHCR as being an integral part of the refugee issue but looks at its action with high scepticism,[5] shapes and limits it.

In the capital city, the UNHCR is responsible for the recognition and the protection of two main groups: the Afghans and the Burmese. They are qualified by the UN as 'urban refugees': individuals and small groups of asylum-seekers who are drawn to the urban centres of host countries in the South.

India and the Refugees

India is neither a party to the international legal framework nor has it enacted a domestic law on refugees. Governed by the Foreigners Act, 1946, refugees are considered as 'foreigners' and defined as 'a person who is not a citizen of India' [Foreigners Act, 1946, Section 2(a)]. The absence of a formal law which would have uniformized the policy on refugees enables India to deal with the refugee populations on a one-to-one basis. Rejecting the internationalization of the refugees management, India unilaterally or bilaterally hosts the massive influx coming from neighbouring States, considering them as part of its sphere of strategic interests and foreign policy while it leaves to UNHCR's protection more marginal movements, non-South Asian, giving to this word a geopolitical meaning.[6]

Oberoi[7] underlines that State interests, rather than to be '"given" to the state by the material structure of the international system', are constructed by the State itself which gives importance and meaning to certain goals, depending on a specific historical period. Added to this, the eventual ethnic, cultural, linguistic and/or religious closeness leads India to treat certain population with more or less sympathy.[8] While hosting a refugee population, India decides what does this host mean for the country in terms of 'security', 'national interest' or 'identity'.

One essential right for refugees is to receive juridical protection that defaults to them in their country. Then, arises the question of their subsistence in the host country. In India, refugees are not allowed to work with the residential permit that they possess. Furthermore, there is no social welfare system. Access to work, health, education and housing will depend on the specific agreements between India and the population or the UNHCR. The measures the guardian institution (the Central Tibetan Administration (CTA) or UNHCR) will take for the refugees will be decisive. We shall now examine the situation for each group.

2. A VOLUNTARISM IN FAVOUR OF TIBETANS

A Tight Collaboration between the GoI and the CTA

Nehru's favourable position towards the Tibetans can be interpreted as a compensation to his political incapacity to support the Tibetan cause at an international level, the expression of his great sympathy for the Dalai Lama and his attraction to Buddhism.[9] A favourable national feeling for the Tibetans, reinforced by the 1962 defeat against China, strengthens this position. Roy[10] adds another element: 'India has been accommodative to the Tibetan refugees all along primarily because of its anti-China stand and also because of politicization of Tibet issue at the world level by the West.'

As a result, the GoI and the Dalai Lama's administration, the CTA developed a common management of the Tibetan community. Particularly, the creation of the settlements has enabled two—complementary—visions to co-exist: Nehru's one to isolate Tibetans and entrust them the exploitation of remote rural areas and the Dalai Lama's one, concerned about keeping its people united to preserve its cultural and religious particularism.

The establishment of a Tibetan education system constitutes the other milestone of the setting up of Tibetans in India. It is jointly administered: the Central Tibetan Schools Administration—which counts 28 of the 80 Tibetan schools—is led and funded by the Indian Ministry of Human Resource Development.

The legal situation of Tibetans in India, defined by the possession of a temporary residential permit, depends on their date of arrival. The Tibetans who arrived during the initial period (before the end of 1979) were issued residential permits (Foreigners Registration Certificates, RC hereafter). Since then, and till 2003, arrivals were not issued permits. The office of the Dalai Lama was regularly providing a list of the new arrivals to the Ministry of Home Affairs. In 2003, the Tibetan Refugee Welfare Office of Kathmandu negotiated with the Indian Embassy in Nepal the issue of a visa called 'Special Entry Permit'. This new development is enabling the legal entry of Tibetans into India and is changing the patterns of the migration into one of neighbouring migration, like for the Nepalese.

The access to the labour market is noteworthy, though non-formalized, except for the case of Tibetans who arrived before 1962, who could enroll in a section of the Indian army: the Establishment 22 or the Special Frontier Force. One needs to notice that the Tibetan labour network is largely community-based: Tibetans work in the settlements, for the CTA or run their own businesses, organized at a community level. In Delhi, where there is no settlement, Tibetans are self-employed people, the youths working in call centres, five star hotels or restaurants or are college and university students. According to the CTA, there are around 5,000 Tibetan refugees in Delhi.

All the above arrangements are testimony to a long-term vision: such structures assume a non-immediate return. They have drawn Tibetans to firmly anchor their network into the local landscape, becoming a part of the Indian society. Yet we shall talk about a *de facto* but not by rights recognition.

A *DE FACTO* BUT NOT BY RIGHTS RECOGNITION

India allowed the CTA to establish in Dharamsala, where the Dalai Lama settled down. This has not lead the GoI to recognize Tibet, which is officially considered by New Delhi as an integral part of China. Here again we can see the ambiguous Indian position which, at the same time, does not allow any refugee to engage in political activities and tacitly tolerates the Tibetan refugee campaign to free their country from Chinese domination, made of demonstrations and spectacular actions (like burning the Chinese flag in front of the Chinese Embassy in Delhi or climbing up buildings where Chinese diplomats are invited and raise the Tibetan flag under their very eyes).

The lack of RC for those who arrived between 1980 and 2003 has two main consequences: in case of an identity control, the person is jailed, but soon released by the intervention of the CTA; s/he cannot apply for an Identity Certificate (IC), the travel document issued by the GoI, the equivalent of a passport. The reasons behind this suspension remaining blurred, one can only express hypothesis. Keeping Tibetans in a precarious status is a way of maintaining them within their group, which protects them. It is also a means to heavily encourage Tibetans to eventually go back, after having seen the Dalai Lama, family, or having done their studies. This is the message the CTA conveys to the refugees, trying to limit the Tibetan exodus. Indeed, the latter, which has been uninterrupted since the 're-opening' of the border in the early 1980s, participates in Tibet's depopulation and 'promotes' the Chinese project of colonization. Moreover, it further increases the weight of this community for which the CTA must bear responsibility. Furthermore, one can believe that the absence of RC, so of IC, is a means for the CTA of not prompting the departure to the West, as there are more and more candidates for expatriation.

The GoI and the CTA jointly administer the Tibetan community in India. All the measures India has taken for the life of Tibetans in India demonstrates its will to take on the role of the country of adoption of the Tibetans. Yet, they remain 'second class citizens.' The assimilation to India, signified by naturalization (for which both governments came to the agreement that Tibetans in India shall not acquire Indian citizenship), by a life outside the settlements or by professional choices going beyond the frame designed by the CTA, is considered a threat to Tibetan identity and is thus opposed.

The situation of the two other groups of refugees is radically different. India's position towards them is far less committed. In this context, UNHCR holds a central place.

3. A *LAISSEZ-FAIRE* TOWARDS AFGHANS AND BURMESE

A Certain Tolerance for the Afghans

Following the Soviet invasion and the conflict that arose between the Russian forces and the Mujahiddin in 1979, the Afghan refugee phenomenon started. Millions[11] of Afghans took refuge in Pakistan and Iran. Some of them, mostly belonging to the middle and upper classes, came directly to Delhi. They had valid travel documents. They stayed in India temporarily on their way to countries of asylum in the West.[12] Those who could not reach these countries stayed in India and asked UNHCR for protection. With India's agreement, UNHCR accorded refugee status to all of those who entered legally. By January 1991, there were 20,000 Afghan refugees in the capital city. In 1993, due to a massive arrival of Hindu and Sikh Afghans, their number reached 25,000. From this time onwards it regularly decreased. In 2006, there were a bit less than 10,000 people registered under the UNHCR, out of whom more than 80 per cent were Hindus and Sikhs.

They got temporary residential permits provided that they possessed a refugee certificate. These residential permits (RP) were temporarily suspended by the GoI, which thus expressed its opposition to the Afghan regime. It happened during the Taliban rule, which was supporting Kashmiri separatists and which had allowed a plane from Indian Airlines, hijacked by Islamist terrorists (1999), to land in Kandahar. In this process, Afghans, a part of whom had fled this regime, were twice penalized. Furthermore, India can refuse the recognition of the refugee status for any given person, reminding UNHCR that it needs its agreement to grant someone refugee status in Indian territory. A circular of the GoI dating back to September 2001 decrees that Muslim Afghans arriving after this date will not get RP anymore. Sikh and Hindu Afghans are not affected by this measure. UNHCR says it has entered into talks with the GoI to negotiate the issue of RP case by case. The discretionary power of the GoI is thus firmly underlined.

Afghans receive different treatment according to their religion. India appears to be the 'natural home of Hindu and Sikh Afghans'[13] while the Muslim Afghans' integration is problematic. But isn't India secular country? Dhavan[14] qualifies this as 'covert communal policies towards particular classes of refugees [that] precipitate hostile discrimination on grounds of religion.' We will see that UNHCR too differentiates between the two. Let us first present the Burmese case.

Camps for the Burmese

The contemporary historical closeness of India and Burma should be underlined to understand the favourable welcome India reserved for the pro-democracy activists who crossed the Indo–Burma border in 1988, after the military coup. The two countries had experienced colonial domination under the British Rule (1858-1947). During this time Indian migrants came to Burma to settle down, but they had to leave; mainly *en masse* in 1964. A few years before, India and Burma were two of the founding members of the Non-Aligned movement. In 1981 India granted asylum to the former prime minister of Burma, U Nu, and his family.

Thus when the Burmese exodus started, India assumed its present position of the 'largest democracy of the world' and took an active but cautious pro-democracy stand on Burma; giving asylum to the few thousands that were reaching the north-east states. The GoI accepted these refugees at camps in Manipur and Mizoram. According to Chakraborty,[15] the Indian authorities provided assistance to the Burmese seeking refuge for political reasons from a humanitarian point of view but they prevent them mixing with political elements on their soil. Some political activists soon reached Delhi to get a recognition of their status by the UNHCR, which recognized the first Burmese refugees in 1990. In 2006, less than 2,000 Burmese refugees were registered in Delhi by the UNHCR, while, according to Indian human rights activists and NGOs, between 30,000 and 50,000 Burmese forced migrants are living in the north-east region.

The GoI did not make any other arrangements for the Burmese except granting them residential permits, in 1999 only, after negotiations with exiled Burmese members of parliament; some of them living in Delhi. Moreover, the preliminary stand India took towards the pro-democratic movement changed.[16] The will to promote economic exchanges and counter the north-east insurrections (as well as China's influence in Burma) has lead the GoI to foster its relations with the Burmese military government.

The Afghan and Burmese refugee's stay in India depends on the goodwill of the host government and is linked with geopolitical relations. It is thus highly precarious. The few arrangements the GoI made for these two populations are more a *laissez-faire* than a real policy in favour of refugees, as the country has for the Tibetans. We shall now tackle the second aspect of the Afghan and Burmese refugee's stay; the issue of their subsistence. The UNHCR being their representative in this juridical vacuum, we shall now explore what the UN agency's policy is.

UNHCR's Policy

According to UNHCR's guidelines, three durable solutions are recommended to solve the refugee problem. The first solution is the 'voluntary return to the country of origin': a reintegration to their nation of birth, which implies the cessation of their refugee status. In this case, only a tiny proportion of Afghans have gone back (1 per cent a year since 2002 according to UNHCR[17]).

The second option, where the host society offers this possibility is 'the integration to the host country'. Refugees enter a juridical process which consist of granting them rights which are more and more similar to the nationals' ones. With time, this process would lead the person to a permanent resident's status and sometimes national citizenship, which is at the discretion of the State. In this process of getting equivalent rights with Indians, two rights appear essential: the right of residence, that we have talked about, and the right to work. Yet, refugees are not allowed to work.

Until 2006 getting the refugee status used to automatically give rights to a six months living allowance, which was then reviewed (and usually renewed). Along with the allowance the agency provided refugees with trainings to help them becoming self-sufficient. For those who have been identified as *Extremely Vulnerable Individuals*, the allowance is maintained. Even if 90 per cent of the workers are employed in the unorganized sector,[18] Delhi is characterized by a highly competitive labour market. To be deprived of a specific protection increases the refugee's dependence on the UNHCR.

The UNHCR does not remain inactive though: health and primary education fees are reimbursed, to a certain extent, up to Indian standards. The institution offers language and computer courses, some vocational training and a placement service has been set up to help refugees find a job. The aim is to reduce the dependence of refugees who do not manage to find their way in Indian society.

Achieving better integration into the local society would take the path of naturalization. Officially, anybody who can prove twelve years of legal residence on Indian territory is entitled to Indian nationality (the person needs a RP as the refugee certificate is not considered as a proof). In fact, only Sikh and Hindu Afghans are given this status. At the end of 2004,[19] 2,744 persons had expressed their interest to start the process but in 2006, 14 refugees gained citizenship; so it is not a major phenomenon yet. But even for those priviledged populations who are the Hindu and Sikh Afghans, one can question the Indian will to see them becoming naturalized citizens if we consider the fee increase: from Rs. 2,000 until 2005 to Rs. 15,000 today.

When the first two solutions are not possible (when the refugee represent a 'protection case' for the UNHCR), the agency proposes a 'resettlement in a third country' (Western countries, especially USA and Canada). It is the continuation of the migration, with an access to the nationality of the resettlement country. Muslim Afghans (whose access to Indian citizenship has not been opened by the GoI) and Burmese refugees (for whom the issue will arise in 2011) are the two populations who can benefit from a resettlement. Proportionally given the size of the groups, a large number of Burmese and Muslim Afghans have been resettled. This has generated a strong hope in these communities for whom resettlement appears to have become the main objective.

By the programmes' orientation one can read the ideology of the UNHCR and its conception of the nation state, taking into account the limitations India imposes on the treatment of refugees. The three proposed options attest the idea of a State based on a common culture, a shared religion, a mutual language. Refugees have to deal with the paradox that stems from the confrontation of ideas of permanent integration to the host society and the temporary state of the refugee. It is particularly felt in India, which keeps them in a precarious condition, and apparently more easily solved in third countries as refugees acquire their host country's citizenship. India appears to these two groups as a transit place, a stop on the migration path.

THE REFUGEES' RESPONSE

New Challenges for the Central Tibetan Administration

One cannot limit oneself to the description of the Indian response to apprehend the Tibetan living conditions in exile. Western political and financial support to the Tibetan cause is essential too: it enables Tibetans arriving in India to benefit from the protection of an administration similar to the one of a Welfare state (which India is far from being). Though the Tibetan state is not formally recognized, it is a very concrete reality for the Tibetans: studies are sponsored for all worthy students, needy families can get social and medical aids, some retirement homes have been opened, subsidies exist to help setting up one's own business.

This Western financial support is widely due to the action of the Dalai Lama who has succeeded in drawing international attention to Tibet's plight by establishing cultural and religious ties with the West. This had led to the constitution of a transnational network of activists, NGOs, political parties and groups of parliamentarians supporting the cause, mainly from America, Europe and India itself. One of the main focus of this international network is to defend the Tibetan interests perceived as threatened by the recent strategic rapprochement between India and China. It provides the Tibetan refugees a window to lobby foreign States, international organizations and consequently to strengthen their political weight and improve their situation in India.

Yet, the model of integration the CTA and India proposes to refugees, which could be qualified as 'integration without assimilation,' is highly challenged by the new generations. They denounce the limitations they are facing with regard to the access to the formal sector jobs and to the Indian citizenship, as most of them do not want to remain in the settlements. The jobs the CTA can offer them, though highly valued in term of service for the community, do not represent a real solution considering the number of candidates.

Furthermore, resettlement programmes have been particularly developed since the 1990s. Western nations, starting with the USA, have been delivering annual scholarships and skilled and non-skilled work permits to Tibetans. Many can then remain in their new host country. On the long-run, these programmes contribute to the group scattering and to the constitution of a larger migratory space within which men and women easily move, as do money and ideas. Remittances sent by the Tibetan expats to their families in India, rapid access to national citizenship act as magnets for the educated youth yearning for white collar jobs. These new challenges will have to be addressed by the CTA.

Waiting for Resettlement: Burmese and Muslim Afghans

According to the Burmese, reaching self-sufficiency is unrealistic in India since the government does not grant them work permit. In the informal sector, their unstable status, their small number, but also their religious, cultural and linguistic differences contribute to marginalize them. As they cannot go back for political reasons, UNHCR must give them a subsistence allowance or guarantee them a resettlement in a third country. Thinking that pursuing integration into the Indian society would ruin their chance to resettle—as UNHCR will first recommend people whose life in India is problematic—they firmly resist to UNHCR's initiatives to lead them to self-sufficiency. It is worth mentioning that they were receiving till recently a monthly allowance from the UNHCR. This has been phased out for most of the group since 2005.

As a consequence, they haven't sought to extend their networks in India, with the exception of the political sphere through human rights activists, political parties and MPs (like the Tibetans). It brings thus the Burmese refugees some sort of political legitimacy, but cannot influence the domestic situation in their home country. Far from being successful too in its Burma policy, the Western political and financial support provides nonetheless the Burmese refugees with a much needed assistance. Despite not benefiting from the same support than the Tibetans, they receive some subsidy to finance their political activities and social projects. But all these initiatives are limited in terms of the people concerned and duration.

To reach Western countries, a largely shared objective among Burmese in Delhi, different options exist. Apart from resettlement through scholarships or under humanitarian programmes led by developed countries, Burmese Christian refugees are offered other opportunities through the support of Churches which act as sponsors. We shall mention here that around 90 per cent of the Burmese refugees group in Delhi consist of ethnic Chin[20] who are Christians. The Western Protestant network appears quite strong in supporting refugees' claim for resettlement, especially in North America. The resettlement programme the United Pentecostal Church managed to open, dealing directly with the Canadian government, is an illustration of its power: 200 persons (which represented 20 per cent of the group) left for Canada in 2002-3. The Burmese expats, who have resettled in the West and who are called by the refugees in Delhi the *diaspora*, are largely Christian.[21] Along with Christian human rights NGOs, the Churches and the Burmese diaspora constitute a transnational actor whose agenda is the resettlement of Burmese refugees in prosperous and Christian lands.

On their side, as far as access to the Indian job market is concerned, local language knowledge or children's schooling, Muslim Afghans are better established in their new territory than the Burmese. This is notably due to the Muslim network (Delhi has a sizeable Muslim Indian minority). Besides, as UNHCR stopped the monthly allowance to the major part of the group around 1994, and as they do not receive any foreign financial assistance, Afghans had thus to find other ways to earn their living. Nevertheless, they too benefit from resettlement programmes: several thousands of Muslim Afghan refugees have migrated to the West (around the half of the group) in the past years. Obviously, the ones who are still in India are waiting for their turn.

But unlike the Burmese, they do not have vocal and organized networks which could advocate for them at a collective level. They have had to develop individual strategies to increase their chances to migrate: through family members who are already resettled and can act as sponsors, through matrimonial strategies, and also sometimes through conversion to Christianity.

A Lonely Way to Become Citizens: Hindu and Sikh Afghans

Called by UNHCR 'Indian Origin Afghans,' Sikh and Hindu Afghans' history is actually linked to India. These Indian migrants shifted to Afghanistan in different waves, the latest having been caused by the British colonial operations in the nineteenth century along the North-West Frontier Province and by the Partition of 1947. These latest Afghan migrants share the fate of the many other refugees who arrived in Delhi in 1947. This common destiny and the shared religions with Indians helped them enter local networks which then could afford them a better integration into the local society. As a consequence, they have an undeniable access to work.

It should be observed that if they benefit from Punjabi networks, by the Sikh and Hindu networks, they have around them some 10,000 Sikh and Hindu Afghans established in the city, who are not (or no more) refugees. Relationships of solidarity have been built between these Afghan Indians and what they consider as the weakest section of their community, the refugees.

Eventually, the UNHCR's programmes—targeting assimilation to the Indian society—do not project them into this transnational world. Their only option, apart from going back, is to become Indian citizens, at a high cost.

CONCLUSION

We have seen that the decision to host certain refugees and accept responsibility for them, as opposed to delegating these responsibilities to the UNHCR, is dependent on geopolitical bilateral relations and on the way India defines its national security, interests and identity. Yet, the GoI does not grant any formal status to anyone, keeping thus a foreign-policy tool. The GoI, the CTA and UNHCR can be seen as central powers, controlling people, defining and standardizing identities. For each distinct category of refugees, a different system is put in place, and it affects in different ways the decision whether to stay in the country or to prolong the migratory adventure by moving on. Thus, for Tibetans, the framework proposed makes India their nation in exile, whereas for Burmese and Afghan refugees it is a country of transit. Refugees are not passive actors in this process. To meet their needs, they mobilize networks, both within the country and across borders.

It is important to emphasize the very paradoxical situation of the Tibetan refugees who, although they are living in exile, benefit nonetheless from the protection of their government. Based on Dufoix's[22] (2003) structural models for the collective experience in exile, Tibetans function, as refugees, in an 'antagonistic mode', making manifest their opposition to the government of the country they come from; in effect, the Tibetan government can be characterized as diasporic. Nonetheless, in this very unusual case, one is tempted to view the Tibetan 'State' in India as the point of reference, to consider the Tibetans living in India as the population of origin, and to view the Tibetans living elsewhere as the diaspora, thus functioning on a 'centro-peripheral mode'.[23] Within this perspective, Tibet exists as an idealized and mythical land.

Tibetans and Burmese refugees follow diasporic rationales. They are scattered in several countries but unified by the existence of trans-nation movements of people, ideas and money. They use transnational networks to put pressure on given countries and the UN. The ties with the country of origin are more affective than material, and highly political. But as far as the concept of diaspora is concerned, one major difference has to be underlined. The economic situation of the Burmese prevents us from considering them, as opposed to the Tibetans, to be a diaspora. In fact, the Burmese in Delhi use the term 'diaspora' to describe those who have succeeded in reaching the West, thus implying a degree of material well-being, while 'refugee' suggests living conditions that are precarious. For refugees under UN mandate in India, to whom integration into the host society is not really a possibility; it is the process of resettlement that allows the creation of a diaspora.

The situation of Muslim Afghans is too unstable for them to be characterized as a diaspora, whereas Hindus and Sikhs can be viewed in this way (especially those holding Indian citizenship). For the Burmese and the Tibetans, diaspora refers to those who enjoy a measure of financial security (notably those living abroad). The transition from refugee to diaspora appears to be dependent on economic factors and to imply a change in status from one that was previously temporary and marginal.

We have seen in this analysis that, like 'diaspora', the term 'refugee' is used to describe very different situations. It is a powerful indication of an individual's identity. It suggests the story of a people and their involvement in the struggle for their homeland; and it allows them as well access to a welfare system. The term diaspora, on the other hand, evokes primarily strong ties to one's country of origin. It must be noted nonetheless, as Dufoix has said, that neither of these concepts serves to describe actual phenomena. They are scientifically useful in that they give visibility to researchers working in these fields, and politically meaningful for those who define themselves in terms of these categories, but remain weak from a theoretical standpoint.[24]

NOTES

1. It is based upon fieldwork conducted in Delhi from 2001 to 2006 which consisted of a 3-months internship at New Delhi's UNHCR Office (2001), followed by regular field trips among the refugee communities in Delhi.
2. Gabriel Sheffer, *Modern Diasporas in International Politics*, London: Croom Helm, 1986, p. 3.

3. Alain Tarrius, *Arabes de France dans l'économie souterraine mondiale*, La Tour d'Aigues: Éditions de l'Aube, 1996, pp. 71-96.
4. Pia Oberoi, *Exile and Belonging: Refugees and State Policy in South Asia*, New Delhi: Oxford University Press, 2006, p. 30.
5. Rajeev Dhavan, *Refugee Law and Policy in India*, New Delhi: PILSARC, 2004.
6. Sarbani Sen, 'Paradoxes of the International Regime of Care: The Role of the UNHCR in India', in Ranabir Samaddar (ed.), *Refugees and the State: Practises of Asylum and Care in India, 1947-2000*, New Delhi, Thousand Oaks and London: Sage, 2003, pp. 396-442.
7. Oberoi, op. cit., p. 3.
8. Dhavan, op. cit.
9. Dawa Norbu, 'The Settlements: Participation and Integration', in Dagmar Bernstorff and Hubertus von Welck (eds), *Exile as Challenge: The Tibetan Diaspora*, New Delhi: Orient Longman, [2003] 2004, p. 192.
10. Sanjay K. Roy, 'Refugees and Human Rights: The Case of Refugees in Eastern and North-Eastern States of India', in Sanjay K. Roy (ed.), *Refugees and Human Rights*, New Delhi: Rawat, 2001, p. 29.
11. Between 1979 and 1992, over six million people left Afghanistan.
12. Manik Chakraborty, *Human Rights and Refugees: Problems, Laws and Practises*, New Delhi: Deep and Deep, 2001.
13. Dhavan, op. cit., p. 7.
14. Ibid.
15. Chakraborty, op. cit.
16. Renaud Egreteau, *Wooing the Generals: India's New Policy on Burma*, New Delhi: Authors Press, 2003, pp. 121-49.
17. *UNHCR India*, 2006.
18. Ashish K. Ghose, 'The Employment Challenge in India', *Economic and Political Weekly*, 27, 2004, p. 5109.
19. UNHCR's figures.
20. Belonging to the Tibeto-Burman ethnolinguistic group, the Chin are one of Burma's minorities. They live in the Chin state, bordering India and Bangladesh.
21. Indeed, there is a over-representation of the members of the minority ethnic groups of Burma among whom many are Christian.
22. Stéphane Dufoix, *Les diasporas*, Paris: PUF, Que sais-je ?, 2003, pp. 72-3.

23. Ibid.
24. Ibid., p. 122.

REFERENCES

Baujard, J., 'La politique du HCR à Delhi (Inde). Mise en oeuvre et évolution,' *Autrepart* (51), 2009, pp. 3-18.

Bernstorff, D. and H. von Welck (eds.), *Exile as Challenge: The Tibetan Diaspora*, New Delhi: Orient Longman, 2004.

Chakraborty, M., *Human Rights and Refugees: Problems, Laws and Practises*, New Delhi: Deep and Deep, 2001.

Chatelard, G., 'Incentives to Transit: Policy Responses to Influxes of Iraqi Forced Migrants in Jordan,' *EUI Working Papers*, RSC 2002/50, 2002, http://www.eui.eu/RSCAS/WP-Texts/06 25.pdf, 29 June 2009.

Danis, D.A., 'Waiting on the Purgatory, Religious Networks of Iraqi Christian Transit Migrants in Istanbul,' *EUI Working Papers*, RSCAS 2006/25, 2006, http://www.eui.eu/RSCAS/WP-Texts/06 25.pdf, 2 July 2009.

Dhavan, R., *Refugee Law and Policy in India*, New Delhi: PILSARC, 2004.

Dufoix, S., *Les Diasporas*, Paris: PUF, Que sais-je ?, 2003.

Egreteau, R., *Wooing the Generals: India's New Burma Policy*, New Delhi: Authors Press/CSH, 2003.

Ghose, A.K., 'The Employment Challenge in India,' *Economic and Political Weekly*, 27, 2004, pp. 5106-16.

Norbu, D., 'The Settlements: Participation and Integration,' in Dagmar Bernstorff and Hubertus von Welck (eds.), *Exile as Challenge: The Tibetan Diaspora*, New Delhi: Orient Longman, 2004, pp. 186-212.

Oberoi, P., *Exile and Belonging: Refugees and State Policy in South Asia*, New Delhi: Oxford University Press, 2006.

Roy, S.K., 'Refugees and Human Rights: The Case of Refugees in Eastern and North-Eastern States of India,' in Sanjay K. Roy (ed.), *Refugees and Human Rights*, New Delhi: Rawat, 2001, pp. 17-60.

Samaddar, R. (ed.), *Refugees and the State: Practises of Asylum and Care in India, 1947-2000*, New Delhi: Thousand Oaks and London: Sage, 2003.

Sen, S., 'Paradoxes of the International Regime of Care: The Role of the UNHCR in India,' in Ranabir Samaddar (ed.), *Refugees and the*

State: Practises of Asylum and Care in India, 1947-2000, New Delhi, Thousand Oaks and London: Sage, 2003, pp. 396-442.

Sheffer, G., *Modern Diasporas in International Politics*, London: Croom Helm, 1986.

Tarrius, A., *Arabes de France dans l'économie souterraine mondiale*, La Tour d'Aigues: Éditions de l'Aube, 1996, pp. 71-96.

5

Reducing the Asymmetrical Labour Relationship in a New Global Order

Prospects for India and Its Diaspora

ERIC LECLERC

The idea of this paper came to my mind while reading Neelakhanda Aiyer's book *Indian Problems in Malaya*.[1] The portrayal of the plantation workers that you find in his book, seem so well fitted for the actual situation of Indian IT professionals in Malaysia, that immediately the question of the changes in the condition of Indian workers since the beginning of the twentieth century arises. Engaged in a research about the latest Indian workers circulating all over the world, the so-called 'Knowledge Workers', I want to draw a parallel between them and the indentured labourers, but from an international relations perspective. I will try to address the issue of workers' migration and its role in affecting relations between India and the receiving countries. Is the asymmetrical labour relationship between India and the receiving countries which started during the colonial period over? Is the new diaspora able to redress the balance, and what is the role of the Indian government in this process?

In the first section, labour migrations will be considered as an issue affecting India's international relations in an historical perspective. We will notice the construction of an asymmetrical relationship and its effects on Indian diplomacy. The examples used in the second section—the Polaris case in Indonesia and the Palm court incident in Malaysia—will raise the question of a new Indian policy towards its diaspora and its effects on its relations with the receiving countries. The third section will highlight the emergence of new actors in the international labour relationship and their effects on the nation state.

1. THE EFFECTS OF ASYMMETRICAL LABOUR RELATIONSHIP ON THE INDIAN DIPLOMACY

India has inherited the asymmetrical labour relationship from the slavery system, which was replaced by the indentured labour system in the second half of the nineteenth century. Even if it was built on a contract basis, it was rightly labelled a 'new system' of slavery by Hugh Tinker.[2]

The Role of Indian Overseas Workers in the Incipient International Relation of India

During this period, the role of the Indian government was caught between the legacies of the colonial power and the advents of the freedom movement. In Malaya, as the Indian labourers were hired in British-owned estates, there was no trade unions, and the wages and living conditions were determined by the manager. An agent of the Government of India, was part of the negotiation process to fix the wages with employer' organizations (United Planters' Association of Malaya) and the Labour Department of the Malayan government.[3] The low wages and the deplorable living conditions in the plantations were a testimony of the very limited bargaining power left in the hand of the Indian government's representative. Even the agent of the Indian government sometimes used to act as an auxiliary of the British power, for example when Indian troops were used in Klang, the port of Kuala Lumpur, in 1941 to put down a strike of 8,000 Indian workers against rising prices.

Such asymmetrical relations got closely linked with the agenda of ongoing freedom struggle. The links between this migrant population and the fight for independence were strong, since the principal figure in the history of this movement, Mahatma Gandhi, voluntarily migrated to South Africa, and initiated its political struggle there. The bad transport and inhuman working conditions of these migrant workers nurtured the denunciation of the imperial system. Racial discrimination against Indians continued unabated throughout this period [the Devonshire Declaration[4] (1923) in East Africa and the Pegging Act[5] (1943) in South Africa], and kept the Indians in a lower social and political position. The Indian National Congress tried to defend the interests of these immigrants in international forums without much success, and reached the conclusion in 1923 that 'unless India became independent, the grievances of the Indian Diaspora could not be properly remedied.'[6] Immediately after Independence the new Indian government sought the assignment of quasi-diplomatic representative in the British colonies where its diaspora had settled. These new 'Indian commissioners' reached Mauritius, Fiji or Trinidad (West Indies) in 1948.

The Indian Worker Abroad as a Subaltern Subject

But the grievances of the Indian diaspora were not remedied, for the policies of independent India defined by Nehru recommended the integration of the immigrant population within the entities created by the dismemberment of the British empire. In the name of the fight against imperialism and with the aim of creating a third path in international relations through non-alignment, India refused to defend the interests of its expatriate community. The auxiliary minority syndrome, which may have been applicable in the case of the merchant or civil servant Indian communities in some part of the British empire, was extended to all its components, irrespective of its social and economical status. After 1947, the radical shift in the relations between the Indian government and its diaspora, reduced the asymmetry with host states while decreasing the relations with its diaspora.

In the wake of the independences of the Third World countries, the Indian workers overseas have played an important role in the decolonization process, in contrast with their previous situation. Hugh Tinker gave numerous examples of Indian workers unions evolving into a political party to participate in the local freedom struggles in Mauritius and Trinidad. In British Guiana, the leaders of the People's Progressive Party (PPP) who won the elections of 1953, were trade union organizers from various background with one Black leader, Forbes Burnham and one Indian leader, Cheddi Jagan.[7] At the end of 1953, when the PPP ministry was dismissed under British military pressure, the two leaders fled to India. But Nehru never brought their plight to the Trusteeship Council of the UN, as promised. The Indian government was unable to extend its help to the overseas Indians under political repression.

A New Asymmetrical Labour Relationship

In the 1970s, a new trend of international migration started—to fill the demand for low skilled workers in the Middle East. The bulk of these workers came on a temporary contract from South Asia, India accounting for 40 per cent of this workforce in 1980[8] and numbering 3 million peoples in 1999.[9] The situation of these Indian workers is in many ways comparable with their ancestors, the indentured labourers. Apart from the fact that they were travelling by plane and not by boat, unless they tried to cross the boundaries of these countries illegally, they were recruited for the same reasons. They were cheap, disciplined and hard workers, qualities required for the employers to hire them for infrastructure and construction tasks. Their situation in the Gulf countries with poor educational or medical facilities, and without proper accommodations, was no better than that of the 'coolies'. At the end of the 1970s, these bad working conditions and the unequal wage structure initiated riots in Bahrain (1974), Saudi Arabia (1976), and Dubai (1977).[10] But their situation has not improved yet. In Oman qualified workers have to live in dormitories for low wages (Rs. 6,000 against 15,000 promised by their recruitment agent). The situation of women (garment company) is the worst as they are rarely allowed to go out of their working place.[11]

This new asymmetrical labour relationship appeared in a post-colonial context even if India has a long tradition of emigration to the Gulf. Compared to the other South Asian countries, India relied more on the private and kinship networks to export its workforce than on public action. On the contrary, the Pakistani and Bangladeshi government created dedicated agencies (Bureau of Emigration and Overseas Employment, and the Bureau of Manpower, Employment and Training, respectively) to promote labour export. As a deliberate foreign policy, the Bhutto government used this emigration to foster its links with other Islamic countries.[12] This asymmetrical relation tied on one hand a receiving country with a deficit of its workforce, and on the other hand, a country that becomes more and more dependent on the remittances provided by its nationals working abroad. India is the largest recipient of remittances in the world with $17.4 billion in 2003. It is equivalent to nearly 30 per cent of its export.[13]

Even, if the Indian government isn't engaged in the migration process of its workers, this asymmetrical relation has an impact on its foreign policy. The Indian government is tied in this relation by geo-economic (oil exports and remittances) and geo-political considerations (to counterweight the relations with Pakistan). As the number of its immigrants is increasing, around 3 million today in West Asia, the Indian government might be afraid of a sudden repatriation of this workforce. When this menace became a reality in 1991 with the invasion of Kuwait and the subsequent first war of the Gulf, the massive comeback of the immigrant population has a disruptive economical and political effect in India and in some specific states like Kerala. For all these reasons, the Indian workers cannot rely too much on their government whose degree of liberty is restricted. As workers' union and strikes are prohibited in most of Gulf countries, the Indian workers can only organize themselves to uphold their situation through NGOs like Peace Trust in Dindigul (India) or Snehathazhvara in Abu Dhabi. The remarks of Weiner in the 1980s are still valid for the present situation: 'The Indian Government is thus willing to tolerate conditions for Indians in the Gulf that it would not tolerate for its citizens elsewhere.'[14]

From the time of indentured labour to the emigration to the Gulf countries, India has been engaged in an asymmetrical relationship with the countries receiving its workers. In contrast with other Asian countries (Pakistan, Bangladesh or Philippines) the Indian government had never tried to elaborate a pro-active migration policy. But even without specific bilateral agreement with the receiving countries, this asymmetrical relationship had decreased its ability to protect these workers.

2. IS THERE A NEW INDIAN POLICY TOWARDS ITS WORKER DIASPORA?

The open door policy of the Indian government on the matter of International migration had been similar in the case of the migration of higher skilled workers to the industrialized countries that gained momentum in the 1970s and 1980s. Besides deploring the effect of this brain drain, the Indian government never attempted to forbid such movements. With more than 1.5 million Indian immigrants in the USA and 1.2 million in the UK, the new Indian diaspora is more and more pre-eminent in the agenda of the Indian government. Portrayed as a model immigrant community in the USA, the Indians settled in the US enjoy the best per capita income among all the expatriate communities ($60,093 per annum, as compared to the American average of $38,885). Although this average may hide inequalities, their economic strength authorizes them to remit more money than the workers in the Gulf. According to a recent survey by the IMF, 51 per cent of the remittances sent to India originate from America (Asia amounting for only 22 per cent).

A More Interventionist Indian External Policy

Some recent events in Indonesia and Malaysia tend to accredit the idea that the Government of India is more assertive to protect its diaspora nowadays. The first incident occurred in Indonesia on 13 December 2002 when the Jakarta police detained the chairman of Polaris Software Labs along with other executives of the company for one week. Their passports were seized and they were able to leave Indonesia after the personal intervention of the Prime Minister A.B. Vajpayee. The official intervention was necessary as an act to counterweight the commercial partner of Polaris, the Artha Graha Bank, that had close links with the Indonesian military.[15]

The second incident occurred three month later on 9 March 2003 in Kuala Lumpur when a combined team of policemen and custom officers raided the Palm Court Condominium in Brickfields where they arrested 200[16] IT professionals to check their work permits. The mistreatment of these Indian nationals triggered a rapid reaction from the Indian High Commissioner, Veena Sikri who lodged a protest against the Malaysian government. A few days later, India pulled out from the Sultan Azlan Shah Cup Hockey Tournament in retaliation to the slow pace of the investigation. The incident was closed when both the Malaysian Home Ministry and Foreign Ministry apologized for it.

Reproducing the Asymmetrical Relation in the Indian Diaspora

The two incidents involving Indian IT professionals demonstrate the new ability of the Indian government to react to the abuse of its nationals abroad. Despite this efficient protection, this incident had sent the signal of departure for some of these software engineers who went back to India or relocated to Singapore or Australia. In the Malaysian case, the Indian government was in a strong position with a trade deficit of $1.8 billion *vis-à-vis* Malaysia, which was also engaged for an equivalent amount in infrastructure projects in India.[17]

In fact, IT professionals from India represented 63 per cent of the foreign knowledge workers in 2004,[18] an important factor for a nascent industry in Malaysia. Even if these foreign workers accounted for only 15 per cent of the total workforce in the IT-related companies, they held key positions as Malaysia suffers from shortage of skilled labour. Despite this valuable contribution to the development of the Malaysian Multimedia Super Corridor, these engineers felt that they never received 'the respect nor the remuneration they might otherwise have expected.'[19] They are assimilated with the old Indian diaspora, a dangerous class in the Malaysian psyche. 1.6 million People of Indian Origin (PIO) live today in Malaysia (7 per cent of the total population), but apart from a small middle-class group (20 per cent), the vast majority has a low economic status (15 per cent of the households were below the poverty level of $130 a month in 1990).[20] This backward community has developed socio-economic problems with the highest rate of crimes (40 per cent) among the Malaysian society, fuelling the racist discrimination that they are bearing.

Far from an Equilibrium Situation

The attitude of the Indian government is more ambiguous regarding this community and also with the illegal Indian workers. For the former, their Malaysian citizenship entrusts the Indian government to keep a low profile even though they are facing racial discrimination or violence. In 2001, racial riots in Petaling Jaya resulted in 4 dead and 34 injured among the Indian community. Numerous Malaysian PIO associations are advocating for the protection from their country of origin, or at least some diplomatic gesture during times of crisis. If the Indian government had been willing to react to the mistreatment of the software engineers, one year later they were unable to stop the flow of expulsion of 'illegal migrants', the second group of NRI. When the Malaysian government decided to deport the illegal foreign workers, the Indian authorities in Kuala Lumpur issued 16,000 'emergency certificates' (three times more than the number of IT professionals) for the illegal workers who opted to go back to India during the amnesty period.

Even for the well off NRI, their protection depends upon the country of residence. In Saudi Arabia, the indigenization of the economy restricts the expatriates to 32 job categories. Travel agency is one of them, in which Indian workers represent 80 to 85 per cent of the manpower. In June 2004, three Indian executives working for a travel agency were arrested and tonsured in Riyadh and Jeddah. Even if their Saudi Arabian employers complained to the highest authority, they faced expulsion like the 3 million foreign workers the kingdom plan to repatriate within 10 years. These massive expulsions are a nightmare for both the receiving and sending countries. The receiving country also has to face a dislocation of its economy, as the substitution of a skilled manpower is not an easy task. The expulsion of PIO in East Africa has been a bad experience for the refugees but also for the Ugandan and Kenyan economies. We might expect that these international issues should be handled in a bilateral dialogue, not through a unilateral national agenda, as it is today.

3. NEW ACTORS AND OLD NATION STATES: PROSPECTS FOR THE ELABORATION OF NEW LABOUR RELATIONSHIP

These examples demonstrate that the diplomatic gestures of the Indian government are still confined to a few cases, and that even for the well off NRI the asymmetrical relationship is a valid notion. In this third section, we will try to see if it is possible to correct this imbalanced relationship between the receiving and sending countries, and which actor could achieve this result?

The Sustainability of an Indian Transnational Middle Class

The first question we will try to answer is: why did these IT professionals need the diplomatic gesture of the Indian High Commissioner in the Palm Court incident? Beyond the fact that they are Indian citizens, one of the main reason lies in the absence of their political power in Malaysia. For the Malaysian authorities, they are guest workers. But they also see themselves as sojourners and they do not invest any time to develop contacts with the local Indian community. Hence during adversity, they didn't find any support in this community.

It was also very difficult to find some support among the IT professionals in Malaysia or from abroad, because this category has not developed a trade union culture. It is the result of a very short history, but it is also the consequences of the liberal values that they are sharing, inherited from the US model. These companies are run with a new paternalistic ideology, more high tech. The manager must be always accessible, at least by email, and non-hierarchical values are promoted. This atmosphere is not very conducive for trade unionism. There are few employees' associations like the IT forum, which is a global association. But they try to enhance the knowledge workers' conditions mainly through lobbying rather than organizing strikes.

Xiang Biao[21] has derived his notion of Transnational Middle Class from the case of the Indian IT professionals. For him 'Transnational Middle Class are those who have no active possession over established global capital, yet actively facilitate the expansion of the global capital'. In this hypothesis, the members of the Transnational Middle Class, deprived of capital, could only offer the globalization of their labour to gain access to the global market. They are selling their labour power wherever they can earn good salaries regardless of the country. For this purpose they have a high level of mobility, and it is also their only bargaining power, to vote with their feet.

In the international arena, they are not depending upon bilateral relations, sending and receiving countries. They are engaged in another asymmetrical relationship between capital and labour power, between the Transnational Capitalist Class and the Transnational Middle Class. Even though, their global mobility has to find a local haven for their sojourn, that's when they are caught in a national situation (the sons of the soil policy of the Malaysian government).

Engaging a New Relationship with the Indian Government

The relationship of the Transnational Middle Class with their government may be quite ambiguous as it is serving the global capital rather than any national economy. In the case of the Indian IT professionals, the most successful entrepreneurs of the Silicon Valley created various associations to replicate their achievement elsewhere on the globe. The Indus Entrepreneurs (TIE) founded by Kanwal Rekhi, is one of the most active associations in this field. They have opened chapters in more than 13 countries, and 18 cities in India.[22] Its members, predominantly entrepreneurs, are controlling the capital of their company, so it is more appropriate to classify them as a part of the Transnational Capitalist Class.

During the TIE annual gathering in Delhi, in December 2004, the scandal of pornographic SMS occurred and the chairman of a service provider was arrested because these images had circulated through his portal. Immediately the TIE members were mobilized to secure the release of their colleague. After intense lobbying and declaration to the media, they were able to obtain from the Indian governement his immediate release. It is not for the first time that this class of IT entrepreneurs was trying to influence the Indian government. At the time of their generous donation to their *alma mater*, the IIT, they were pushing hard for the privatization of these elite public institutes.

Obviously the Capitalist Class has more bargaining power than the Middle Class, but they have in common to be new actors in the international migration process and their logic is transnational. It is more difficult to assess their ability in the international relation arena, because most of the immigration policies of the receiving countries are defined under a national agenda, in the nation state framework.

Prospects for a More Balanced Labour Relationship

During this analysis, we observed that the Indian government was in an asymmetrical position with the receiving country for its unskilled workforce in at least two cases, the Gulf countries and in Malaysia. But if we take into account the situation of the skilled and even the knowledge workers, the assessment is no better. For the latter, this weakness lies in the temporary status of these migrations. These movements were organized through body-shopping to the USA, Australia or Malaysia. In this scheme, a body-shop company recruits IT workers from overseas and farms them out to clients on a contract basis. The body-shop firm manage, at a global level, the workers on behalf of the employers. It's a very flexible system, because if there is a downturn in the IT sector, the jobless employees have to flee the receiving country. That's what happened in the USA after the dotcom burst under the H-1B visa scheme. At that time, the Indian government was unable to exert any diplomatic pressure on the US government, even though thousands of IT professionals, had to leave this country.

Meanwhile, the emigration, even temporary, of the knowledge workers may be an opportunity for India, the sending country, to re-evaluate its foreign policy on the issue of international migrations. These workers might be a valuable asset. In the USA, more precisely in the Silicon Valley, the foreign knowledge workers from Taiwan, China and India had filled the shortage of brain power. From the beginning of the 1980s, they participated also in the dynamic development of this area. They created 3,000 companies, and 70,000 jobs. The second asset of the Indian government might be its student population. The brain drain is not over. On the contrary if 15,000 students from India were going to the USA in 1990, they are now 50,000 (2001).[23] But this emigration of young students comes with a heavy financial cost. If the flow of remittances from the receiving countries to the sending countries has been highlighted, there is today a counter flow of education fees in the reverse direction. *The Economic Times* estimated in 2004 that the American universities were able to collect $13 billion every year from half a million foreign students.

In these two examples, the shortage of brain power and the collection of fees from foreign students to finance their private higher education system, the receiving country need the immigration of foreign workers or future workers as much as the sending country. With the demographic evolution of the European countries, more and more receiving countries will have to hire immigrant workers. In this conjuncture, may be the time has come for the sending countries to regain some bargaining power in international relation to reverse the asymmetrical labour relationship. If we take into account the Gulf countries, the situation is more complex. The influx of skilled and highly skilled workers from India has increased, and the Indian government may be more responsive to their living and working conditions than before. But the political situation is more difficult with autocratic regimes because without public sphere, the immigrants cannot hope for any support to improve their life or change their political situation, locally. With 25 years of circular migration between India and the Gulf countries, the position of the Indian government is less precarious than described by Weiner in 1982,[24] and it is the only actor to be able to have a political impact. Thus, the Indian government should consider that these emigrants are Indian citizens, and protect them wherever they work.

CONCLUSION

As Graziano Battistella put it, 'The study of international relations has largely neglected the issue of migration and its role in affecting relations among states.'[25] In this paper we tried to concentrate on aspects of 'low politics.' May be our background in geography, is responsible for this orientation. Our first conclusion will be that the asymmetrical labour relationship has not weakened with the advent of the high skilled worker migrations. A new circulation regime with an increasing mobility has started during this phase of the globalization process, changing the rules for the old actors (nation state) and creating opportunities for new actors—the transnational classes (capitalist or middle class). Their respective agenda might be different. For the nation state, the goal is to mobilize its diaspora. That is what the Indian government is trying to do since 2000, in order to foster its international position. For the new transnational classes, the goal is to gain access to the global market, wherever it is, but it is always through local circumstances.

NOTES

1. K.A.N. Aiyer, *Indian Problems in Malaya: A Brief Survey in Relation to Emigration 1900-1938*, Kuala Lumpur: GOPIO International, 2004, p. 91.
2. H. Tinker, *A New System of Slavery: The Export of Indian Labour Overseas, 1830-1920*, London/New York: Oxford University Press, 1974, p. 432.
3. Ibid., pp. 98-9.
4. A declaration recognizing that the interests of native Africans were superior to those of the Indian immigrants, M.C. Lall, *India's Missed Opportunity*, London: Asghate, 2001.
5. The Pegging Act prohibited Indians from owning any land or enterprises that were previously owned by a European, until 1946, Lall, op. cit., pp. 83-4.
6. Ibid., p. 85.
7. Tinker, op. cit., pp. 66-8.
8. Cf. Knerr Béatrice, Tab 8.3, in C.G. Clarke et al., *South Asians Overseas: Migration and Ethnicity*, Cambridge/New York: Cambridge University Press, 1990, p. 179.
9. P.C. Jain, in B. Parekh et al., *Culture and Economy in the Indian Diaspora*, London: Routledge, 2003, p. 105.
10. L. Ling, cited by Knerr, op. cit., p. 181.
11. Press Trust of India, 17 May 2005.
12. Knerr, op. cit., p. 190.
13. M. Debabrata and M. Kapur, 'India's Worker Remittances: A User's Lament About Balance of Payments Compilation', *Committee on Balance of Payments Statistics*, 2003.
14. Weiner, cited by Jain, op. cit., pp. 12-13.
15. The Chief Managing Director of the bank, Letjen Tni Kiki Syahnakri was the deputy chief of staff of the Indonesian Army, G. Shrikanth 2002, 'Friday, the 13th', *Dataquaest*, 31 December 2002, p. 62.
16. 165 according to police sources, but nearly 270 from Indian High Commissioner sources.
17. Balan Moses, 'PM Expected to Visit India as Part of Efforts to Boost Ties', *The Nation*, March 2004, p. 14.
18. These figures were valid for the companies with an MSC status, but the proportion should be extended to the rest of this activity. *Source:* Multimedia Super Corridor Impact Survey, 2004, p. 9.

19. Reshma Patil, 'Grim Indian shadow under Kuala Lumpur's Petronas Towers', *Indian Express*, 12 April 2005, pp. 1-2.
20. T. Chakraborti, 'Minority Underclassed: Negating a Sociological Truism in Malaysia', in L. Ghosh and R. Chatterjee (eds.), *Indian Diaspora in Asian and Pacific Regions: Culture, People, Interactions*, Jaipur: Rawat, 2004, p. 197.
21. B. Xiang, 'Indian Information Technology Professionals' World System', in *State/Nation/Transnation: Perspectives on Transnationalism in the Asia-Pacific*, New York: Routledge, 2004, pp. 161-78.
22. TIE website http://tienewdelhi.org/tatg.htm, as of 22/09/05
23. B. Khadria, 'Migration of Highly Skilled Indians: Case Studies of IT and Health', in *Directorate for Science, Technology and Industry*, Paris, Organisation for Economic Cooperation and Development, 2004.
24. M. Weiner, 'International Migration and Development: Indians in the Persian Gulf', *Population and Development Review*, vol. 8, no. 1, 1982, pp. 1-36.
25. Graziano Battistella, 'Asian Migrations and International Relations in the Face of the Challenges of a New Century', SIMI.

REFERENCES

Aiyer, K.A.N., *Indian Problems in Malaya: A Brief Survey in Relation to Emigration 1900-1938*, Kuala Lumpur: GOPIO International, 2004.

Battistella, G., 'Asian Migrations and International Relations in the Face of the Challenges of a New Century', paper presented at the Workshop on Migration and International Relations between Asia and Spain: Philippines, China and Pakistan Case Studies, Barcelona, 2004.

Chakraborti, T., 'Minority Underclassed: Negating a Sociological Truism in Malaysia', in *Indian Diaspora in Asian and Pacific Regions: Culture, People, Interactions*, ed. L. Ghosh and R. Chatterjee, Jaipur: Rawat, 2004, pp. 193-232.

Clarke, C.G., C. Peach and S. Vertovec, *South Asians Overseas: Migration and Ethnicity*, Cambridge/New York: Cambridge University Press, 1990.

Debabrata, M. and M. Kapur, 'India's Worker Remittances: A Users' Lament About Balance of Payments Compilation', in *Committee on Balance of Payments Statistics*. IMF, http://www.imf.org/external/pubs/ft/bop/2003/03-20.pdf. (accessed on 09/02/2004).

Irudaya Rajan, S. and P.R. Nair Gopinathan, 'Saudi Arabia, Oman and the Gulf States', in *The Encyclopedia of the Indian Diaspora*, ed. B.V. Lal, P. Reeves and R. Rai, Honolulu: University of Hawaii Press, 2006, pp. 222-33.

Jain, P. C., 'Culture and Economy in An "Incipient" Diaspora: Indians in the Persian Gulf Region', in *Culture and Economy in the Indian Diaspora*, ed. B. Parekh, G. Singh and S. Vertovec, London: Routledge, 2003, pp. 102-22.

———, *Indian Diaspora in West Asia*, New Delhi: Manohar, 2007.

Khadria, B., 'Human Resources in Science and Technology in India and the International Mobility of Highly Skilled Indians', in *Directorate for Science, Technology and Industry*, Paris: Organisation for Economic Cooperation and Development, 2004.

Knerr, B., 'South Asian Countries as Competitors on the World Labour Market', in *South Asians Overseas: Migration and Ethnicity*, ed. C.G. Clarke, C. Peach and S. Vertoveé, Cambridge/New York: Cambridge University Press, 1990, pp. 173-96.

Lall, M.C., *India's Missed Opportunity*, London: Ashgate, 2001.

Ling, L.M.H., 'East Asian Migration to the Middle East: Causes, Consequences and Considerations', *International Migration Review*, vol. 18, 1984, pp. 19-36.

Tinker, H., *A New System of Slavery: The Export of Indian Labour Overseas, 1830-1920*, London; New York: Published for the Institute of Race Relations by Oxford University Press, 1974.

———, *The Banyan Tree: Overseas Emigrants from India, Pakistan, and Bangladesh*, Oxford (Eng.)/New York: Oxford University Press, 1977.

Weiner, M., 'International Migration and Development: Indians in the Persian Gulf', *Population and Development Review*, vol. 8, no. 1, 1982, pp. 1-36.

———, 'Labor Migrations as Incipient Diaspora', in *Modern Diasporas in International Politics*, ed. G. Sheffer, Londres: Croom Helm, 1986, pp. 47-74.

Xiang, B., 'Indian Information Technology Professionals' World System', in *State/Nation/Transnation: Perspectives on Transnationalism in the Asia-Pacific*, ed. B.S.A. Yeoh and K. Willis, New York: Routledge, 2004, pp. 161-78.

Zachariah, K.C., P.R. Gopinathan Nair and S. Irudaya Rajan, *Return Emigrants in Kerala: Welfare, Rehabilitation, and Development*, New Delhi: Manohar, 2006.

6

Diaspora and Foreign Policy

A Case Analysis of Indian American Influence on Indo–US Relations

P.V. RAO

Foreign policy-making process by the American establishment is a sum of a variety of inputs. Such inputs are externally induced as well as intrinsic to the system. The first category, the external inputs, largely represent the lobby groups, legislative bodies, ethnic interests, diplomats, etc. The second category is drawn from the civil service, intra- and inter-departmental committees, leading personalities and presidential choices. Indo–US relations, as a domain of foreign policy, in recent decades is influenced by the Indian American community (IAC) which has factored itself as a dynamic ethnic group in American politics today. Major Indian American associations active in the US public life profess their stated objectives as: to gain identity as an ethnic group in the American public life; safeguard and promote the rights and interests of Indian Americans; educate the community about the professional and business opportunities and help enhance their competitive abilities; build India's image in America and articulate Indian interests in the public domain; and, campaign for better Indo–US understanding. What follows is an analysis of the role of the IAC and its ability to influence the major issues that dominated the bilateral relations between the two democracies.

THE ECONOMIC DIMENSION OF INDO–US RELATIONS

The Growing Wealth of the Indian American Community

IAC certainly is not a homogeneous community and is composed of different linguistic, religious, professional and even caste groups. Prominent among the Indian interest groups in the US are American Indian Association (AIA); Association for the Defence of Indian Americans (ADIA); Indian American Forum for Political Education (IAFPE); Federation of Indian Associations (FIA); National Federation of Indian American Associations (NFIA). During the first half of 1980s, the NFIA encouraged several regional affiliates and towards the end of the decade it became a formidable force with more than 200 branches. In the following years the IAC, reflecting the rise of Hindutva political force in India, came to be sharply divided over religious lines. Though such schism manifested itself on the IAC's participation in American politics, its impact on Indo–US relations has not been serious.

The IAC's role in the domain of Indo–US relations is more of a recent origin. During the heydays of the Cold War when bilateral relations of India and the US were frequently prone to the ideological divide between the opposite poles of global power, IAC had hardly intervened. The dominant issues of Indo–US relations during this period—non-alignment, disarmament, US economic and military aid to India and Pakistan, Indo–Pakistan relations, relations with China, nuclear proliferation—failed to draw the attention of IAC. One main reason for the low key interest of the IAC during the 1960s and the 1970s in the above issues or foreign policy in general was that the IAC was in its formative phase. That generation of Indians who emigrated to the US during this period was more concerned in securing its stay in the US and obtaining the legal status under the Immigration and Naturalisation Act. Obviously, it lacked the numerical strength and political identity to constitute themselves into an organized group to lobby for issues other than their immediate concern of survival in an alien land.

But the IAC's profile in the host country changed much ever since the 1980s. It has grown in numerical strength, wealth and occupations. According to the 2000 US census report, the Indian population has more than doubled between 1990 and 2000 reaching around 1.6 million, the highest recorded increase in the Asian American community. Legally identified as Asian Indians, the Indian community has earned the distinction of being the highest income group in America and 'has practically acquired a critical mass in terms of economic clout'.[1] As early as mid-1970s, records Myron Weiner, the 'incomes of members of the Indian community are higher than the national average and a significant percentage (16 per cent) earned more than $50,000 annually . . . .'[2] With the rise in income levels came a corresponding, perhaps greater, rise in political visibility. An empirical study of the growing political role of the IAC thus concludes that 'substantial contributions to Democratic as well as Republican candidates by Indian Americans has led to increasing clout of Indians in American politics, far beyond their slender electoral strength entitles them'.[3] It is therefore not surprising to see the Indian Americans displaying an impressive measure of interest in American politics, at the State and federal levels. They actively participated in the electoral politics, contested the legislative seats on party lines, mobilized funds for the governor and presidential candidates and lobbied on the Capitol Hill. Thus, testifying to their political clout Senator Brownback would remark: 'By their engagement and their aggressiveness they are able to influence things beyond their numbers.'[4]

The Cold War Period and US's Aid Policy

But the Indo–US relations depend not only the economic weight of the IAC, the perception that the US have of India is a key factor. The US interest in India, rather in South Asia during the Cold War period, was minimal. The region remained peripheral to the global geo-strategic interests of the US and hence her policy orientation and reaction to the regional issues was a fallout of its interests elsewhere, say, West Asia or China. India's policy of non-alignment and pro-Soviet foreign policy choices distanced New Delhi from Washington. Aid debates in Congress were normally the occasions to assess India's foreign and economic policies, its support or lack of it to US policies. The US Administration's aid proposals to India were almost always met with cuts and conditions, obviously coloured by the Congress' political perceptions of India. Surjit Mansingh aptly captured the Congressional mood in determining the bilateral relations between the two democracies as follows: 'US Congressional opinion on Indian economic development was a determining factor in US policy. Congressional opinion fluctuated in response to a variety of stimuli during the period under review (1966-82); different forces pulled in indifferent directions.'[5] The Congress, for example, exerted enormous influence on the settlement of Indian Rupee debts to the US under the PL 480 loans. India negotiated in 1973 with the Nixon Administration a complete moratorium on the PL 480 debts which was a major irritant in Indo–US relations. But the Congress was very critical of the Administration's grace and was in no mood to write off the debt burden on India which amounted to about $3 billion. Congressional opposition to a liberal settlement of the PL 480 counterpart funds was mainly on political grounds. Following the Administration's usual floor tactics but in particular the influential role played by the then US ambassador to India, Daniel Patrick Moynihan in persuading the Congressional members, Congress relented.[6] The agreement finally reached between India and the US was a compromise between complete moratorium on PL 480 debts and an unending schedule of payment by India. Congressional assertion thus spared India with only a part of the PL 480 debt burden.

Paradigm Shift in Economic Relations

It was with the beginning of the 1980s, following the fall of Shah of Iran, Soviet invasion of Afghanistan and the subsequent collapse of the Soviet Union that American interest grew in South Asia. There was a conscious rethinking on the US policy towards India with definite positive overtones. Such a shift in the focus was obvious not only at the executive level but in the Congress too which for a variety of reasons including the Indian community's interest articulation on the Capitol Hill. For the first time, 'members of the Senate, and especially the House of Representatives, concluded that increased attention to the Indian subcontinent could bring benefits in the American political arena'.[7] The mood of expectation out of the improved Indo–US relations was significantly propelled by the shift in India's national economic and strategic perspectives too. The early 1990s saw India embarking on a major departure from the State-regulated economic management to a market-driven policy regime. A middle-class dominated consumer market of 300 to 350 million and vast investment potential on the Indian subcontinent lured the American business interests toward India as an attractive economic destination. Interestingly it was around the same period that the Indian diaspora in the US, by now large and assertive, began to take active interest in Indo–US relations. With a liberalized economic climate in India which opened up opportunities for capital flow, American as well as Indian American entrepreneurs expanded the range of their economic engagement with India. The IndUS Entrepreneurs (TIE) is a good example of the organized business initiative by Indian Americans who moved to capitalize on the investment opportunities extended by post-reform India. It is a broad network of Indian entrepreneurs, mainly IT professionals, which established several chapters in India, sponsoring business conferences, interface between Indian and American investors and other interested parties. Such networking effort represents 'a small fraction of the potential opportunity for professionals in India, in view of the high rate of entrepreneurship of Indian professionals in the US as well as the breadth and size of the Indian economy'.[8] Not only the IT but many other sectors including engineering services, education, biotechnology, health, banking, capital services, real estate and energy are sought after in India by US-based Indian business groups. Commensurate with its increasing economic engagement with the native country, the Indian community has been active in influencing the economic policy-making by the US government *vis-à-vis* India.

Just to illustrate the IAC's lobbying for the purpose at the highest level, the US–India Business Council and IAFPE worked together to persuade President Clinton to visit India in February 2000. The Indian community actively took part in fund-raising for Clinton and claimed to be close to the Clinton administration. The Indo–American Political Foundation, during its fund-raising campaign, reportedly obtained positive response from Clinton to the Indian case for UN Security Council membership. The issue is not whether it signalled 'Clinton's real mind, but how passionately Indians lay down before the administration something that, they perceive, would add to the prestige and dignity of India.'[19] The IAC members who accompanied Clinton to India interacted with the President and his senior staff including the Secretary of State, Secretary of Commerce and members of the India Caucus, and others. They were party to the trade discussions with leading Indian business groups and individuals. The US–India Business Council, formed in 1975, represents about 180 enterprises and functions as the facilitator for the American business interests in India. In fact, in the recently signed July 2005 controversial US–India Civil Nuclear Agreement between the Indian Prime Minister Manmohan Singh and President Bush, the Council was actively involved.[9]

THE INDIAN AMERICAN COMMUNITY AS AGENT OF FOREIGN RELATIONS

A Weak Indian Diplomacy

In the American system decision-making in the domain of foreign relations involves a network of policy interactions between several agencies, primarily the presidency, State department,

Congress and its committees, and the lobby groups. Although the State department is the direct and visible government agency to deal with the foreign governments, it is not necessarily the only institution which is always the source of policy formulation. Depending upon the importance and relevance of a foreign country to US foreign policy goals, a maze of executive and legislative processes are involved in policy formulation. For a foreign country it is not always easy to comprehend these processes, and dealing only with the State Department is not a desirable way to advance its interests in the US. It needs to influence the concerned departments, individuals within the executive branch and the parties, committee leaders and prominent congressmen on the Capitol Hill. According to its strengths, 'each of the foreign policy lobbies seeks to influence Congress through standard techniques of political influence—campaign contributions, public information or disinformation, and mobilization of voting blocs'.[10]

Traditionally, India had been poor on influencing the various policy agencies in the US. Until the early 1980s Indian foreign policy establishment in Delhi and Washington mostly preferred to deal with the executive branch, the State Department to be specific. This was partly because Indian diplomacy was averse to lobbying among the concerned channels and partly due to ignorance. There was a certain degree of moral disdain in the Indian reluctance to influence the congressional groups and parties, a disdain which contributed to the popular American perception of Indians as assertive and argumentative. But the American leadership, the lawmakers in particular, expect a foreign country to take its case to the groups and enlighten at various levels on the issues of its concern. In other words, 'if a foreign country does not lobby, the Congress may take it as a sign of indifference toward what America decides, and its concerns are likely to be ignored, to the detriment both of the foreign interests and to the quality of the American policy which is defined in their absence'.[11] In fact, several congressional staffers this author spoke to were unanimous that Indian lobbying was poor and occasional. They lobby, as Richard Cronin, a well-known researcher on the Congressional Research Service told this author, only for 'defensive' or 'negative' purposes such as stopping arms aid to Pakistan, and tend to be 'argumentative' in their approach. On the other hand, Pakistan's lobbying was organized and regular.[12] It employed lobbying companies and attorneys in Washington during the Cold War years and after a while India mostly lobbied through its own highly resourceful press counsellor in the Indian Embassy, Janki Nath Ganju, who cultivated every important person in the executive and Congressional circles. But, 'no matter how resourceful, Ganju could not bridge major differences on the Soviet Union or Pakistan. Neither was his one-man exercise an adequate substitute for a streamlined professional lobbyist with contacts in the State Department and Pentagon, in the White House or on the Hill.'[13]

The Construction of an Indian Lobby

It is in this background that the Indian community's articulation of the Indian interests in the US assumes significance. It is interesting to recall that Congressional interest in India almost coincided with the IAC's organized activity in the political establishment. An important issue of foreign policy concern taken up by the IAC during this period was to reverse the Administration's idea of supplying of military hardware to Pakistan. In 1981 the Reagan Administration was seriously considering the sale of 40 F-16 war planes to Pakistan. But the Senate strongly objected to the deal arguing that the deal would escalate arms race in the subcontinent and that some Pakistani political sections too were opposed to their sale to the military regime of Zia-ul Haq. But many Pakistanis also believed that the Indian lobby was actively working against the F-16 proposal on the Capitol Hill. Similarly, in mid-1980s the US Administration was considering a request by Pakistan for sale of three E-3A AWACS planes to counter the Soviet attack from Afghanistan. When the Congress was debating the Administration's proposal, the Indian community was actively working on the Capitol

Hill to tilt legislative position against the Pakistani request.[14] The NFIA also mobilized the Indian community to campaign against the sale of sophisticated AWACS planes to Pakistan and together with other Indian Communities even organized a demonstration on the Capitol Hill. Eventually, the Senate rejected the proposal to sell war planes to Pakistan.

The Indian community initially acted mainly through the Solarz Committee, named after Stephen Solarz, the Democratic representative from New York who, as chairman of the House Sub-Committee on Asia-Pacific, ardently championed the India cause in the Congress. The Solarz Committee, soundly backed by the contributions from the Indian community, voiced the Indian interests in America as much as what Chester Bowles had done in the 1950s. The only subtle difference being that while Bowles, the Connecticut Congressman who twice served in New Delhi as ambassador, was a lone champion in the Cold War years, Solarz spoke for India as the Cold War was waning. His India-cause coincided when the American establishment was beginning to shed its Cold War images of India as well as when a visible Indian community was asserting its role in American public life. Labelled as the 'eyes and ears of India' in America, Solarz argued that as the world's largest democracy India deserves to be taken seriously and that the US should adequately support the Indian development programmes. In fact, when the Herger Amendment aimed at cutting the annual aid to India was moved in the House on grounds of violation of Sikh rights in Punjab, Solarz persuaded the House to defeat it and convinced the Reagan Administration to take India seriously.[15]

Stephen Solarz's defeat in the Congressional elections of 1992 was definitely a blow to India on the Capitol Hill. Nevertheless, his absence was equally substituted by the fellow Democratic, Frank Pallone, representative from New Jersey. Pallone, backed by the IAC, was instrumental in establishing the India Caucus in the Congress with the able support of other Congressmen, particularly Gary Ackerman (Democrat) and Benjamin Arthur Gillman (Republican). With a modest strength in the mid-

1990s, the strength of India Caucus soon rose to 130, the largest for an ethnic community.[16] Composed of the House members and a few senators from both parties, the India Caucus provides India for the first time with an institutional base of support on Capitol Hill and 'aggressively argues the case for better US–Indian relations'.[17] The India Caucus, a more recent legislative player on the Capitol Hill, is modelled on the other ethnic lobby groups working in Congressional circles to promote the interests of their native countries. Some of these influential groups are the American Hellenic Institute (AHI), American Israel Public Affairs Committee (AIPAC), American Jewish Committee and the Anti-Defamation League. It is a commonly accepted American political reality that the Jewish lobbies, backed by business interests, are the most powerful on the Hill to advance the interests of Israel. In fact, the newly formed US India Political Action Committee (USINPAC) is known to be working closely with the Jewish groups on the Hill to push Indian interests.

The India Caucus is regularly interacted by the Indian Americans and the leading organizations representing them. Such interactions serve variously in updating the legislators on India affairs, inviting their political positions, guiding legislative initiative on issues of concern, mobilizing wider congressional support through the Caucus and influencing decision-making in the executive branch. The IAFPE was instrumental in organizing internships for Indian–American youth on Capitol Hill resulting in about 200 young Indians in the US serving with various Congressional and Senatorial offices. Engaging the younger generation of Indians in such roles on the Hill would greatly serve the India cause in America. It may be noted that the average American politician's knowledge of India is very poor. Most recently, Gary Ackerman was quoted as saying, 'most members of US Congress believed that "IndiaPakistan" was a single word'.[18] Not very long ago the visiting Indian Prime Minister Rajiv Gandhi was introduced by the speaker of the House to the joint session of the Congress as Indira Gandhi's younger son. Associating Indians as internees with

Congressional offices will, therefore, help educate the political class more about India as well as creating a bridge between the native and Indian Americans.

The Role of IAC During the Sikh Insurgency

The measure of the Indian community's growing clout was perhaps judged by its successful efforts in thwarting Congressional attempts to ban American aid to India. As mentioned earlier, annual debates on foreign economic assistance by the US Congress are exercises in political assessment of the recipient country. Aid debates on India were hardly favourable either during Cold War or the post-Cold War period. Though there were never serious aid cuts to India, the annual Congressional debates on foreign assistance were usually critical of India's foreign policies and her relations with the US. Aid debates through the 1980s and 1990s were embarrassing for India as the Khalistan and Kashmir groups gathered considerable sympathy on the Hill to condemn India's human rights record in Punjab and Kashmir.

Secessionist groups found an easy access to their cause on the Capitol Hill. The US-based Khalistan and Kashmir secessionist groups effectively carried their case against India to force American pressure on New Delhi to meet their demands. Sections of Congressmen across the party lines lined up against India to articulate the Sikh and Kashmiri causes. The well-known Burton Amendments to the India aid bills seeking ban became annual exercises moved by Dan Burton, the representative from Indiana. Though the Republican Congressman never succeeded in his anti-India motions, he mobilized enough supporters across the party lines to condemn India and embarrass the administration. The State department supported India and in fact, State and the Indian embassy, as this author was informed by Richard Cronin, collaborated in their lobbying on the Hill to counter the Sikh campaign. Indian ambassador Narayanan was very active during this period on the Hill to muster Congressional support to the Indian case. The Indian dissident groups in their political campaign questioned the legitimacy of India to exercise her sovereign power over the Sikh and Kashmir states. Alleging ethnic discrimination and abuse of human rights by the central government, the separatists advocated secession of the Sikh and Kashmir-dominated states from the Indian Union. A political discourse of this kind which militates against the territorial integrity and sovereignty of the Indian Republic is against the law and spirit of the Indian constitution. Moreover these groups enjoyed the moral, political and material support of Pakistan whom India had been constantly accusing of encouraging cross-border terrorism. Hence on constitutional grounds and political grounds of seeking extra-territorial support from Pakistan, the Sikh and Kashmir activities in America against India amounted to anti-India campaign.

The Sikhs directly lobbied with the Hill and the Congressmen who supported them argued their case did so more for constituency reasons. In fact, there was no Congressional office on the Hill that was not visited by the president of the International Sikh Organisation, Dr. Gurmit Singh Aulakh and his colleagues. It is well known that Burton and others received funding from the Khalistani sources. Not only Burton but the Congressman from North California Wally Herger whose constituency consisted of the largest Sikh population was a vocal champion of the Sikh rights. The former chairman of Khalistani World Sikh Organisation, Darbara Singh belonged to Herger's constituency. As noted above, Herger's move to cut aid to India was defeated by Solarz.

It was during this period of strong anti-India campaign in the US carried by the dissident Indian ethnic groups that the IAC became active to undo the damage to the Indian interests and her image. 'The India Caucus and the community need to be credited for defeating many anti-India bills and amendments (Burton, Brown, Rowling, etc.) introduced in the US Congress in the last 10 years. The Indian American community can be proud that those anti-India Congressmen do not even attempt to introduce such bills now,' claims Dr. Abraham, founder of NFIA and president of Global Organization of People of Indian Origin

(GOPIO).[20] His claim was right as, after successive defeat of his anti-India amendments, Burton failed to draw support of his own Republican members to propose suspension of American annual aid to India.

Evolution of the Situation about Nuclear Proliferation

These were also the decades which witnessed worldwide ethnic and secessionist wars and the internationalization of human rights discourse. The US too, following the Soviet collapse, advocated human rights protection as one of the cardinal principles of her New World Order. But the early 1990s and the aftermath of Cold War was also a crucial period in Indo–US relations. Both the governments were busily redefining their respective global and regional roles and objectives in a radically changing world. At bilateral level, both India and the US were shedding the Cold War perceptions of each other to draw a new roadmap of mutual engagement in a world dominated by two broad potent forces: globalization and global terrorism. Successive American administrations began to see India as a rising Asian political and economic power. A rising India could serve the American strategic objective of countering China, the other Asian giant. India can also be a valuable partner in combating terrorism, the common enemy of both countries. In such a prevailing mood of mutual accommodation and political and economic bonhomie between India and America, the IAC factored itself into the bilateral foreign policy domain. Its growing presence in mainstream American public life as well as interest in Indo–American relations added a positive input to the evolving relationship between the two democracies.

The issue of nuclear proliferation has always been a constant source of friction in Indo–American relations. Both the countries represented opposite poles of the proliferation regime, the US insisting on Indian adherence to Nuclear Non-Proliferation Treaty (NPT), while India refusing to commit on ground of discrimination built into the NPT. India's first nuclear test in 1974 expectedly sparked off stringent criticism of her nuclear programme with both the government and Congress calling for the suspension of nuclear fuel being supplied to India under the 1963 agreement between Washington and New Delhi. Congressional reaction went further in calling for suspension of annual economic aid extended by the US to India.[21] Relations between the two democracies tended to become acrimonious as India also refused to sign CTBT, went ahead with her nuclear ambitions and finally tested nuclear bombs in 1998. Sharply reacting to the Indian atomic tests, a reaction reminiscent of the 1974 test, the Clinton Administration imposed severe sanctions on India as also Pakistan. International sanctions regime, like the nuclear non-proliferation regime, is not a foolproof one. Given the fluidity of international politics and the growing interdependence of States, no major power can sustain its punitive measures on a country or group of countries longer. Nor the domestic interests of the imposing country would let their government maintain the sanctions indefinitely. Nuclear raw materials, technology, fuel, reactors and reprocessing machinery are as much a domain of big business as steel and petroleum.

Neither the US nuclear industry nor the Indian community tolerated the Clinton Administration's sanctions on India after the Pokhran-II atomic tests. If the Indian community's reaction to the sanctions was sharp, its efforts to revoke them were relentless. Through regular media campaigns, public debates, postal and telephone contacts and rigorous lobbying in Congress and administration, the Indian community mollified the American furor over the Indian tests and worked for the relaxation of sanctions. The Clinton Administration did relax the severity of sanctions on India to the possible extent and it could be surmised the American reaction could have been far more severer had 'the Indian community remained unconcerned or nonchalant in pleading for repealing sanctions . . . .'[22]

The latest US penal sanctions against India are not the first such punitive measures. Washington exercised such option by banning the supply of nuclear fuel to Indian atomic reactors after the 1974 test. The US Congress in order to strengthen the non-proliferation regime passed the Nuclear Non-Proliferation Act (NNPA) in 1978, the so-called Glenn Amendment. NNPA was a rigid and sweeping legislation which mandated the American government to strictly ensure a foolproof non-proliferation regime. Though the apparent objective of NNPA was global in scope, India was its immediate target. Yet, despite India's refusal to honour the NNPA, the Carter Administration issued licenses in 1980 for the export of two nuclear fuel shipments and spare parts to the nuclear reactor at Tarapur.

The credit for this should go to the Federation of Indian Associations in America (FIAA) which exerted pressure on the Carter Administration to supply nuclear fuel to the Tarapur nuclear power plant and the goal was successfully achieved under the Reagan Administration.[23] Could it be surmised that the sanctions relief by Clinton due to the Indian community's pressure snowballed into further waiver by the Bush Administration culminating in the latest offer of nuclear technology under the Indo–US agreement of July 2005!

CONCLUSION

The IAC is no longer a small ethnic group of Asian Indians struggling to better its economic status in the US. It is now economically sound, politically conscious and professionally and technologically competitive. As it rose in its stature, the IAC has constructively translated and directed its clout toward bettering India's relations with the US. Instead of playing such role in a reactive manner, the Indian community has assumed a proactive, even lead role. Thus IAC does not wait for reactions, rather it initiates and leads the situations. Its ability to persuade Clinton to tour their country of origin and force the Congress repeatedly to avoid aid cuts to India and deny advanced weapons to Pakistan are manifestations of the IAC's desire to assert its role in the domain of Indo–American relations and protect India's interests.

Through its active interaction with key institutional determinants of Indo–US relations—the White House, the State

Department, the Congress and the Indian Embassy—the IAC has emerged as an important factor in the decision-making process. No major issue area of Indo–American relations can escape its network and interest, be it family reunification, dual citizenship, BPO, dual-technology supplies, nuclear cooperation, VIP visits or FDI between India and the US. The IAC and its various congregations have, over the decades, groomed themselves into a matured non-governmental constituency (third force) in the host society which today eminently qualifies it to play Track-II role in Indo–American diplomacy. Civil society participation is a dominant norm of modern diplomacy and the two major democracies have demonstrated a track record of involving their concerned sections in foreign policy negotiations. The IAC, given its interest and stake in almost every area of serious concern to Indo–American relations—trade, services, IT, health, immigration, etc.—can be a very useful partner in Track-II deliberations. The governments on either side have implicitly recognized the IAC's potential for such task.

POST-SCRIPTUM

The agreement on civil nuclear cooperation between the US and India that was signed on 18 July 2005, ends the embargo in place since the first Indian efforts of 1974. This derogatory agreement, because India had not signed the NPT, illustrates a deep change in the international relations between both countries that took place after the attacks of 11 September 2001. India's partnership in the war against terrorism was sought for by the Bush Administration. The agreement constitutes a counterpart not divested of economic interests for the US, with the sale of technologies and nuclear raw materials. For its part, India will have to place under the supervision of the International Atomic Energy Agency (AIEA) its civil installations and ban new nuclear tests. Considering the internal political opposition, from the BJP to the CPI(M), India had to wait till the end of the George W Bush's second mandate to see the agreement succeeding. It seems that it is the traditional competence of the diplomacy directed by the Secretary of State Condolezza Rice which played a more important role in this strategic alliance than the Indian Diaspora. The search for a second ally in Asia with Japan, with the rise of China, and the reshaping of the role of its traditional military ally, Pakistan, were determining factors in this American paradigm shift. By this agreement, India hopes to confirm its role as a major power to obtain finally a seat of permanent membership to the Security Council of the United Nations, same as China.

NOTES

1. Tanmay Kanjilal, *Indian Americans and India: An Analysis of Mutual Relations*, Delhi: Kalinga Publications, 2004, p. 6.
2. Myron Weiner, 'The Indian Presence in America: What Difference Will It Make?', in Sulochana Raghavan Glazer and Nathan Glazer, (eds.), *Conflicting Images: India and the United States*, Glenn Dale, Md.: Riverdale Company, 1990, p. 244.
3. Sonalde Desai and Rahul Kanakia, 'Profile of a Diasporic Community', special issue 'The Diaspora', *Seminar*, no. 538, June 2004, p. 49. The authors calculated that the 'median income of Indian American households is substantially higher than that of the white or African-American population'.
4. Quoted in Robert M. Hathway, 'Coming of Age: Indian-Americans and the US Congress', *in* Ashok Kapur et al. (eds.), *India and the United States in a Changing World*, New Delhi: Thousand Oaks; Calif.: Sage, 2002, p. 392.
5. Surjit Mansingh, *India's Search for Power: Indira Gandhi's Foreign Policy, 1966-82*, New Delhi: Sage, 1984, p. 107.
6. Daniel Patrick Moynihan, defending the waiver of the $3 billion PL 480 debt by India to the US, argued in 1973 that the single largest contingent of foreign students in America was from India and that the US was its largest trading partner. The ambassador concluded with a passionate note: 'We may all hope that this exchange of goods and services and people will grow and grow and grow. There is no one thing more important for the future of our two countries.' *U.S. Congressional Record*, 93rd Congress, vol. 119, part 12, p. 14767. Moynihan rightly recorded that the Indian Rupee Settlement was his 'most enduring success in India.' See. Surjit Mansingh, p. 115.

7. Hathway, op. cit., n. 4, p. 399.
8. Ignatius Chithelen and Val Souza, 'Public Capital Markets and New Generation of Entrepreneurs: Success of Indians in the US and Potential in India,' *Economic and Political Weekly*, vol. 40, no. 4, 2005, p. 4375.
9. A *Washington Post* story reports that the US–India Business Council hired top lawyer and lobbyist Graham Wisener's firm Patton Boggs as well as Vickery International to push the nuclear deal through the Congress for approval. Other lobby firms on the Business Council's list include the American multinational farm seeds company Monsanto, arms contractor Lockheed, and Barbour Griffiths. See, Seema Mustafa, 'US-India Deal Big Business for US Lobbyists,' *Deccan Chronicle*, 20 July 2006.
10. Hoyt Purvis and Steven J. Baker (eds.), *Legislating Foreign Policy*, Boulder: Westview Press, 1984, p. 204.
11. 'Lobbying in Washington,' policy tract, Neill and Company, Washington, p. 5.
12. Richard Cronin's interview to the author, 17 December 1990. In the same vein, P.M. Kamat, comparing the Pakistani and Indian lobbying in the American system, reaches the following conclusion: 'India had been very slow in realizing the Pak tactics in fully utilizing the American system of decision-making which is very much prone to be influenced by lobbies and groups. . . . They have been fully able to influence various groups in Congress to gain the foreign policy goals, while India has done very little positive or negative lobbying not only in the context of Indo–Pak relations as a factor in the Indo–American relations but on the other foreign policy issues affecting Indo–US relations as well.' See. P.M. Kamat (ed.), *Indo-US Relations: Dynamics of Change*, New Delhi: South Asia Publications, 1985, p. 180.
13. Sunanda K. Datta-Ray, *Waiting for America: India and the US in the New Millennium*, New Delhi: HarperCollins, 2002, p. 116.
14. Thus when the Senate Foreign Relations Committee debated the issue in March 1987, Dr Jagat Motwani, Executive Director of National Federation of Asian Indian Organizations in America, testifying before the Committee, argued that 'the intended transfer of highly sophisticated United States military technology to Pakistan, combined with its growing capability to produce nuclear weapons, pose a potential danger to the Indian subcontinent. We Indian Americans are seriously concerned about its

various consequences.' US Senate, Foreign Relations Committee, Hearings, *Security and Development Assistance*, March 1987.

15. Author's interview with the Solarz Committee Staffer, 9 January 1991.
16. See, http://www.gopio.net, 8 March 2003.
17. Hathway, op. cit., p. 399.
18. Ibid., p. 386.
19. Kanjilal, op. cit., p. 46.
20. Keynote address delivered at the 40th Anniversary of India Association of Nashville, 8 March 2003. http://www.gopio.net.
21. Immediately following the Pokhran test, a bill was moved in the House of Representatives, which holds the power of purse, to suspend aid to India. Introducing the Bill (no. 15347) on 12 June 1974, which prohibited foreign assistance to India until she signed the NPT, House Representative Paris said: '. . . the suspicion and fear that surrounds the Indian motives for the recent nuclear detonation could set off a wave of nuclear proliferation around the world if left unchecked. . . . I believe it is time for the United States, which between 1950 and 1971 contributed over $10 billion in foreign assistance to India—and in 1972 and 1973 an additional $400 million—to cut-off all economic assistance of any sort to that country until it signs NPT.' *US Congressional Record*, 93rd Congress, vol. 120, parts 13-14, May-June 1974, p. 18896.
22. Kanjilal, op. cit., p. 48.
23. Gabriel Scheffer, *Modern Diaspora in International Politics*, New York: Croom Helm, 1986, p. 56.

REFERENCES

Ahrari, M.E., *Ethnic Groups and U.S. Foreign Policy: Contributions in Political Science*, New York: Greenwood Press, 1987.

Babu, B.R., *Minorities and the American Political System*, New Delhi: South Asian Publishers, 1989.

Chandrasekhar, S., *From India to America: A Brief History of Immigration, Problems of Discrimination, Admission, and Assimilation*, La Jolla, California: Population Review Publications, 1982.

Datta-Ray, S.K., *Waiting for America: India and the U.S. in the New Millennium*, New Delhi: HarperCollins, 2002.

Desia, S. and R. Kanakia, 'Profile for a Diasporic Community', *Seminar*, no. 538, 2004, p. 49.

Dodd, L.C. and B.I. Oppenheimer, *Congress Reconsidered, Praeger University Series*, New York: Praeger Publishers, 1977.

Horowitz D.L., *Ethnic Groups in Conflict*, Berkeley: University of California Press, 1985.

Iyengar S., *A Checklist on Indians in the U.S.A.*, Hyderabad: ASRC, 1983.

Jayaram, N., *The Indian Diaspora: Dynamics of Migration, Themes in Indian Sociology*, New Delhi: Sage, 2004.

Jensen, J.M., *Passage from India: Asian Indian Immigrants in North America*, New Haven: Yale University Press, 1988.

Kanjilal, T., *Indian-Americans: Participation in the American Domestic Political Process*, Calcutta: Anuradha Kanjilal, 2000.

———, *Indian-Americans and India: An Analysis of Mutual Relations*, Delhi: Kalinga Publications, 2004.

Kapur, A., *India and the United States in a Changing World*, New Delhi: Sage, 2002.

Kondapi, C., *Indian Overseas, 1838-1949*, New Delhi: Indian Council for World Affairs, 1951.

Lessinger, J., *From the Ganges to the Hudson: Indian Immigrants in New-York City*, ed. N.I. Series, New York: Allyn and Bacon, 1995.

Mansingh, S., *India's Search for Power: Indira Gandhi's Foreign Policy, 1966-1982*, New Delhi/Beverly Hills: Sage, 1984.

Min, P.G., *Asian American: Contemporary Trend and Issues*, Sage Focus Editions, Thousand Oaks, Calif.: Sage, 1995.

Polsby, N.W., *Congress and the Presidency*, 4th edn., Prentice-Hall Foundations of Modern Political Science Series, Englewood Cliffs, N.J.: Prentice Hall, 1986.

Purvis, H.H. and S.J. Baker, *Legislating Foreign Policy: A Westview Special Study*, Boulder: Westview Press, 1984.

Schechterman, B. and M.W. Slann, *The Ethnic Dimension in International Relations*, Westport, Conn.: Praeger, 1993.

Sheffer, G., *Modern Diasporas in International Politics*, Londres: Croom Helm, 1986.

Sheth, P., *Indians in America: One Stream, Two Waves*, Jaipur: Rawat, 2001.

Sundquist, J.L., *The Decline and Resurgence of Congress*, Washington, D.C.: Brookings Institution, 1981.

Tinker, H., *The Banyan Tree: Overseas Emigrants from India, Pakistan and Bangladesh*, Oxford (Eng.)/New York: Oxford University Press, 1977.

Waters, M.C., *Ethnic Options: Choosing Identities in America*, Berkeley: University of California Press, 1990.

7

Diasporic Politics of Hindu Nationalism in the United States

PRALAY KANUNGO

The Rashtriya Swayamsevak Sangh (RSS), the fountainhead of Hindu nationalism, is no more confined to India; its ideology, politics and organizational network have gone transnational transcending India's territorial boundaries and forging lateral links among dispersed Hindus across nations. Now its mission is not just to unite Hindus of India; 'Hindus of the world unite' has also become its new clarion call in order to achieve global Hindu unity. This paper attempts to understand how the RSS and its family—the Sangh Parivar—disseminates Hindu nationalism among the 'Hindu' diaspora in the United States (US) and mobilizes their support in order to achieve its political mission at home.

HINDU NATIONALISM GOES OVERSEAS

As the story unfolds, in the late 1940s, there was an accidental meeting between two *swayamsevaks*, while separately reciting the RSS prayer aboard a ship carrying them to Kenya. As both belonged to the saffron brotherhood, they became friends during the voyage. After their arrival they started the first over seas *shakha* (branch/unit) in Kenya.[1] As organization always remains supreme in the RSS agenda, it could not afford to allow the formation of overseas units to accidents and chances. Soon the RSS made its entry into those countries where Arya Samaj, Sanatan Dharma Sabhas, Ramakrishna Mission and other Hindu organizations had already gained foothold. After experimenting with a few names like Bharat Swayamsevak Sangh, it finally chose Hindu Swayamsevak Sangh (HSS), perhaps for strategic reasons; emphasis on religion than nationalism would be more appropriate in the overseas context and be attractive to the expatriates.

Though the RSS claims to have pursued a more proactive strategy *vis-à-vis* the Indian diaspora, its overseas engagement was almost non-existent during the 1950s and 1960s as its primary objective was to expand in India. However, some *pracharaks* (professional organizers) like Bhaurao Deoras, Laxman Rao Bhide occasionally visited overseas and opened branches. Its overseas activities took a new turn in the mid-1970s when Balasaheb Deoras, the third chief of the RSS, sent many RSS leaders abroad seeking support for anti-Emergency struggle. Rajendra Singh became instrumental in setting up of the Friends of India Society International (FISI) in 1976 in UK, and subsequently in the US, mobilizing overseas Indians against Indira Gandhi's authoritarian and anti-democratic rule.[2] With the coming of the Janata Party to power in 1977 and Atal Behari Vajpayee's heading the Ministry of External Affairs, the RSS enhanced its presence as well as credibility abroad. During the 1990s, the RSS actively mobilized overseas Hindus, particularly those in the US and UK, seeking support and raising resources for the Ramjanmabhoomi movement.

The BJP became the only political party that included issues concerning overseas Indians in its election manifesto. After coming to power at New Delhi the BJP-led NDA government pursued a proactive agenda for the Indian diaspora. Vajpayee appointed B.K. Agnihotri as ambassador-at-large for non-resident Indians (NRI)/Peoples of Indian Origin (PIO). Agnihotri, an American green card holder, has been one of the front-ranking leaders of the HSS, FISI and the Overseas Friends of BJP (OFBJP). He was also instrumental in the campaign undertaken by the Sangh Parivar in the wake of nuclear tests and during the Kargil conflict to mobilize public opinion in the US. The RSS wanted someone who could further its diasporic agenda; as per the RSS strategy, Agnihotri's diplomatic status would not only accord him legitimacy, but would also make available the government resources at his disposal.[3] In pursuance of its diasporic agenda the BJP government appointed a High Level Committee on the Indian Diaspora in 2000 under the chairmanship of L.M. Singhvi. The Committee gave some significant recommendations[4] for overseas Indians including the granting of dual citizenship. Vajpayee government endorsed these recommendations. In 2003, it started an annual congregation of overseas Indians named Pravasi Bharatiya Diwas on a regular basis on 9 January, the day Mahatma Gandhi returned to India from South Africa in 1915.

During the tenure of the BJP government the Sangh Parivar expanded its global network further. At present, HSS, the overseas affiliate of the RSS, dedicated to promoting global unity of Hindus, claims to have established contacts in more than 100 countries, out of which it has active branches in 34 countries where it runs 570 *shakhas* including the US, England, South Africa, Fiji, Mauritius, Kenya and various countries in Africa, Caribbean and Europe.[5] The HSS claims to have set up 84 chapters in the US.[6] Other prominent members of RSS's American Parivar are Vishwa Hindu Parishad of America (VHPA), Hindu Students Council (HSC), American Hindu Against Defamation (AHAD), India Development and Relief Fund (IDRF) and OFBJP. The RSS's British Parivar is equally impressive.[7] The sprawling global network of the RSS is co-ordinated by its world wing (*Vishwa Vibhag*).

Indian Political Parties and the Indian Diaspora

In contemporary India, major political forces compete with each other for transnational connections and desire to have relationship with the Indian diaspora. Congress, Socialists, Communists, and Hindu nationalists have established their respective overseas networks cultivating the Indian diaspora.

The nature of this inter-connection and relationship differs, however.

Demolition of every facet of Nehruvianism has always been part of the RSS agenda, hence, it predictably criticizes the Congress government for being indifferent towards the overseas Indians and accuses that during the Burmese crisis Jawaharlal Nehru advised the Indians in Burma to get assimilated in Burmese society forgetting their Indianness. If Congress changed its approach towards overseas Indians, it argues, it was only because of their emerging financial potential.[8] However, it would be incorrect to suggest that Congress was apathetic towards overseas Indians and Nehru was indifferent to their ill-treatment. On the contrary, Indian National Congress passed number of resolutions concerning overseas Indians and sent its emissaries to different countries to understand their problems; thus, C.F. Andrews visited Fiji in 1915 to take stock of the plight of the Indian indentured labourers and one of the objectives of Lala Lajpat Rai's visit to the US in 1914 was to know the conditions of the Indians settled there. And with regard to Nehru's refusal to get involved in the Burmese affairs, his response was not only in consonance with his visionary foreign policy of non-alignment, non-interference and peaceful co-existence, but more importantly, was the most pragmatic decision at that juncture.[9]

In case of Congress, the legacies of freedom struggle and Mahatma Gandhi defined the nature of its overseas relationship, which has by and large been fraternal and flexible. During the post-Independence period, the Congress leadership under Jawaharlal Nehru, Indira Gandhi and Rajiv Gandhi stressed on the 'Indianness' of the diaspora which was primarily cultural; their overseas cultural policy celebrated secularism and inclusiveness as the hallmarks of modern India. Indian socialists, influenced by variants of Socialism, particularly the European ones, attempted to indigenize them in theory and practice and kept only a limited global connection; however, their diasporic connection got disrupted due to intermittent fragmentation and their periodic absorption into other political parties. For Communists, ideological and intellectual inspiration primarily came from outside—either from radical thinkers or from revolutionary movements. They not only got organized on foreign models, but also subjected their parties to overseas scrutiny for a long time; however, now there has been a decisive shift in their relationship with overseas communist parties and movements which have become more fraternal and reciprocal. Communists were proud of their Ghadar (mutiny)[10] lineage and consistently championed radical, secular and class agenda *vis-à-vis* Indian diaspora; with the onset of liberalization at home some of them have started wooing the prosperous diaspora to invest in the States ruled by them.

In contrast, Hindu nationalists have supposedly designed a different model of overseas linkage which is exclusive; they neither acknowledge any external source of inspiration nor follow any external model. As they claim, it is only *Bharat* which is their reference point and it is only Hindutva which provides ideological succour to the Hindus across the globe. Hindu nationalism has created a transnational network of Hindus, which not only follows its prescribed ideological and organizational model but also keeps this complex network under its total tutelage.

HINDU NATIONALIST PROJECT OVERSEAS

The objective of RSS's transnationalism is clear: 'What we need today is a model Hindu society, which is better organized, strong, assertive and the one that speaks in one voice.'[11] In this model, one finds an interesting interplay of 'foreignness' and 'nativeness', of 'nationalism' and 'transnationalism'; the marginality felt by migrants in other parts of the world makes them into important agents of innovation at home.[12] The RSS, calls its transnational project of uniting all Hindus, who supposedly possess a common cultural identity based on Hinduism, as cultural. However, it should be clarified at the outset that the Sangh Parivar's global 'cultural' agenda has deep political implications; its transnational nationalism innovatively engages Indian diaspora in the long-distance politics back home in India.

Globalization being a complex process, generates contradictory manifestations. While making the nation state porous with large flows of people, capital, information, ideas, and images,[13] it has simultaneously brought back nationalism of various kinds to the very centre of the contemporary world. While opening up new frontiers of pluralism, diversity, co-existence and tolerance, it has also seen the resurgence of radical religious-nationalisms and fundamentalisms, which travel beyond the nation at a much faster speed and intensity, capturing the imagination of diaspora communities. South Asian diaspora, like any other, has become enamoured by their fervent appeal.

As the Sangh Parivar's mission is to create a syndicated Hindu identity overseas, it realizes that syncretism is prelude to such an exercise. Hence, demonstrates enough flexibility and pragmatism in order to bring together diverse cults and sects under a broad Hindu umbrella. In order to realize this objective it has entered into the overseas temple network in a big way as temples have emerged as the key sites for the socio-cultural life of Hindu diaspora. Besides, it is also aware about their growing search for spiritualism, particularly the second and third generation American-Hindus. However, it understands well that rejecting the realm of the material world and scientific knowledge would not be the appropriate strategy to capture their attention. Hence, it espouses 'pragmatic spiritualism' by discovering scientific, therapeutic, and management principles in every aspect of Hinduism. As Vasudha Narayan would explain, idol worship is interpreted as abstract forms of contemplation; burning camphor is thought to be a symbolic purification of the self; and cow-dung is said to have antiseptic properties. Moreover, a workshop demonstrating 'Vedantic principles of self-enquiry' may be described as 'a supreme stress management spiritual workshop' and a *vratam*, a ritual fasting, may become 'human resource management'.[14] Thus, Sangh Parivar's 'packaged Hinduism' ideally combines elements of conservative traditions and culture with open narratives of science, modernity and globalization in appropriate measures to attract overseas Hindus.

The RSS understands it well that in order to attract overseas Hindus towards its political project, the best tactic would be to address the core problem that bothers them the most, i.e. protection, preservation and strengthening of family values. Though they usually look down upon American family life and take pride in the strength of their family relationships, in reality, Indian Americans have to grapple with the increasing problems of marital tension, wife abuses, and waywardness of children. Hence, they employ home and family values as ideal tools for reinforcing hierarchy, control, obedience and authority. The RSS recognizes that erosion of parental authority of Hindus in the West has been leading to a 'cultural and spiritual crisis' and hence, the language of rights should be discarded in the upbringing of Hindu children.[15] H.V. Seshadri, the RSS ideologue, laments that children in the West 'are told at every step that they enjoy as much rights as their parents or teachers. Corporal punishment even by parents—let alone by teachers—is considered a crime'.[16] A soothing discourse for immigrant parents indeed!

H.V. Seshadri prescribes a common behavioural pattern for overseas Hindus: At the individual level, a Hindu should try to imbibe Hindu moral and spiritual values, practise meditation, yoga, etc., insulating himself against the prevalent permissive, competitive atmosphere. At the family level, he should aim at preserving a Hindu home and bring about a devotional atmosphere through *bhajans*, reading of scriptures, etc., with all members of the family participating in them. At the social level, they should strive for Hindu unity and offer part of their time, energy and resources in the service of Hindu community. The cultural and religious discourse soon turns political when Seshadri underscores the urgency of 'forging a strong

Hindu lobby to protect Hindu interests anywhere in the world.' He proceeds: 'Hindus abroad should consider Bharat as their spiritual motherland and visit Bharat occasionally. They should also take care not to indulge in any kind of disparaging talk about Bharat.'[17] He calls upon the Hindu diaspora to play an active political role imbibing Sister Nivedita's 'aggressive Hinduism.'[18] Thus, in Seshadri's paradigm, the overseas Indians have a significant role in the affairs of India.

'Hindu Diaspora' and Hindu Nationalism

To what extent has the 'Hindu diaspora' in the US become 'saffronized'? Why does it support Hindutva and contribute generously for its advancement? To answer these complex questions one needs to understand that diasporic politics takes shape as a response to the racial, social and economic marginalization experienced by immigrants. Hindu nationalism of Indian Americans is a response to their experience of racial marginalization in the United States.[19] Religious identity 'becomes a way of evading racial marginality, and of appearing to side-step the great chain of being that has whites above and blacks beneath.'[20] Prema Kurien,[21] in her study on the rise of Hindutva movement in Southern California, observes that Indians in this area experience a greater degree of marginalization than in other area of the country. This in turn has heightened the importance of religion and religious organizations and the need for ethnic affirmation giving Hindu nationalism a much stronger appeal to Hindus here.

Moverover, unlike the post-1965 generation of Indians, who were products of secular Nehruvian India, the recent immigrants are more exposed to the politics of Hindutva in India. Since the 1990s many immigrants with a small town background have come to the US; some of them have already been Hindutva activists and sympathizers in India, and hence, obviously get into the fold of the Sangh Parivar in the US. Moreover, when the new immigrants feel marginalized while negotiating with the stress of immigration and settlement, they are more likely to look towards region, religion, homeland involvement, and the company of fellow Indian immigrants to feel secure. The Sangh Parivar ideally pitches its activities in terms of religion and culture to attract these immigrants. The focus on religious identity provides them relief to overcome marginalization.

This is not to suggest that Indian Americans are innocent victims of Hindu nationalist politics. They are certainly not mere passive recipients of Sangh Parivar's homeland politics. They also manoeuvre homeland resources to elevate their status and respect in the host society. For instance, India's nuclear explosion created euphoria among overseas Indians as it gave them a great sense of pride. And naturally, Sangh Parivar received a big applause as it always favoured a nuclear India. At the same time, VHP's version of a strong Hindu state offers compensatory gratification for the experience of exile and marginality and promises redemption.[22] Likewise, Sangh Parivar's Aryan theory has many takers among Indian immigrants as it elevates their racial status. This theory provides them ammunition to argue that India and Hinduism were the cradle of European civilization and that Indians are if not racially identical to the whites, are at least closer to Euro–Americans (they enjoyed Caucasian status till 1922) than other American minorities.

Closely related to this theme is the myth of model minority. Indian Americans, particularly the educated professionals, being enamoured by the concept of model minority, consciously nurture a desire to achieve such status. Dinesh D'Souza,[23] argues that model immigrants are a special breed demonstrating the finest qualities of hard work and an impatience to succeed. The success story of Indian Americans has been spectacular, as it has the highest per capita income, much above the national average. In 2000, the white households of the US had a median income of about $44,500, the African American households had $29,000, and the Indian American households had a median income of $63,500, the highest among all racial and ethnic groups in America. However, there is another side of the reality—a growing percentage of Indian immigrants do not have advanced level degrees, do not speak English well, and live below the poverty line.[24]

As long as their pursuit of capital accumulation goes uninterrupted, Indian Americans don't mind working silently at the margins receiving approbation from white Americans. D'Souza further asks: Why can't an African American be more like an Asian? For him, the oppressive condition of black Americans is more a result of their civilizational collapse than of the persistence of racist structures. The crisis of black America, he claims, is made more acute by the embarrassing fact of Asian American success. As Vijay Prasad argues, 'D'souza's racism is premised upon a faulty analysis of Asian success in the United States. Those attainments are not caused by natural or cultural selection; rather, they are the result of state selection inherent in the 1965 Immigration Act.'[25] Despite Hindutva's discourse on 'Hindu Superiority' and a general attitude to run down the West, it neither takes up the issue of racial discrimination nor it makes any effort to build any alliance with other marginalized ethnic groups, particularly the Black Americans; it silently endorses the myth of model minority, observes Vijay Prasad.

It would also be naïve to suggest that all those Hindus who find solace with Hinduism do necessarily support Hindutva. After all, Hinduism is much beyond and even antithetical to Hindutva. The Sangh Parivar's ability to conflate the two concepts as well as its persistent attempt to collapse Indian with Hindu makes many of them vulnerable. Sangh Parivar's mission 'is to propagate the idea among identity-insecure Indian immigrants and their vulnerable offspring that Indian=Hindu=supporter of Hindutva.'[26]

The Sangh Parivar in the US: HSS, VHPA, HSC, AHAD, IDRF, OFBJP

RSS's American odyssey started soon after professional Indian immigrant wave to the US began in 1965. It founded the VHPA in 1970, which was incorporated in New York in 1974 as a nonprofit, tax-exempt volunteer-based organization serving the needs of Hindu community in the USA. Unlike the UK, the HSS remained in the background allowing the VHPA to take the lead role. However, the HSS quietly and slowly organized *shakhas* and gave directions to the American Parivar. It divided the US into five organizational zones and started using temple premises to conduct its weekly *shakhas*. It brought some *pracharaks* (preachers/professional organizers) from India to do its organizational work in different zones. Some of these *pracharaks* were educated professionals.[27] Subsequently, it trained some Indian Americans as *vistaraks/pracharaks*. As the Gujarat episode forced the VHPA to be defensive, the HSS came to the forefront taking over the baton from the former.

The VHPA projects a grand vision of building a dynamic Hindu society inspired by the eternal values of Dharma and the lofty ideal of *vasudhaiva kutumbakam* (the entire creation is one family). Its growth was slow in the 1970s as it added only two more offices—Connecticut and Illinois. The VHPA organized the World Hindu Conference (WHC) in 1984, New York, with the objective to bring all Hindu organizations to a common platform under the banner of Hinduism and hegemony of the Sangh Parivar. Between 1980 and 1990 the VHPA established 10 more offices and now claims to have branches in 40 States with active 'member families'. The Sangh Parivar grew rapidly in India during the Ramjanmabhoomi agitation. All of its overseas front organizations became very active, undertaking different programmes like *shila pujan* (consecration of bricks to be used in the construction of the Ram Temple at Ayodhya), etc., generating enthusiasm among Hindus in America, and seeking their support for its homeland project. In the US the period also witnessed a rapid expansion of the Sangh Parivar. The VHPA organized its World Vision 2000 conference in 1993 eliciting an endorsement from the diaspora for the razing of the Babri Masjid. Its supporters in the US called upon 'brothers and sisters in India' to pressurize the government to lift the ban that had been imposed on 'nationalistic organizations' such as the VHP and the RSS. The VHPA organized *Dharma Sansad*

(Parliament of Religion) in 1998 and 1999 which advised Hindus in America to call themselves 'Hindu Americans' instead of Indian Americans and prescribed a model code for them. The VHPA also organized Vishwa Dharma Prasar Yatra (VDPY) in 1999. VHPA's Hindutva politics got a further push with the 9/11 attack. While strongly condemning the 9/11 terrorist attack the VHPA reminded American authorities that Hindus have been victims of terrorist violence in Jammu & Kashmir and hoped that now America will join India and other nations in the fight against this global plague. It called for a global alliance against terrorism and brings 'the perpetrators of this ghastly crime against humanity to justice'.[28] Expressing solidarity with the Americans it appealed Indian Americans to provide all possible assistance to the local and federal authorities in this hour of crisis.

The Hindu Students Council (HSC) functions in many ways as the most visible flagship organization of Hindutva. Founded in 1990, in New Jersey, the HSC has grown very rapidly in North America. It focuses on four ideals: Dharma, Knowledge, Unity and Progress. Its goals are: to provide opportunities to learn about Hindu heritage and culture; foster awareness of issues affecting Hindus; and provides services (*seva*) to the community. The HSC had grown to have 50 chapters spread all across the US and Canada. Initially, the first generation immigrant graduate male students who had some direct connection with the Sangh Parivar in India ran the HSC in most cases. Gradually, the second generation Hindu Americans, who have links in the VHPA, took over the leadership. The HSC is organized along hierarchical lines, thereby confirming that for the Sangh Parivar, organization and hierarchy are inseparable. It organized the Global Vision Hindu Conference in 1993 and Freedom Festival in 1997.

The VHPA has created another organization called AHAD, which acts as a Hindu watchdog group, dedicated 'to preserve the sanctity of Hindu symbols, icons, culture and customs'. Believing in the principle of *dharmo rakshati rakshitah* (those who defend the Dharma are defended by it), it is committed to counter 'Hindu bashing' through writing protest letters, sending e-mails and fax, organizing demonstrations, etc. AHAD had protested the distortion of Lord Krishna's picture on Aerosmith's *Nine Lives* cover, inclusion of Hindu deities at the Karma Club in Chicago, and improper portrayal of Hindu deities in Universal Studio's *Xena: Warrior Princess* show, inclusion of a Hindu *shloka* (verse) in the movie *Eyes Wide Shut.* If protests do not work, AHAD uses even economic threat 'to guard the honor of Hinduism'. For instance, a Seattle-based firm that had been selling toilet seats with the pictures of Hindu deities, such as Lord Ganesha and Goddess Kali, had to apologize and stop marketing the product under AHAD's threat of economic boycott by Hindus worldwide.

The IDRF was founded in 1988 by Vinod Prakash, a *swayamsevak* and a former World Bank employee, and has been running 'as an all-voluntary, tax-exempt, NGO with zero overhead', which is also eligible for corporate gift-matching and gift of appreciated stocks. Its motto—'India is our mother, not just a nation, and it is our duty to serve her'—strikes an emotional chord with the Indian Americans and propels them to contribute liberally. As the IDRF claims, it has been supporting a residential higher secondary school, more than 200 one-teacher schools in tribal areas, each providing non-formal education at an annual cost of only $350 per school, mobile medical vans in rural/tribal areas, and women's vocational training centres. The IDRF has actively supported when natural calamities struck India. In 1993, it raised more than 3 million dollars for the victims of Latur earthquake in Maharashtra and reconstructed a devastated village. In 1999, it raised $315,000 for the rehabilitation of victims of Kargil crisis. It also raised money for the victims of Orissa cyclone. However, 'Foreign Exchange of Hate' accuses that IDRF has been 'funding sectarian groups in India from its inception' and has been raising funds to support RSS activities from US corporations and NRIs there. To prove its case, the report has systematically set out the links between the IDRF and the Sangh Parivar.[29] On the other hand, the Sangh Parivar and the IDRF have denied these charges. Even some academics also dismiss that the Indian diaspora is largely pro-Hindutva and its financing has empowered the Sangh Parivar to perpetrate heinous acts of communal violence against minorities as they do not find enough empirical evidence or analytical reasoning to substantiate these charges.[30]

The OFBJP-US has ten chapters in the US: New York, New Jersey, Connecticut, Los Angeles, San Francisco, Houston, Chicago, Washington, Atlanta and Tampa. It not only promotes the BJP's ideology and politics in the US but also highlights the concerns of overseas Indians to the Indian and overseas authorities. It often plays host to the many visiting party leaders from India. During the general elections in India, party leaders like L.K. Advani have visited different states in the US and the OFBJP raised money for the Indian elections. It also interacts with the cultural and business delegations from India. However, the organization has been plagued by acute factionalism compelling its president to step down in 2005 before the expiry of his term.

Though one may agree with the proposition that the RSS has not yet established its hegemony over the Hindu diaspora in the US, there is no doubt that it has systematically penetrated into the Indian diasporic public sphere in the US particularly during the last two decades. Its agenda at home had definitely got sustenance and support from its diasporic presence; its overseas network is organically linked with its ideology and politics back at home.

Disseminating Hindutva in America

How does the Sangh Parivar propagate its ideology and politics? The innovative mediums include 'Sunday Schools', summer 'Heritage' camps, seminars and conferences, and comic books like *Amar Chitra Katha*; every organization of the Parivar has its own newsletter and publications. VHPA runs *Val Vihar* for imparting 'informal education of Hindu Dharma (religion), culture, music, Indian history and language for children mostly of Indian descent. The main goal is to pass on our rich heritage to the next generation of Americans of Indian origin.'[31] The summer camps run by the VHPA have been able to rope in 'many unsuspecting second-generation Indian Americans so that they emerge into young adulthood with a very narrow definition of what it is to be an Indian.'[32] When a young Syrian Christian from Kerala went to a meeting of one of the South Asian students club at New York University, she was surprised to hear: 'How can you be Indian with a name like "Abraham"? That's not an Indian name.'[33] This is very much in tune with Sudarshan's prescription for Indian Muslims and Christians to adopt Indian/Hindu names.

Hindu nationalists have opened Hindu University of America in Florida in 1989 to teach 'all aspects of Hindu thoughts, life, traditions, religions and culture.' Moreover, the Internet has emerged a powerful tool in dissemination of the ideology and politics of Hindu nationalism overseas. Anita Khandelwal has made a detailed study to understand the manner in which 'diaspora nationalism' is propagated and enacted, particularly with the aid of the Internet.[34] The HSC sponsors Global Hindu Electronic Network (GHEN), which connects to different Hindutva websites, such as *hindunet,* the Hindu Vivek Kendra, archives of *Hinduism Today*, etc. These websites, in the name of Hindu history, not only disseminate myths and misinformation on Hinduism, but also consistently preach hatred against Islam and Muslims.[35] Many professional Indians, particularly the Hindus, quite readily and uncritically accept the culture of the Internet.

Besides *Hinduism Today*, which openly takes up Hindutva causes, Hindu nationalists in the US have cultivated cordial relationship with the two well-circulated Indian American newspapers: *India Abroad* and *India West.* For instance, Sonal Shah, who has been allegedly promoting the cause of Hindutva in the US, got India Abroad Person of Year (2003). Thus, the RSS has been able to saffronize the Indian American media to some extent. An American journalist of *Houston Chronicle* revealed that Hindu nationalist activists in Houston never appreciated his reports on Hindu–Muslim bonhomie and cooperation.

Growing Political Clout of Indian Americans and the RSS

Indian American population in the US has dramatically increased by almost 106 per cent from 1990 to 2000, comprising 1.678 million of the US population, rising more than twofold from 815,447 in 1990. The Indian American community is now the third largest Asian American group in the US behind Chinese and Filipino Americans. With their growing number and economic clout the community is now gearing to flex their political muscle. Influential community members have a direct link with many Senators and Congressmen in New York, Washington, Chicago and the West Coast. Indian Americans have been very active in raising funds for both presidential as well as Congressional elections. Almost after a gap of five decades Bobby Jindal has become the second Indian American to enter the Congress and later he also became the Governor of Louisiana; few Indians have got elected to state legislatures as well. President Barak Obama's administration has had an impressive number of Indian Americans: while Sonal Shah heads White House's Office of Social Innovation and Civic Participation, and Vivek Kundra is the federal Chief Information Officer (CIO); subsequently, Rajiv Shah has been appointed as the chief of US Agency for International Development (USAID). There has been strong allegation that both Sonal Shah and Vivek Kundra have Hindutva connection.

The growing presence of Indian Americans in the White House suggest that Indian diaspora has now mastered the art of political and business lobbying. The largest caucus on Capitol Hill is the India Caucus with a membership over 180. Despite Golwalkar's appreciation of Hitler's purging of Jews, the RSS has always remained close to Israel because of its anti-Muslim ideology and the Sangh Parivar in the US has always appreciated the aggressive lobbying skills of the Jews. During the NDA regime it got the opportunity to collaborate with the Jewish lobbying groups in the US, including American Israel Public Affairs Committee (AIPAC). The Indian Ambassador started celebrating Hanukkah inviting American Jews. Emulating them, a new lobbying forum called US Indian Political Action Committee (USIPAC) was launched in September 2002 with the motto: 'Let Indian American Voices be Heard'. A joint meeting of Capitol Hill Forum was organized in 16 July 2003 in which US Indian Political Action Committee (USIPAC), American Jewish Committee (AJC), and AIPAC participated. Tom Lantos, Democratic Congressman from California, explained the logic of such collaboration: 'We are drawn by mindless, vicious, fanatic, Islamic terrorism' receiving standing applause by Indians. Gary Ackerman, another Democratic Congressman from New York, observed that while Israel was surrounded by 120 million Muslims while India has 120 million (within).[36] All the speakers used Muslim and terrorist interchangeably. Compulsion of American politicians might have been contextual, but this helps the diasporic politics of the RSS quite well.

Resistance to Hindu Nationalism in the US

Hindu nationalism does not go unchallenged in the US, however. Politically progressive groups and individuals who celebrate diversity, plurality, peace, tolerance and mutual respect challenge its monolithic, hegemonic and divisive discourse. Various small groups have sprung up advocating rights for the marginalized and oppressed Indian Americans: taxi-drivers, workers, women, gays, lesbians and so on.

A strong solidarity among these groups is shaping up. More importantly, all these organizations vociferously condemn the communal politics of the Sangh Parivar. Some activists and academics brought out a detailed report on the source of Sangh Parivar's American funding and their disbursement and making appeal to the Indian Americans to stop funding the 'Hate Campaign' in India. Organizations like EKTA outrightly condemned the 2002 Gujarat massacre.

After the Gujarat carnage, Coalition Against Genocide (CAG) was formed consisting of students, self-employed, professionals, artists, Hindus, Muslims, Christians, Sikhs, and Atheists. In an aggressive campaign by e-mail, phone and fax it opposed Narendra Modi's invitation by Association of Indian Americans of North America (AINA) to New York in March 2005. Modi was also to attend the annual convention of the Asian American Hotel Owners Association (AAHOA) in Florida. CAG called on Chris Mathew, the host of AAHOA, to pull out; the Institute of Religion and Public Policy wrote to Condoleezza Rice; 125 faculty members of different South Asian Studies Programs wrote to the state department. Citing UN Genocide Convention they argued that the Gujarat case was genocide and referred to the US Congress Resolution 156 and 160 which condemned persecution of Muslims and Christians in Gujarat. As a result of this aggressive campaign Narendra Modi was denied diplomatic visa by the State Department under the International Religious Freedom Act. This might have been a temporary setback to Hindu nationalism in the US, but it is unlikely to compel the RSS to change the contours of its diasporic politics.

CONCLUSION

Hindu nationalism does not represent the entire Indian American community, which though predominantly Hindu, also comprises Muslims, Sikhs, Christians, and Parsis of Indian origin. It does not even represent the entire Hindu community which is diverse in terms of region, language, class, caste, gender and generation. However, Hindu nationalism in the US has been successful in constructing and consolidating a religious and cultural Hindu identity to some extent, primarily due to its efficient organizational ability, its eclectic approach to bring all Hindu organizations under its own canopy and its skill to manoeuvre diasporic anxiety and marginalization. Moreover, transnational politics of Hindu nationalism got a major boost in the US during the years of the BJP rule in India, which not only endeared the Indian Americans by pursuing a proactive diasporic policy, but also greatly facilitated the entry of the Sangh Parivar into the US diplomatic circle thereby resulting in its collaboration with the Jewish lobbies and other right wing forces, against 'Islamic Terrorism', particularly after 9/11. Though the fall of the BJP government held back the political march of Hindu nationalism, it still continues to work quietly for Hindu consolidation in the US.

NOTES

1. Jai Prakash, 'The Sangh Fraternity Bringing the World Within its Fold', *Organiser*, vol. XLVI, no. 40, 7 May 1995, pp. 51-2.
2. Many overseas sympathizers of the Congress joined FISI in the US. Gaurang Vaishnav, the present General Secretary of VHPA was one of them. *Interview* with Gaurang Vaishnav, New Jersey, December 2003.
3. The US government put a condition on Agnihotri to forego his green card to be eligible for diplomatic status. However, Agnihotri was not ready to surrender that privilege and continued to run his office at New York without any diplomatic standing. The Comptroller and Auditor General of India has criticized the NDA government for opening Agnihotri's office without assigning any mandate and incurring an 'avoidable' expenditure of Rs. 15.95 crore. There was overlapping of functions between this office at New York and the Indian Mission in Washington.
4. See *Report of the High Level Committee on the Indian Diaspora*, New Delhi: Indian Council of World Affairs, 2001.
5. *Interview* with Shyam Parande, *Sah-Sanyojak*, Vishwa Vibhag, July 2005, New Delhi. One can see the growth of the HSS between 1995 and 2005; in 1995, the HSS conducted only 178 *Shakhas* in 18 countries. See Jai Prakash, op. cit.
6. Khanderao Kand, PR Coordinator, HSS, USA, quoted in *Organiser*, vol. LVII, no. 7, 28 August 2005. During the last decade the HSS in the US has grown fivefold by enhancing the number of *shakhas* from 17 to 84.
7. See Chetan Bhatt, 'Dharmo rakshati rakshitah: Hindutva Movements in the UK', *Racial and Ethnic Studies*, vol. 23, no. 2, May 2000, pp. 559-93.
8. For Hindutva's critique of Nehru on Burmese crisis, see *Organiser*, 5 May 1991, p. 12, quoted in Arvind Rajagopal, *Politics, After Television: Hindu Nationalism and the Reshaping of the Public in India*, Cambridge: Cambridge University Press, 2001, p. 243.

9. Hugh Tinker, *The Banyan Tree*, London and New York: Oxford University Press, 1977, p. 10.
10. During the First World War, the radical Ghadar Party mobilized the Indian diaspora in the US to overthrow the British government in India.
11. S.V. Tatwavadi, 'Hindus Abroad', in *Vishwa Mangal Hetave*, Souvenir published on the occasion of Vishwa Sangh Shibir, Mumbai: Vishwa Adhyayan Kendra, 2000, p. 119.
12. Peter van der Veer, *Religious Nationalism: Hindus and Muslims in India*, New Delhi: Oxford University Press, 1996, p. 134.
13. Arjun Appadurai, *Modernity at Large*, Minneapolis: University of Minnesota Press, 1996.
14. Vasudha Narayanan, 'Creating the South Indian "Hindu" Experience in the United States', in Raymond Brady Williams (ed.), *A Sacred Thread: Modern Transmission of Hindu Traditions in India and Abroad*, Chambersburg: Anima Publications, 1992.
15. H.V. Seshadri, *Organiser*, 4 November 1984, p. 9.
16. H.V. Seshadri, *Hindus Abroad: The Dilemma, Dollar or Dharma?* New Delhi: Suruchi, 1990, p. 58.
17. Ibid., p. 65.
18. Ibid., p. 39.
19. Rajagopal, op. cit., p. 268.
20. Arvind Rajagopal, 'Hindu Nationalism in the US: Changing Configurations of Political Practice', *Ethnic and Racial Studies*, vol. 23, no. 3, 2000, p. 472.
21. Prema Kurien, 'Constructing' "INDIANNESS" in the United States: The Role of Hindu and Muslim Indian Immigrants', http://www.usc.edu/ dept/ LAS/SC2/images/top_page.jpg.
22. Rajagopal, op. cit., p. 47.
23. Dinesh D'Souza, *The End of Racism: Principles for a Multiracial Society*, New York: Simon and Schuster, 1995.
24. Mira Kamdar, 'Lights, Camera, Action', *Seminar*, 538, June 2004.
25. Vijay Prasad, *The Karma of Brown Folk*, Minneapolis: University of Minnesota Press, 2000, p. 4.
26. Kamdar, op. cit., p. 81.
27. For example, Manohar Sindhe, who was in charge of the West Zone of the US, is a qualified doctor. *Interview* with Manohar Sindhe, *Artesia*, Southern California, December 2003.
28. http://www.vhp-america.org/press/vhpa_pr_091101.htm

29. See *The Foreign Exchange of Hate: IDRF and the American Funding of Hindutva,* Mumbai, India, and The South Asia Citizens Web, France: Sabrang Communications & Publishing Pvt. Ltd., 2002.
30. Devesh Kapur, 'Firm Opinions, Infirm Facts', *Seminar,* 538, June 2004, pp. 32-5.
31. *Chaitanya Bharati,* Special Bala Vihara Publications, 2004, VHPA, Inc., Metropolitan Washington (DC) Chapter, editorial.
32. Kamdar, op. cit., p. 81.
33. Ibid.
34. See Stanley J. Tambiah, 'Transnational Movements, Diaspora, and Multiple Modernities', *Daedalus,* pp. 163-93. Tambiah refers to Anita Kandelwal's unpublished essay on 'Nationalism on the Net: An Analysis of the Internet in the Creation of Diaspora Nationalism.'
35. For a detailed account of virtual Hindutva, see Vinay Lal, 'The Politics of History in the Internet: Cyber-Diasporic Hinduism and the North American Diaspora', in Makarand Paranjape (ed.), *In Diaspora: Theories, Histories, Texts,* New Delhi: Indialog, 2001, pp. 179-220. On virtual Islam, see Peter Mandaville, 'Communication and Diasporic Islam: A Virtual Ummah?', K.H. Karim (ed.), *The Media of Diaspora,* London, New York: Routledge, 2003, pp. 135-47.
36. *Ghadar,* vol. 7, June 2004.

REFERENCES

Appadurai, A., *Modernity at Large: Cultural Dimensions of Globalization,* Minneapolis, Minn.: University of Minnesota Press, 1996.

Bhatt, C., 'Dharmo Rakshati Rakshitah: Hindutva Movements in the UK', *Ethnic and Racial Studies,* vol. 23, no. 2, 2000, pp. 559-93.

Kapur, D., 'Firm Opinions, Infirm Facts', *Seminar,* no. 538, 2004, pp. 32-5.

Narayanan, V., 'Creating the South Indian 'Hindu': Experience in the United States', in *A Sacred Thread: Modern Transmission of Hindu Traditions in India and Abroad,* ed. R.B. Williams, Chambersburg, PA: Anima, 1992.

Prakash, J., 'The Sangh Fraternity Bringing the World Within its Fold', *Organiser,* vol. XLVI, no. 40, 1995, pp. 51-2.

Report of the High Level Committee on the Indian Diaspora, New Delhi: Indian Council of World Affairs, 2001, p. 576.

Seshadri, H.V., *Hindus Abroad: The Dilemma, Dollar or Dharma?*, New Delhi: Suruchi, 1990.

Tatwavadi, S.V., 'Hindus Abroad', in *Vishwa Mangal Hetave*, Mumbai: Vishwa Adhyayan Kendra, 2000, p. 119.

The Foreign Exchange of Hate: IDRF and the American Funding of Hindutva, Mumbai, India, and The South Asia Citizens Web, France: Sabrang Communications & Publishing Pvt. Ltd., 2002.

Tinker, H., *The Banyan Tree: Overseas Emigrants from India, Pakistan, and Bangladesh*, Oxford (Eng.)/New York: Oxford University Press, 1977.

van der Veer, P., *Religious Nationalism: Hindus and Muslims in India*, Berkeley, CA: University of California Press, 1994.

PART II

Sub-National Indian Diaspora in International Relations: Beyond Long-Distance Nationalism

8

Legacies, Trajectories, and Political Fortunes

Aspects of the Hindu Sindhi Diaspora

MARK-ANTHONY FALZON

Hindu Sindhis are a most remarkable lot. Since at least 1860 they have been involved in large-scale migration—to trade, in response to shifting political situations, and as part of a wider post-War migration from the Indian subcontinent. Their shops and businesses are to be found in well over 100 countries, selling and trading in anything from textiles to groundnuts to Oriental handicrafts. Sindhi names feature regularly on the various lists of the world's richest Asians. And yet, this group is all but absent from the academic literature. The notable exceptions are Thakur (1959), Anand (1996), Markovits (2000), and Falzon (2004). Even in broad-sweep surveys such as *The Cambridge Survey of World Migration* (Cohen, ed., 1995), or *The Penguin Atlas of Diasporas* (Chaliand & Rageau, 1995), there is no mention of this group.

I suspect that the reason why Sindhis are so 'invisible' as a group has to do with their approach to the politics of diaspora. There is very little mobilization of resources and ideas to mobilize the group as a transnational political entity. Further, in their various countries of settlement Sindhis tend to keep a low profile and to steer clear of (national) politics. The exception is India itself, where Sindhis constitute a rather well-known group, politically and economically.

In this paper I shall be looking at the main types of political articulation within the Sindhi diaspora: cosmopolitanism, visions of a new homeland, and involvement in Indian national politics. On the one hand, Sindhis exhibit a marked degree of group corporacy; closer inspection, however, reveals that there are important and historically-rooted disjunctures, primarily along the lines of *jati* and their specific histories of mobility.

THE HINDU SINDHI DIASPORA

Hindu Sindhis (henceforth 'Sindhis') originated in the province of Sind which from 1843 to 1947 was the north-western most province of British India; it became part of the newly-formed nation state of Pakistan with the Independence of India and the Partition of the country in 1947. When the British conquered and annexed Sind to their Indian possessions in 1843, the province had for several hundred years been ruled by a series of Muslim dynasties. The population was mainly Muslim but roughly one out of every ten was a Hindu—this proportion varied according to state and locality. The Hindus of Sind were mostly employed in trade and small business, although a very small number of them served as administrators to the Muslim royalty and aristocracy, and later to the British.

In terms of religious practice, Sindhis are the result of the confluence of cultures and ideas that was pre-Partition Sind, and which of course has continued in the manifold localities where they are settled. Most Sindhis are Nanakpanthis. This means that they follow the teachings of Guru Nanak (the first guru of Sikhism) and perform various rituals associated with Sikhism (not with Khalsa though); at the same time they have not abandoned their devotion to the Hindu pantheon or to the rituals of mainstream Hinduism. In addition, Sindhis today cultivate to a decreasing extent one religious legacy of pre-Partition Sind: Sufism and personal devotions to Sufi *pirs* (holy men).

The term 'Sindhi diaspora' in effect subsumes a number of processes of migration each of which took place within a particular historical and social context.[1] In a nutshell, there were three major waves of population movement out of Sind and South Asia. The first, which originated with the British annexation of the province in 1843 and the subsequent incorporation of Sind into an expanding world-system, was confined to a group of merchants from the small town of Hyderabad. It was a trade diaspora in—Abner Cohen's (1971)—sense of the term. Leaving their families behind, men struck out in search of business opportunities to places as far apart as Panama and the Straits Settlements (today's Singapore). These migrants were known as 'Sindworkis' and the type of long-distance translocal commerce they practised as 'Sindwork' (I should also point out that Sindwork was in the main a prerogative of the *bhaiband jati*).[2] To a lesser extent, the spread of the Sindworkis was mirrored by the mobile banking practices of traders from the town of Shikarpur to the north of Hyderabad, who themselves spread across central Asia and later the Indian subcontinent (Markovits, 2000). The earliest migrations, therefore, were centred solely around trade and existed within the economic and administrative structures of the British colonial enterprise; they represent the type of migrants that Parekh (1994) has called 'passenger Indians' who followed the economic opportunities created by indenture and other projects of empire.

The second migration, on the other hand, was a direct result of the political and social strife that came with the Partition of India in 1947. Sindhis left their homes in the fledgling Pakistan *en masse* and moved to India or to locations in which they already had considerable business interests (It ought to be mentioned, however, that small populations of Hindus still live in Sind, Pakistan). My informants (see also Anand, 1996) gave various reasons why Bombay (Mumbai) attracted more than its fair share of Sindhi Partition refugees—why it became, in fact, the major centre of relocation in post-1947 India. First, the relation between Sind and the city of Mumbai had its historical roots in the British period. Sind had been part of the Bombay Presidency up to 1936, and its colleges had been affiliated to Bombay University. This meant that Sindhis who wanted to further their education, notably Hindus from the *amil jati* of Hyderabad and Karachi, often did so in Mumbai. There was therefore a relation between the educated elites of

Sind and Mumbai as the centre of the Presidency. In addition, many Sindwork firms from Hyderabad had established business branches in Mumbai well before 1947; these were in the main sourcing branches intended to supply a growing global trade.

Apart from this longer-term historical relation, there was the issue of communication during the events of Partition. The safest way to travel out of Sind at Partition was by ship to Mumbai; within the context of the violence of the time, train journeys were deemed unsafe and prone to attack. Last but not least, it must be remembered that most Sindhis in pre-Partition Sind were traders, and that therefore Mumbai—which has always been the commercial hub of the subcontinent—held a special attraction to them. In any case the 1951 census of India showed that of the 0.8 million or so Sindhi-speaking people settled in India, 36 per cent had set up home in Mumbai. Today several hundred thousand Sindhis live in the city and its satellite towns—notably Ulhasnagar, formerly a refugee camp and now a town which is synonymous with Sindhis and business activities.

Many Sindhis who settled in India in 1947 have since participated in a third migration: the so-called 'Indian diaspora' that has seen millions of people move out of the subcontinent in search of opportunity. From the early 1950s but mainly since the 1960s, a number of them started moving to the industrialized countries of the West—the United States, Canada, and Britain—as well as to Australia. This was part of a wider immigration movement from South Asia into these countries, which were and are seen as 'lands of opportunity' and good employment—Britain has taken at least 1.5 million immigrants in the last thirty years or so, and the US and Canada almost 0.8 million (Chaliand and Rageau, 1995: 154). This trend has today been fuelled by the labour requirements of the information technology sector. The countries of the Gulf (notably the United Arab Emirates and in particular the city of Dubai) have also attracted a large number of Indians among whom Sindhis are strongly represented. Again, these countries offer much opportunity because of their economic position as countries of great wealth, low populations, and labour shortages; they encourage migration by presenting themselves as places where one can make money. Sindhis dominate the textiles trade in Dubai, and they are also known to be involved in 're-exporting' (smuggling) consumer items from South Asia and East Africa via Dubai to India and other places (most recently Russia) (Weiner, 1982).

One has to add to the list of population movements of Sindhis, the 'numerous small partitions' (as my informants called them) that have accompanied political changes, the most notable of which took place in East Africa where 'Africanisation' by the Kenyan and Ugandan governments from the late 1960s to the early 1980s forced Sindhis (all Indians in fact) out of the countries where they had been living for generations. These people are what Bhachu (1985) calls 'twice migrants.' One should note, however, that this term appears to be conservative when one considers the stories of Sindhi traders such as one Tekchand Mirpuri dispensing free medicine at his private charity in Ulhasnagar: 'Our family has been through so many partitions. We lost property in Lagos, and Cambodia and Saigon in Indo–China. Now we are operating mainly from Manila in the Philippines.' Tekchand would perhaps more properly be described as participating in 'multiple experiences of rediasporization' (Boyarin, cited in Clifford, 1994: 305).

As a result of this series of migrations, Hindu Sindhis today are dispersed in well over a hundred countries; they retain a degree of cohesion that manifests itself in marriage and kinship practices, in the politics of group identity and, most notably, in the types of business networks they engage in. It is important to point out that this cohesive tendency has a history; until Partition, what really mattered was not so much the abstract and generic designation of 'Sindhi' as the heavily connotated details and particularities of *jati* and regional origin. Even if as an anthropologist one is not too surprised to learn that the notion of a Hindu Sindhi identity followed rather than preceded the time when Hindu people were effectively living in Sind, it is nevertheless important to stress the point that Partition as a common historical trajectory with its baggage of unifying Partition memories had a profound effect on the formation of contemporary understandings of 'Sindhi identity'.

SINDHI COSMOPOLITANS

The first way in which Sindhis approach the politics of diaspora is through the idea of cosmopolitanism. The prime characteristic of Sindhis as an ethnic group is their cosmopolitanism; Sindhis have immediate relatives living in other countries, from Panama to Dubai to Singapore, and there is an exchange of goods and a marked movement of people between them, across space. Harry, a Sindhi trader living in London, illustrates this cosmopolitan way of life. First, his real name is Hardas but he prefers to call himself 'Harry' because he feels it sounds more cosmopolitan, more 'Western', possibly more sophisticated. He runs his own small import-export company from a small office in a London suburb. Harry's father, who spent his life in three different countries, was born in Hyderabad, initially worked with a Sindwork firm in East Africa; eventually he set up his own small business and moved there permanently with his family after Partition. In 1975, when the situation of Indian traders in East Africa became precarious, the family moved to London. Even today, Harry moves between London and Mumbai. Every year in December, Harry and his wife spend a few weeks in Mumbai, meeting their relatives and other Sindhis. Harry's ambition is to make enough money to buy a flat in Mumbai, preferably in one of the posh suburbs of the city, in order to spend longer periods in the city after retirement. They will also be seen as true cosmopolitans, with homes in London as well as in Mumbai.

It is necessary here to qualify the word 'cosmopolitanism', which, judging by the spate of books and scholarly articles that include it in their title, has of late experienced something of a revival. As its etymology (Greek *cosmos*, 'world' and *polites*, 'citizen') suggests, to be cosmopolitan originally meant to be a 'citizen of the world', a human being (dis)located above all attachment to the particular—be it tribe, native town, religious group, or nation. In this sense, for the Soviets, for instance, the term implied a disparagement of Russian traditions and culture and was equated with disloyalty to the State.[3] Its frequency in late twentieth-century popular discourse, however, has prompted a broadening of its meaning. The fact that a growing number of groups claim cosmopolitan status is, to paraphrase Deshpande (1998: 279, emphasis in original), '*accompanied by* the growth of particularistic cultural identities of all kinds'. From 'world citizen', therefore, 'cosmopolitan' has come to signify a transnationally-situated subject who is nonetheless rooted in particular histories, localities, and community allegiances—'world' has become 'worlds', that is. Robbins (1998) points out that what we see around us is a plurality of cosmopolitanisms—alternatively, as Pollock et al. (2000: 588) put it, 'cosmopolitanism is infinite ways of being'. A detailed discussion of this shift in understanding is outside the scope of this paper, but suffice it to say that 'cosmopolitanism' for Sindhis means three things: dispersal, interconnectivity, and adaptability. It means the world (or a substantial chunk of it) as a potential field of interaction—not least along the historically-established lines of particular allegiances to community, locality, nation.

Cosmopolitanism is therefore one of the main feature in the imagination of the Sindhi ethnic group. The phrase 'we Sindhis are everywhere' is constantly used. Further, not only do Sindhis see themselves are dispersed all over the world, but they also visualize themselves as being connected via kinship. This is, of course, a common feature of all ethnic groups, but it becomes especially striking when the web of real and/or imaginary kinship encompasses over 100 countries around the world. Sindhis tend to believe that, 'if you keep on going back, you will make the connection somewhere'. That somewhere could mean the Sindhi family living down the road in suburban London or, equally, one settled in Singapore or Ghana. Crucially, the kinship 'connection' invariably has commercial overtones as Sindhi surnames stand for particular families and, almost without exception, particular business engagements.

The conquest of geographical space is an important component of Sindhayat (Sindhiness). Vernacular histories, for instance, tend to come up with narratives that, accurately or not, emphasize the mobility of the group and its sense of adventure in search of trading opportunity. As Buxani (cited in Panjwani, 1987: 95, my parenthesis) writes,

> [i]t has been asked, perhaps naively, in what countries Sindhuvarkis [Sindworkis] are to be found. A more appropriate question might be: where are they not to be found? A Sindhwarki post has not yet been set up in the new Antarctica settlements of scientists but a Shikarpuri who operates gold business in Alaska is believed to be working on it.

Eager to impress upon his readers the idea of the conquest of space, Malkani (1984: 169) assures us that '(o)thers had found a Sindhi enterprise even on Falkland Islands near the South Pole.' Note the exaggerated southerly position of the Falkland Islands, which highlights the idea of exploration and wide-ranging mobility—this is also present in Buxani's quote (above), which portrays a Sindhi from Alaska thinking of setting up business in Antarctica no less. Moreover, this notion of mobility and ubiquity is presented as an ancient phenomenon. One popular theory is that the Phoenicians were in fact Sindhis (ibid.: 153), while a more ambitious one maintains that '(r)esearch indicates there must have been Sindhvarkis in the ports where Ulysses called in the course of his 30 years Odyssey . . .' (Buxani in Panjwani 1987: 94).

Travel, therefore, is the logical counterpart of the idea that Sindhis are a cosmopolitan group. This holds especially for Sindworkis, who run translocal businesses and who have widely-dispersed families. As Mohan, a well-established lawyer in Mumbai, said 'Sindworkis are so difficult to meet, because they are always on the move.' This mobile lifestyle of successful Sindhis extends to their more popular gurus. Dada J.P. Vaswani has 'been around the world several times' and is known as an 'international saint.' Typically, Vaswani gives a talk (sometimes attended by hundreds of people), spends some time meeting people at semi-private events and *satsangs*, and moves on.

Dada Ishwar Balani, who operates the Holy Mission of Guru Nanak in London, travels frequently and widely, conducting *satsangs*, delivering sermons, and establishing local *tikanas*. A guru who aspires to recognition by the Sindhi community must be sensitive to the cosmopolitan realities of his would-be followers. He 'must go around'. And yet, both these gurus constantly exhort their audiences to preserve their culture. For them, Sindhis were isolated from their own land, like Jews. Like Jews, they should remain united and preserve their language and traditional values. This discourse, coupled with the geographical spread of its context, beautifully sums up the idea of an 'actually-existing' cosmopolitanism.

Hand in hand with this notion goes that of adaptability—clearly, if such a mobile group is to thrive, it has to be able to adapt to local circumstance. This idea of adaptability takes on various guises. The first concerns religious practice. *'Ba Brahman "Ram Ram", ba Mullah "Allah Allah"'* (When among Brahmins say 'Ram Ram', when among Mullahs 'Allah Allah'), goes a Sindhi proverb. Indeed, apart from the rise of Jhulelal, the only constant factor of Sindhi religious practice is its variability. Of course, like the lack of a 'homeland', this religious eclecticism is a source of some vexation among the cultural entrepreneurs of the community, and is partly the reason why the devotion to Jhulelal was reinvented after Partition as a unitary force bringing all Sindhi devotions together.

If we take into account these three characteristics (i.e. cosmopolitanism, multi-sited locations and religious eclectism), Sindhis appear as a group of people for whom geographical distance is a challenge but never an obstacle—indeed, it is an essential aspect of their being as a community.

THE POLITICAL PROJECTS OF THE SINDHI DIASPORA

The Necessity of a Homeland

The second way in which Sindhis approach the politics of diaspora is through the idea of a 'new homeland', a place over which

Sindhis would hold sovereignty and where they would inscribe notions of local 'community', 'culture', and 'people'. Sporadically the idea is peddled in Sindhi magazines, internet sites, books, etc. Two suggestions have been a corner of Rajasthan (Anand, 1996) and the Andaman and Nicobar Islands (Advani, 1997).[4] What is interesting about these cultural entrepreneurs, whose products find few takers among Sindhis and who constitute the exception rather than the rule, is that they represent the contemporary phenomenon of a 'diasporic language' (see Clifford, 1994; Vertovec, 2000)—not least through a continuous process of self-comparison with groups such as the Kurds, the Lebanese, and, of course, the Jews. 'There were three communities in the history of humanity that lost their land', one rather ill-informed publisher of a 'community magazine' explained, 'the Palestinian Muslims, the Jews, and the Sindhis. The Muslims got their land back as did the Jews—we are the only bloody community that didn't.'

It is important to understand why these imagined Sindhi homelands do not coincide with the territory of Sind in Pakistan. In this respect there are two important observations to be made. First, Sind is now a part of Pakistan which is not merely a different nation state but an Islamic one which is perceived as hostile and threatening by many Hindus—especially those under the influence of Hindutva groups such as Rashtriya Swayamsevak Sangh (RSS) which, broadly-speaking, view Pakistan as a terrorism-sponsoring State doing its best to infiltrate India and undermine Hinduism.[5] Although a very few, particularly those influenced by Sufism, felt a bond of kinship and language with Muslim Sindhis living in Sind, most of them held very strong opinions about Pakistan and its alleged anti-Hindu activities. This is hardly surprising, given the extent to which Hindutva has been exported or 'transnationalized' by Hindu nationalist organizations in India (see for instance Raj, 1999). Sind as a primordial homeland with which to continue to cultivate ties, therefore, is seen as an increasingly unviable *political* prospect by Sindhis in diaspora.

Second, since Sindhis are mainly involved in business and notably in transnational trade, very few of them seriously imagine a future for themselves trading in or from an isolated valley in Pakistan. For a number of Sindhis, Partition was 'a blessing in disguise', a historical watershed which saw the formation of translocal networks of family and trade, or at least the consolidation of the networks established by Sindworkis in the nineteenth and early twentieth centuries. In an *economic* sense, therefore, the idea—whether embodied in myth or political projects—of a return to the homeland seems highly implausible to Sindhis.

Sindhis and the Indian Nation State

My depiction of Sindhis classifying their religion as 'open' and incorporative of many elements may come as a surprise to readers acquainted with Indian politics. Indeed, some Sindhis have emerged as key players in the Hindu nationalist movement—the most prominent of whom is of course former Deputy Prime Minister L.K. Advani, a Sindhi Hyderabadi amil who is widely regarded as one of the hardliners of the BJP. Another amil, K.R. Malkani, was recognized as a significant exponent of Hindu nationalism, particularly through his various writings on the subject (1980, 1993, 2002). The RSS, India's most prominent Hindu nationalist organization, was certainly very active in Sind from the 1920s until Partition. The organization was introduced locally by 'Shriji' Rajpal Puri, and by the 1940s had strong roots all over Sind. Advani himself, for instance, joined RSS in 1934 when, at age 14, he was approached by the *prant pracharak* (regional head) for Sind.[6] It is not surprising that amils, who of course had a profound legacy of literate culture and structural proximity to the State, have been most active in this nationalist discourse and rhetoric. Since they are also historically less mobile than the *bhaibands*, the discourse of openness and adaptability to local circumstance rings somewhat hollow to them.

The romance with the Hindu Right, however, is not exclusive to amils. In India and especially in Bombay, a good number of Sindhi traders stake their claim within Hindu nationalism through the Shiv Sena. This association is resented by a small group of leftist Sindhi writers, who are keen to point out the kinship between Muslim and Hindu Sindhis, and that at Partition it was Muslim *mohajirs* (refugees) from India who caused trouble; even so, the leftist writers I met turned out to be vigorously nationalistic and, although they could 'never fully subscribe' to the BJP–RSS agenda, felt 'a certain admiration' towards it. One should also note that the relation between the Shiv Sena and Sindhis in Mumbai has not always been a pleasant one; initially in fact, the Shiv Sena targeted Sindhis, among others, as not being 'sons of the (Maharashtrian) soil'. By the 1990s, however, relations had greatly improved. Many of the businessmen, and particularly the more prominent ones, had a photo of themselves with Bal Thackeray displayed in their offices. There is a logical explanation for this which should not be too difficult to decipher considering that commercial activity is always dependent on well-lubricated relations with political parties. 'Of course they like Thackeray', a Sindhi engineer said, 'when you're in trade, you need to be able to get things done'.

One Sindhi organization that is relevant to the current argument is Bharatiya Sindhu Sabha (BSS). Formed in 1978, its explicitly nationalist agenda is the establishment of Sindhis as one of the essential linguistic and regional groups of Hindu India. Its objectives are to foster an awareness of Sindhi roots and cultural heritage, to build 'sociocultural unity' among Sindhis, to promote the 'educational achievements' of Sindhis spread all over the world, and to 'restore' the Sindhi language.[7] In terms of set-up the BSS has a number of branches around India (up to 350 according to one informant)—often little more than a tiny office with a local representative. It also functions as a marriage bureau for Sindhis; the BSS branch in Chembur, Mumbai, had 600 'candidates' on its books when I visited in 1999. It is clear that BSS is inspired by the BJP and RSS—many of its leaders are BJP supporters, in fact. The autumn issue of the magazine had a picture of Ram on the front cover, and the editorial was fiercely nationalistic in tone, eulogizing the nuclear tests carried out by India, the Agni missiles, and the victory over Pakistan at Kargil.

This proximity to the Hindu right is usually justified by the idea that Sindhis were 'the worst sufferers of Partition.' This narrative of Muslim eviction clearly legitimates their claim to a place of honour in the Hindu nationalist movement.

It is interesting to note that Sindhis often portray themselves as some sort of aboriginal and primordial Hindus. As a BSS editorial[8] put it,

> We are not only part of India but we are the root part of India. The very name India comes from Indus. Hindu and Hind is derived from Sindhu and Sindh. Even Bharat was a Sindhuputra, after whom the whole country has been named. Pandit Nehru categorically refused to delete the name of Sindh from national anthem of India. Although Sindh is no more a part of India.

This type of discourse, often blended in with vague references to Mohenjo-Daro[9] as the dawn of Indian civilization and the Aryan ancestry of Sindhis [about which a Sindhi has written a book (Gidwani 1996)], is not uncommon among Sindhis.

If Sindhis in India readily involve themselves in politics, the opposite is the case with Sindhis living outside of the *matribhoomi* (motherland). The *Statute of the Indian Merchants Association of Malta*, published in 1955, states that '(t)he association is a non-political association and therefore shuns politics. It is loyal to the Queen and the British Commonwealth of which Malta forms a part.' This stance is a very typical one indeed and of course there are solid reasons behind it. First, politics is fickle business and 'outsiders' become particularly vulnerable when the tide turns. Second, especially Sindworkis are drawn from the trading *jatis* of Sind, that traditionally were much less intimate with statecraft than amils. To most bhaiband traders the encounter with politics seldom goes beyond a donation to charity, or a word with the local politician at a Diwali ball.

CONCLUSION

The case of the Sindhi diaspora, which we hope is more visible at the end of our paper, is fascinating for two reasons. First it raises the question of the definition of the Indian diaspora, what are its contours? Does it include the Sindhis? Second, the political dimension seems totally absent from the life of this diaspora and beyond the game of international relations as it is a real transnational network. We have restricted the definition of the Sindhi diaspora according to a religious criterion, the Hindu Sindhi. But religion is not a central criterion in defining the diaspora, taking into account the religious adaptability they profess. The main criterion is related to the event of Partition, and the flight from Pakistan. The question of membership of Sindhis to the Indian diaspora, is not specific to them. We can ask the same question to all the PIOs who have left the country before Independence. One reason for Sindhi invisibility is their distance in terms of policy both in the countries where they stayed and also within their diaspora. This characteristic shared by many trade diasporas is remarkable because their history could inspire them to seek a homeland. But apart from a few cultural entrepreneurs, this political claim has not found its place in this community. This is not a de-territorialized community since it found a centre in Mumbai. The answer given by the Sindhi diaspora, lack of homeland, upsets the approach in terms of country of origin and destination so often cited in diaspora studies. The Sindhi diaspora demonstrate that diasporic communities are not homogenizing entities but rather groups that manage to draw boundaries around a heterogeneous reality and across space.

NOTES

1. For a broad discussion of the different phases of migration from the subcontinent, see for instance, C. Peach, 'Three Phases of South Asian Emigration', in *Migration: The Asian Experience*, ed. J.M. Browns and R. Foot, Oxford: St. Martin's Press & St. Antony's College, 1994, pp. 28-55.
2. In this paper, the Hindi word *jati*, is taken to mean a 'community or caste group' (*Oxford Hindi Dictionary*). The basic meaning of *jati* is simply 'type'. Thus Hindu Sindhis themselves, as a group,

may be termed a *jati*, but within the group there are other, smaller, regional/linguistic *jatis*.

3. *The Oxford English Dictionary*, 2nd edn., Oxford: Clarendon, 1989.
4. The only reason I can think of as to why anyone would choose these localities as sites for a homeland is that there are no competing claims.
5. The escalation of tension over Kashmir, for instance, was triggered off by an armed attack on the Indian Parliament on 13 December 2001, which the Government of India blamed on cross-border terrorist groups. On a popular level, the belief that Pakistan sponsors terrorism in India is widespread among Hindus, both in India and among Indians of 'the diaspora'.
6. Interview with L.K. Advani on www.rediff.com, 7 June 2003.
7. BSS mission statement.
8. *Bharatiya Sindhu Sabha* (magazine), Mumbai, October-November 1998.
9. An archaeological site in Sind, where remains of a complex urban civilization date back to over 4,000 years.

REFERENCES

Advani, M.G., *A Saga of Trials and Triumphs of Sindhis, 1947-1997*, Bombay: Indira Ghanshyam Mirchandani Service Centre, 1997.

Anand, S., *National Integration of Sindhis*, New Delhi: Vikas, 1996.

Bhachu, P., *Twice Migrants: East African Sikh Settlers in Britain*, London; New York: Tavistock Publications, 1985.

Brown, J.M. and R. Foot, *Migration, the Asian Experience*, St. Antony's/Macmillan Series edn., New York.: St. Martin's Press in association with St. Antony's College, Oxford, 1994.

Chaliand, G. and J.P. Rageau, *The Penguin Atlas of Diasporas*, New York: Viking, 1995.

Clifford, J., 'Diasporas', *Cultural Anthropology*, vol. 9, no. 3, 1994, pp. 302-38.

Cohen, A., 'Cultural Strategies in the Organization of Trading Diasporas', in *The Development of Indigenous Trade and Markets in West Africa*, ed. C. Meillassoux, London: Oxford University Press for the International African Institute, 1971, pp. x, 444.

Cohen, R., *The Cambridge Survey of World Migration*, Cambridge; New York: Cambridge University Press, 1995.

Deshpande, S., 'Hegemonic Spatial Strategies: The Nation-Space and Communalism in Twentieth-Century India', *Public Culture*, vol. 10, no. 2, 1998, pp. 249-83.

Falzon, M.A., *Cosmopolitan Connections: The Sindhi Diaspora, 1860-2000*, International Comparative Social Studies, V. 9, Leiden; Boston: Brill, 2004.

Gidwani, B.S., *Return of the Aryans*, New Delhi; New York: Penguin Books, 1994.

Malkani, K.R., *The RSS Story*, 1st edn., New Delhi: Impex India, 1980.

———, *The Sindh Story*, New Delhi: Allied, 1984.

———, *The Politics of Ayodhya & Hindu-Muslim Relations*, New Delhi: Har-Anand, 1993.

———, *India First*, New Delhi: Ocean, 2002.

Markovits, C., *The Global World of Indian Merchants 1750-1947: Traders of Sind from Bukhara to Panama*, Cambridge Studies in Indian History & Society, Cambridge: Cambridge University Press, 2000.

Panjawani, R., *Sindhi Ain Sindhyat*, Bombay: the author, 1987.

Parekh, B., 'Some Reflections on the Indian Diaspora', *New Community*, vol. 20, no. 4, 1994, pp. 603-20.

Pollock, S., H.K. Bhabha, C.A. Breckenridge and D. Chakrabarty, 'Cosmopolitanism', *Public Culture*, vol. 12, no. 3, 2000, pp. 577-89.

Raj, D.S., '"Who the Hell Do You Think You Are?": Promoting Religious Identity Among Young Hindus in Britain', *Ethnic and Racial Studies*, vol. 23, no. 2, 1999, pp. 535-58.

Robbins, B., 'Actually Existing Cosmopolitism', in *Cosmopolitics: Thinking and Feeling Beyond the Nation*, ed. P. Cheah and B. Robbins, Minneapolis: University of Minnesota Press, 1998, pp. 1-19.

Thakur, U.T., *Sindhi Culture*, Bombay: University of Bombay, 1959.

Vertovec, S., *The Hindu Diaspora: Comparative Patterns*, New York: Routledge, 2000.

Weiner, M., 'International Migration and Development: Indians in the Persian Gulf', *Population and Development Review*, vol. 8, no. 1, 1982, pp. 1-36.

9

Migration, Ethno-Religious Symbolism and State Policy

Sikh Mobilization for the Turban in the UK and France

CHRISTINE MOLINER

The notion of a Sikh diaspora has emerged forcefully over the past twenty years in the social sciences. I wish here to analyse how it has also become a social reality for diasporic Sikhs through the study of their mobilization for the turban in their diasporic homes, which has been a major tool in their identity-building process.

In a crowd, Sikhs are easily identifiable, thanks to their turban, that projects the image of a homogeneous community with well-defined boundaries.

In India where many communities and individuals sport it in various shapes, the turban has nonetheless become their sole emblem, after a long and complex historical process. Indian Sikhs are allowed to wear the turban at work, at school, in the army . . . and this right is guaranteed by the Constitution.

In Western countries, where Sikhs migrated *en masse* in the second half of the twentieth century, their turban challenges cultural practices and national political models. In that respect Great Britain and France offer two sharply contrasting case studies: in the former, Sikh mobilization arises in a post-war political context shaped by colonial legacy, in particular by a specific set of representations of the Sikh body and within a multi-culturalist framework valourizing the public expression of cultural difference. In the latter, the very absence of colonial relations entails a specific migration history (Sikhs migrated much later and in much lesser numbers to France) and a very different response to Sikh demands, seen as incompatible with the *laïcité*. These two examples point to the crucial importance of national contexts in shaping diasporic social formations.

After a semiology of the turban highlighting its multiple meanings, I shall examine how British colonial policy has reinforced the process through which the turban becomes the ethno-religious symbol *par excellence* of the Sikhs and how this process has evolved in the diaspora: in Great Britain, with the turban campaigns of the 1970s and in France since 2004.

A POLYSEMIC SYMBOL

Symbolic Value and Social Function of the Turban

Foremost, the turban for the Sikhs endorses a spiritual meaning. In that respect it goes with the long hair, protecting and sanctifying them. Both the turban and long hair materialize continuity between mankind (through an intact human body) and the divine. Long hair is part of the 5 Ks,[1] those bodily and dress injunctions imposed, according to Sikh tradition, by the tenth and last Guru, in 1699 when he created the Khalsa, a religious and military order. *Amritdhari* (literally those who took *amrit*, during the initiation ceremony to the Khalsa) are to follow a specific code of conduct and carry five symbols: *kesh* (keeping one's hair unshorn), *kangha* (comb), *kara* (iron or steel bangle), *kirpan* (sword) and *kaccha* (knee-length underwear). According to tradition, one of the aims of the tenth Guru was to ensure that every Sikh would be easily recognizable and thus unable to hide in the face of the oppressor.

Interestingly, the turban is not part of the 5 Ks, but was used as early as the sixteenth century by Sikhs. Closely linked to political power, as it symbolizes royalty in Mughal India, it further endorses a multiplicity of meanings that add to its primary spiritual dimension.

One has to mention its gender dimension. Indeed, although the 5 Ks apply equally in theory to men and women, the turban is in fact a male attribute. Very few women, mostly in the diaspora and mostly belonging to the third generation, wear it: they belong to the *Akhand Kirtani Jatha*, a religious group claiming that the turban (*keski*) is indeed one of the 5 Ks.

But for the vast majority of Sikhs, the turban appears as a major marker of male identity. It is a lifetime companion for those Sikh males who sport it. A turban is tied, offered or exchanged according to the life-cycle ritual celebrated. It is therefore heavily loaded emotionally, at individual and collective levels, hence its strong mobilization potential and the impassioned and controversial nature of the debates surrounding it.

A Problematic Symbol

Because of its multiple meanings, the Sikh turban produces both distinction and ambiguity.

Within the Panth, it is a bone of contention between two competing visions of Sikh identity: the dominant one, emphasizing a normative, monolithic and orthodox definition of Sikhism—the product of a historical evolution that I describe briefly bellow—confronted to a vast array of practices, beliefs and ways of being Sikh, at home and abroad. Multiple identities, defined by varying degrees of religious observance, have always coexisted:[2] *amritdhari* Sikhs embody the ideal-type that every Sikh should emulate; *keshdhari* Sikhs wear the visible symbols (turban, kesh and beard) but, not being initiated, they are not submitted to the same code of conduct (mostly, they don't follow the ban on meat and alcohol); finally *mona* (literally shaven), who cut their hair and beard and don't sport the turban. *Amritdharis* constitute a small minority, both in the Punjab and in the diaspora; *keshdharis* are a majority in the Punjab, while *mona* Sikhs are dominant in the diaspora.

These categories are in practice extremely flexible, especially in the diaspora, where one can switch, according to circumstances, from one to the other. Hence one individual can be in his lifetime a *keshdhari* then a *mona* then an *amritdhari*, depending on his migration history, his age, or following political or religious motivations.

But this fluidity is problematic in a Western context, that is characterized by its dualist and fixist approach of religion. For instance in Canada, plurality within Sikh beliefs and practices has been used to delegitimatize Sikh demand to wear the turban in the Mounted Police. Those opposing Sikh demand—that was ultimately accepted—were quick to oppose 'pluralism within any one tradition versus the hegemonic authority of one dominant orthodox community',[3] and to assert that if so many Sikhs do without the turban (which is true), it is therefore not an essential article of their faith (but who else than the Sikhs themselves is to decide what is or not essential to their faith?).

Finally this ambiguity also appears in the demarcation of boundaries with other communities. Outside India, Sikhs are frequently mistaken for Muslims because of their turban. It was true before 11th September, but it has taken a tragic course since then: in England, racist attacks have been targetting gurdwaras (lit. the door of the guru, the Sikh places of worship), in the US three Sikh males were killed, immediatly after 11 September, during a wave of attacks targetting Muslims, or more exactly, people looking like them. Beyond its practical consequences, this ambiguity surrounding ascribed identities is problematic for Sikhs, whose popular imagery has constructed the Muslim (particularly under the disguise of the Mughal oppressor) as the Other *par excellence*.[4]

The Turban, Sikh Reformism and Colonial Representations[5]

To understand the process through which the turban has emerged as a core element in Sikh diaspora identity construction, one has to take a sharp turn back to colonial history. Colonial narrative and policy regarding Sikhs were a great deal fashioned by the concept of martial races. Inspired by European biological determinism, it relies on a hierarchical ordering of human races. Only a few of those races, Gurkhas, Pashtuns and Sikhs, were perceived as gifted with inbred martial characteristics, that can be corrupted, lest colonial power preserves them in their purity and prevents them from deteriorating through contacts with non-martial groups. British obsession with purity are translated, as far as Sikhs are concerned, into the recurring theme of Sikhism in danger of reabsorption into Hinduism-finding an echo in the preoccupations of the Singh Sabha, the contemporary Sikh reform movement. According to a famous phrase by Macauliffe:

> Hinduism . . . is like the boa constrictor of the Indian forests. When a petty enemy appears to worry it, it winds round its opponent, crushes it in its folds and finally causes it to disappear . . . in this way it is disposing of the reformed and once hopeful religion of Baba Nanak . . . [that is] making a vigorous struggle for life, but its ultimate destruction is [. . .] inevitable without State support.[6]

And State support to prevent Sikhism purity from Hindu 'contamination' has first and foremost been translated into a specific military recruitment policy. Only 'proper' Sikhs, i.e. baptized Sikhs, were enlisted into the Imperial army. Baptism, the 5 Ks and the turban were made compulsory for Sikh recruits.

Colonial policy has therefore promoted and legitimized one particular set of socio-religious identity, that of the Khalsa, that was until then competing with other identities, thereafter termed as heterodox.

The Singh Sabha, the socio-religious reform movement operating among the Sikhs from the 1880s, has also been a major actor in this process. Influenced by colonial representations and policy, as much as its Hindu and Muslim counterparts, the Singh Sabha aimed at restoring their community's pristine purity and past glory, in sharp contrast with what they perceived as its present decline. Oberoi has analysed in detail how reformist Sikh intellectuals worked at shaping a distinct, homogeneous community with well-defined boundaries.[7] They focused on the terrain of practices and attitudes towards human body, that according to Oberoi has always been used in Sikh tradition as a powerful symbolic system:[8] their project of 'sikhizing the Sikhs', according to Oberoi's phrase, entailed the enforcement of external symbols, in particular the *kesh* and the turban and specific life-cycle rituals.

But it is important to stress that this does not mean at all that neither the Singh Sabha, nor the British 'invented' the turban (or Singh identity for that matter): they have in fact borrowed from an existing cultural repertoire and invested the turban with new meanings, as a pillar of collective identity and last resort against decline.

ETHNO-RELIGIOUS SYMBOLISM AND DIASPORIC IDENTITY CONSTRUCTION IN GREAT BRITAIN

Sikh Migration to Great Britain: Historical Background

Sikh migration history started in the second half of the nineteenth century as it was linked to British colonial expansion and preferential recruitment of Sikhs into the army that took them to South-East Asia first, then to North America, Australia, New Zealand and East Africa.

Sikh migration to Britain became a mass movement during the post-war economic boom of the 1950s. It came to a halt once a very restrictive immigration legislation was adopted in 1962 (Commonwealth Immigrant Act) but was revived in the 1970s with the arrival of Sikhs from East Africa. There are an estimated 4,50,000 Sikhs in the UK today.

In the extent literature, British Sikh community construction follows four major phases, with varying degrees of religious observance. After the pioneer phase of the 1920s, the chain migration of the late 1940s and 1950s entailed a major redefinition of religious identity, with the shedding of the beard and turban as part of an adaptation strategy to the host society. The arrival of their families in the 1960s, then of East African Sikhs a decade later, led to major changes: besides a tightening of social linkage, strong internal cleavages (socio-economic, political, caste-based) emerged, and third a renewed religiosity was expressed, with for instance men re-adopting the turban, through the double influence of their families (specially the women who play a major role in religious transmission) and of East African Sikhs (whose specific ethno-religious identity has been reinforced in Africa by their status of intermediaries between the British and the local population).

A fourth phase in the 1980s witnessed the emergence of a second and third generation, in a context that I describe below of rising Sikh fundamentalism, that invested the turban with a new political meaning.

The Context of British Sikh Mobilization for the Turban

This unique context is characterized by an intertwining of three elements, of which I will develop the last two: first, the evolution of British ideological and political framework regarding immigration, that culminates in the 1980s in differentialist multiculturalism, where ethnic groups are regarded by the authorities as homogeneous and discreet communities on the basis of religious affiliation; second, the emergence of a second diasporic generation and the ensuing fear of assimilation to British society; third an acute political crisis in the home country starting in 1984.

The emergence of a second and third generation of British Sikhs in the late 1970s gives way to a feeling of insecurity, of threat posed by Westernization, perceived as ineluctable, of the youth. The shedding of the turban, of the 5 Ks, of 'traditional' norms and values (elders' authority, arranged marriage . . .) seemingly embodies the 'identity crisis' of the youth. Popular media are replete with references to a so-called 'between two cultures' syndrome, characterizing a migrant youth caught in a cultural vacuum, neither British (in particular because of a persistent racism) nor anymore Asian/Indian/Sikh.

This questioning specific to the diaspora is made even more acute by the political crisis the Punjab has gone through during the last 20 years. The issue of an independant Sikh state (Khalistan), settled in India through State repression, has remained at the centrestage of the diaspora where it monopolized until recently socio-political space and created deep-rooted disjunctions. During the conflict with the Indian State perceived as a Hindu state, a Sikh neo-fundamentalist narrative has been fashioned, using the 'Sikhism in danger' motive and identifying two enemies: outside, the Hindu enemy, dominating and aggressive, and inside, the corruption of values, the foresaking of external symbols.

In this context of crisis, both in the home society and the receiving country, the turban has again been perceived as a symbol and safeguard of an identity undersiege, threatened by assimilation in the West and State repression in India.

Sikh neo-fundamentalist discourse has been all the more successful among diaspora Sikhs that they have been deeply shocked, at both individual and collective level, by the traumatic event that took place in 1984 (desecration of Harmandir Sahib, massacres of Sikhs in Delhi and around). A lot of them, beyond generation, caste or class rifts adopted or re-adopted the turban and the other external symbols, which took on a new political dimension.

Inner and Outer Dynamics of the Mobilization for the Turban

Before analysing the major mobilization of the 1970s and the 1980s, it is necessary to mention briefly the earliest turban campaigns of the 1950s and 1960s that involved Sikh bus drivers or postmen from Manchester and Wolverhampton who, with the support of local Sikhs, fought for the right to wear the turban as part of their company uniform. These first mobilizations are quite remarkable: although they take place in a very adverse political climate (characterized by an assimilationist policy regarding immigrants) they set the tone of later ones and in a way foresee ethnic minority's political and religious activism of the 1980s and 1990s, with British Sikhs and later Muslims at the forefront.

I will here focus on the 1970s and 1980s turban campaigns that have greatly contributed to the fashioning of public policy regarding ethnic minorities.

It started in 1973, following the adoption by the Parliament of the Motor-Cycle Crash Helmet Act that makes helmet compulsory on motorcycles, including for turban-wearing Sikhs. A Sikh based in Southall enlisted the support of the local Sikh community, of the Akali Dal and that of the Labour MP for Ealing and Southall, Sidney Bidwell. Bidwell, who gives a detailed account of this 'turban victory' in a pamphlet published by the Sikh Missionary Society,[9] presented in 1975 a bill, adopted in 1976, exempting Sikhs from wearing a crash-helmet (Motor-Cycle Crash Helmets [Religious Exemption] Act, 1976). Parliamentary debates surrounding the reading of this Act are surprisingly fascinating. A peculiar vision of the Sikhs surfaces, monolithic and essentialist, deeply influenced by colonial representations and fashioned by a kind of nostalgia for the Empire. Sikhs are described as 'loyal, law-abiding and devout people', 'the Empire inspired their idealism and harnessed all the noblest instincts of a warrior race . . .'[10] To win his colleagues' approval, Bidwell referred to the Anglo–Sikh military past, and to the well-established tradition of toleration of the turban in the British army.

The next mobilization took place in a 1979 in school, instigated by Gurinder Singh Mandla, a solicitor from Birmingham, who had come to Britain in the mid-1970s from East Africa. The headmaster of a local private school refused to admit Mandla's *keshdhari* son unless he removed his turban to comply with school uniform. With the support of the local Sikh community (based at the biggest gurdwara in England, just opposite his office), Mandla referred this case to the newly-created Commission for Racial Equality (CRE), that appealed to the House of Lords, after the case was dismissed twice, by the County Court and the Court of Appeal.

In 1982 Mandla's appeal was allowed by the House of Lords on the basis of the notion of indirect discrimination. The scope of this decision went well beyond its original stake, since it granted Sikhs with the status of an ethnic group.

Dowell Lee was found guilty of 'indirect discrimination against a member of a racial group' by reference to the 1976 Race Relations Act, which introduced this new legal concept. But the whole issue was not in fact to prove whether there was indirect discrimination or not but to establish whether Sikhs were an ethnic/racial group or not, as only groups defined on an ethnic, and not merely religious, basis could benefit from the 1976 Act prohibiting discrimination in employment, social services and education. The headmaster contended that Sikhs do not have the characteristics of an ethnic group, as they share with Muslim and Hindu Punjabis common ethnic patterns.

Helped by the CRE, the Sikhs contended that the parliament meant them to benefit from the new legislation as they fit the definition of an ethnic group as construed by the Act:

> For a group to constitute an 'ethnic group' . . . it had to regard itself, and be regarded by others, as a distinct community by virtue of certain characterisitics, two of which were essential . . . : a long shared history, of which the group was conscious as distinguishing it from other groups, and the memory of which it kept alive, and second . . . a cultural tradition of its own, including family and social customs and manners, often but not necessarily associated with religious observance.[11]

Here the Lords appear as major brokers in British Sikh identity building process. Their proceedings are permeated with the same colonial representations as described above, on which is superimposed a sociological reflexion on ethnic identity. Further, they concede that Sikhs are more than a religious group, 'almost a race, a nation.'[12] This 'almost a nation' echoes both nineteenth-century orientalist contructions, where Sikhs constitute a distinct political community and a more contemporary Sikh separatist politics in India.

Their decision is crucial: for Sikhs of course, who benefit since then from the legislation against discrimination (whereas

British Muslims do not, still today) and have gained in visibility in British society; it also confirms a new turn in British policy towards minorities, with the politicization and ethnicization of minority religious affiliations.[13]

Let us now analyse the complex internal dynamics of this mobilization, especially in the 1979-82 campaign.

As I said, Mandla is an East-African Sikh from a service caste, a Ramgarhia. This caste has a specific socio-economic profile and migration experience: they are twice-migrants,[14] who migrated from the Punjab to East Africa, where, as a minority group, they developped a strong sense of their religious and ethnic specificity. After being expelled from Kenya and Uganda, they migrated to the UK, where they joined other Sikhs who had come directly from the Punjab, most of them belonging to the dominant caste of Jats. A lot of Jats had shed external symbols. Roger Ballard, talking of a Sikh version of Sanskritization, shows how Ramgarhias chose to emphasize their religious orthodoxy, trying to subvert caste hierarchy that granted them in Punjab a much lower position than Jats.[15] It is in this context that Puran Singh, a religious leader most respected by Ramgarhias, coming also from East Africa, was instrumental in the campaign supporting Mandla that culminated in a demonstration of 40,000 Sikhs in Hyde Park.

Once again, the ambiguity of the turban is striking, at once a powerful vehicle of group cohesion and mobilization and of internal competition.

THE TURBAN, *LAÏCITÉ* AND EXCLUSION DYNAMICS IN FRANCE

Sikh Migration to France

Whereas Sikhs in Britain are a visible, numerous (3,36,000 according to the last census in 2001) and prosperous community, Sikhs in France are a tiny minority (10,000 at most), whose settlement is recent and very precarious.

Sikh migration to France and continental Europe started in the early 1980s, after migration to Britain had become almost impossible. France, then Belgium, Germany, Italy and more recently Spain, Portugal and Greece appeared as substitutes for prospective migrants. These pioneers called their families in the 1990s and were supplemented by asylum seekers. A lot of them ended up in France before crossing the Channel illegally.

Sikh migration experience in France and more generally continental Europe is characterized by high levels of mobility, precariousness and clandestineness that form the basis of very strong community solidarity but also of its marginalization in the host society. Like elswhere in the diaspora, the gurdwara[16] is a lot more than a place of worship: main arena of socialization for all generations, for men and women alike, it is also the focus of community politics.

The Turban and French Administration

One has to wait until the 1990s for the first turban cases: the 1980s pioneers were mostly *mona* Sikhs (either they had shorn their hair in India, or they did so when they reached France, anticipating problems to find a job). The first cases involved two categories of immigrants: the asylum seekers and political refugees who were asked to provide, for the renewal of their driving license or *carte de séjour*, an ID photo *tête nue*, and refused to comply; the second the *keshdhari* pupils newly arrived from India.

Long before the 2004 mobilization, the turban became an issue the French administration (mostly *préfectures* and *tribunal administratif*) had to cope with, leading to several lawsuits. And most administrative decisions seem strikingly inconsistent, inflexible or arbitrary (some prefectures, mostly that of Paris and Seine St Denis, rejecting photos with turban, others accepting them).

At school, a handful of *keshdhari* children were concerned. Following a *Conseil d'Etat* ruling in 1991 (stating that 'students wearing signs by which they mean to demonstrate their adherence to a religion is not by itself incompatible with the principle of *laïcité*') a case-by-case settlement was adopted: so turban was accepted in some schools, not in others, but no student was excluded until 2004, and a few chose private schooling.

The French *Laïcité* and Sikh Mobilization Against the 2004 Act

French historians and intellectuals such as Jean Baubérot[17] have cautioned us to distinguish between the several and evolving meanings of the concept of *laïcité* that were confused in the debate surrounding the adoption of the Act. The original definition of *laïcité* refers to a legal and ideological framework that guarantees, through the separation of Churches and the State, the independence of religious organizations *vis-à-vis* political power and secondly freedom of conscience (in particular religious freedom) by that same power. *Laïcité* implies that religious affiliation and citizenship are dissociated and that all are equal before law. In that sense, French *laïcité* is not very different from the Indian notion of secularism as it was portrayed in the Indian media (see for instance 'Secularism Unwrapped', *Hindustan Times*, 22 September 2004).

To put it schematically, the third Republic designed this framework at the beginning of the twentieth century as an attempt to limit the power of the Catholic Church that, with the Royalists, was trying to destabilize the young and fragile regime. One should stress that this was done not in a militant spirit (there was no intent to crush organized religions) but in a compromising one.

The 2004 Act banning the wearing of religious signs in State-run schools departs therefore from the original notion of *laïcité*. It marks the historical evolution of the latter in a context where the public expressions of faith by Muslims are increasingly perceived as the new opposite of *laïcité*—after catholic clericalism. The wearing of Islamic headscarves in school has agitated French society from 1989, and has been constructed as a threat to the whole Republican framework, to be safeguarded by the act.[18] It is an irony that, while primarily targetting Muslim girls wearing *hijab*, it mostly affected Sikh males sporting the turban.

In December 2003 the Stasi Commission, appointed by President Jacques Chirac to prepare the ground for the new legislation, gave its report . . . without having interviewed any Sikh. Understanding only then the impact of the proposed legislation for their children, Sikhs organized on 31 January 2004 a demonstration in Paris—their first in France—gathering 3,000 of them, who came from all over Europe.

The bill was then discussed by the National Assembly, in a confused political and media context: some prestigious members of the Commission disowned the Bill, so did some leaders of the majority, the education minister proposed a ban on beard and in lieu of the turban 'an invisible net' for Sikhs ! All these remarks and debates were widely covered and commented by the Indian media (and to a lesser extent by the British media), at some points with a daily coverage by the press.

Sikh mobilization gathered momentum, through support in India and the diaspora. British Sikhs for instance were prominent in the Paris demonstration and the ensuing meetings with French authorities. They also organized a demonstration in front of the French Embassy in London, and actively lobbied their government to discuss this issue with the French government. Under the pressure of the Indian government (and notably under the new leadership of a Sikh prime minister since May 2004), France promised on several occasions (the latest being President Jacques Chirac's visit to India in February 2006) to take into account the demands of Sikhs.

Following talks with the education authorities, an agreement was achieved in June 2004: students would be accepted in school, providing they compromised on the length and shape of their turban. But in early September, several kids were not accepted in their school, most notably in Louise Michel High School in Bobigny. After another round of negotiations, this time unsuccessful, three students were shut out from High School, and again several of them in September 2005.

This 'turban affair' has had contradictory consequences for French Sikhs. While enhancing their minority complex and their sense of marginalization in the host society, it has also dramatically increased their visibility, nationally and internationally. French and foreign media discovered Bobigny Gurdwara and shed light on the plight of turbaned Sikhs. Until 2004, Sikhs in France were invisible despite their turban (only a small minority are *keshdhari*) or rather because of its ambiguous nature. Because of the lack of collective representations borrowed, as in the case of Britain, from the colonial past, Sikhs are probably the least known minority group in France. Well before 11 September *keshdhari* Sikhs were routinely mistaken for Muslims.

As noticed in England, this mobilization has helped to legitimize some political brokers, appointed through their regular contacts with the government and the press as community leaders. Without debating the question of their legitimacy to represent their community (whose vast majority was not affected by the new legislation, since they and their children are *mona* Sikhs), it is interesting to observe how this unprecedented exposure to the most courted authorities and media has created new divisions and conflicts for a share of power. These tensions have been enhanced by outside interventions, particularly those of British Sikhs. The generational divide also played a role: because of the lack of proficiency of their elders in French, the youth has become for the first time spokesmen of their community. It might be under their influence and due to their understanding of the French ideological context that Sikh discourse has shifted: to circumvent the ban on 'ostensible religious signs', the turban has been at times presented as a 'cultural' symbol, rather than a religious one, to the disapproval of Sikhs abroad. But this demonstrates once again the adaptability of diasporic identity narratives to the various national frameworks.

The transnational, diasporic dimension of this campaign is worth noting. If it continues, this mobilization will be the most important one since the Khalistan movement. Incidentally, there is a sort of continuum between the two: some of the actors, networks and *modus operandi* (demonstrations, lobbying techniques and protest use of internet) of the latter are 'recycled' in the turban campaign, but with a major difference: this time they benefit from the support of the Indian government. Even if it has not met with great success so far, it reinforces the expanding Sikh diasporic space that includes France now, in a more peaceful manner than the Khalistan movement.

CONCLUSION

The case of the Sikh turban presented here underscores several points in the articulation of migration, religion and collective identity. First, it offers an example of the adaptability of migrant strategies to local contexts, or even of migrants fashioning these as in the case of British Sikhs. Whereas in India the turban is clearly identified as a religious symbol, it becomes an ethnic one in the West—in the UK because racial or ethnic identity only is acknowleged in the anti-discrimination legislation, in France, because the public expression of religious affilition is rendered illegitimate by the evolution of the *laïcité*. The ensuing observation points at the ethnicization of religion, as a marker of ethnic identity, in response to the migration experience, all the more so in the case of Sikhs, they have been engaged in a political struggle in their country of origin that enlisted the support of some sections of the diaspora.

Third, the case illustrates the tensions between the local and the global that structure all transnational religious movements, in respect of patterns of mobilization, emergence of a leadership, and issues of representation or legitimacy.

NOTES

1. See J.P.S. Uberoi, 'Five symbols of Sikh Identity' for a complete analysis of their ideological meaning and social function.

2. See the work of H. McLeod, specially his classic *Who is a Sikh*, New Delhi: Oxford University Press, 1989.
3. See on this question 'The Turban Issue: Question of Orthodoxy?', *The Sikh Reformer*, 1 June 2004.
4. See my paper 'Frères ennemis? Relationship between Sikh and Muslim Punjabis in the Diaspora', *South Asia Multidisciplinary Academic Journal*, 2007, online since 14 October 2007.
5. On colonial representations, see Richard G. Fox, *Lions of the Punjab: Culture in the Making*, Berkeley: University of California Press, 1990 and Thomas Metcalf, *Ideologies of the Raj*, The New Cambridge History of India, New Delhi: Cambridge University Press, 1995.
6. M.A. Macauliffe, *The Sikh Religion*, Oxford: Clarendon Press, 1909.
7. Harjot Oberoi, *The Construction of Religious Boundaries: Culture, Identity and Diversity in the Sikh Tradition*, New Delhi: Oxford University Press, 1994.
8. Oberoi, op. cit., Chapter 6.
9. Sydney Bidwell, *The Turban Victory*, n.d.
10. Bidwell, op. cit.
11. For a detailed account of the appeal, see 'Mandla and Another *vs* Dowell Lee and Another', *All England Law Reports*, 1983.
12. Ibid.
13. See John Crowley, *Immigration, 'relations raciales' et mobilisations minoritaires au Royaume Uni*, Thèse de doctorat, Institut d'Etudes Politiques de Paris, 1995.
14. Parminder Bhachu, *The Twice Migrants: East African Sikh Settlers in Britain*, New York: Tavistock, 1985.
15. R. Ballard, 'Differentiation and Disjunction among the Sikhs', in R. Ballard (ed.), *Desh Pardesh*, London: Tavistock, 1994, pp. 88-116.
16. There are in fact five gurdwaras, created, according to well-established patterns, when personal/political/caste conflicts divided the group controling the main gurdwara in Bobigny.
17. See among their several publications on that subject: Jean Baubérot, *Laïcité 1905-2005: entre passion et raison*, Paris: Seuil, 2004.
18. This is in contradiction with the Conseil d'Etat ruling mentioned above, where a pluralist and open definition of *laïcité* was privileged as opposed to the defensive one imposed in 2004.

REFERENCES

All England Law Reports, 'Mandla and Another *vs* Dowell Lee and Another', 1983.

Ballard, R., 'Differentiation and Disjunction Among the Sikhs', in *Desh Pardesh*, London: Tavistock, 1994.

Bhachu, P., *The Twice Migrants: East African Sikh Settlers in Britain*, New York: Tavistock, 1985.

Bidwell, S., *The Turban Victory*, Southall: Sikh Missionary Society, n.d.

Baubérot, J., *Laïcité 1905-2005: entre passion et raison*, Paris: Seuil, 2004.

Crowley, J., *Immigration, 'relations raciales' et mobilisations minoritaires au Royaume Uni*, Thèse de doctorat, Institut d'Etudes Politiques de Paris, 1995.

Fox, R.G., *Lions of the Punjab: Culture in the Making*, Berkeley: University of California Press, 1990.

McLeod, H., *Who is a Sikh*, Oxford: Oxford University Press, 1989.

Metcalf, T., *Ideologies of the Raj*, The New Cambridge History of India, New Delhi: Cambridge University Press, 1995.

Moliner, C., 'Frères ennemis ? Relationship between Sikh and Muslim Punjabis in the Diaspora', *South Asian Multidisciplinary Academic Journal*, 2007.

Oberoi, H., *The Construction of Religious Boundaries: Culture, Identity and Diversity in the Sikh Tradition*, New Delhi: Oxford University Press, 1994.

Uberoi, J.P.S., 'Five Symbols of Sikh Identity', in *Religion, Civil Society and the State*, New Delhi: Oxford University Press, 1996.

10

Nationalism Beyond Borders

A Comparative Study of Sikh and Mohajir Long-distance Nationalisms

LAURENT GAYER

> Although we talk in English
> For the sake of our homeland
> We are ready to place our lives on our palms
> We feel extreme sadness and pain
> When there is disruption in our homeland.
>
> DCS, *Dil Phirbi Panjabi* (Our hearts are still Punjabi)[1]

Nationalism, which contributed to the re-definition of political and social boundaries worldwide from the nineteenth century onwards, spread itself transnationally (Dieckhoff, 2000). From its European cradle, it travelled to the colonies,[2] where it was appropriated and reinvented through a process of 'vernacularization'. Throughout this process, overseas students and political exiles played a crucial role. They acted as go-betweens, by mediating the norms of the colonial agent and translating them into local parlance. Thus, 'long-distance nationalism' (Anderson, 1995; 1998) is nothing new, at least if we look at is as an ideology of exile. Yet, as a form of transnational mobilization, it has greatly benefited from the revolution of transportation and communication that the world has witnessed since the 1960s and even more so since the advent of the internet. The democratization of international travel and transnational communication has facilitated 'social remittances' from migrants to their nation state (Levitt, 2001) and they are partly responsible for the 'stretching, fragmenting form of the contemporary nation' (Jeganathan, 1998: 515).

This paper is based on a comparative study of two such long-distance nationalisms: that of the Sikhs and that of the Mohajirs settled in Europe and North America. This comparison shows that, in casual times, political exiles experience difficulties finding an audience. But political upheavals affecting the homeland provide nationalists abroad with a golden opportunity to mobilize their ethnic brethren. When such political crisis reach a critical level, they may even produce 'moral shocks' (Jasper & Poulsen, 1995) in the diaspora, by brutally upsetting the political attitudes of its members and leading them to mobilize themselves in favour of their homeland. However, once this moment of trauma is overcome, factional politics usually comes back with a vengeance. Structures of mobilization set-up by nationalist organizations then play a crucial role, by determining the movement's fate in the international arena and, ultimately, in its homeland. The comparison of Sikh and Mohajir nationalisms is particularly eloquent in this regard and provides us with two models of 'long-distance nationalism'.

Sikh long-distance nationalism may be defined as a 'diffuse' or 'multicentric' form of trans-nationalism. Even if it takes its roots in the social and political changes which took place in the Indian Punjab in the course of the 'Green Revolution', the movement for Khalistan only grew in the Sikh diaspora after the attack on the Golden Temple in 1984. Until then, the demand for Khalistan (which was originally formulated in the 1940s as a response to the Pakistan movement) remained a source of mockery among overseas Sikhs, *Khalistan* literally meaning 'the empty country' in Hindi. The events of 1984 led many overseas Sikhs to think of Khalistan more seriously. However, in the diaspora (as in the Punjab), the movement for Khalistan quickly suffered from fissiparous tendencies and Khalistani organizations competed for the representation of the Sikhs in their countries of residence and in the international public sphere. This fragmented diasporic movement quickly became estranged from its subcontinental counterpart and ultimately disconnected itself from Punjabi politics. It ended up articulating Sikh expatriates' aspirations and grievances in their host societies rather than expressing their desire to 'go home'.

The spread of Mohajir nationalism among Pakistani expatriates followed a similar pattern. The repression of the Mohajirs by the Pakistani army during 'Operation Clean Up', in 1992, produced a 'moral shock' among many Urdu-speaking Pakistani emigrants. However, after this initial phase, during which many of these migrants 'discovered' their Mohajir identity, the transnational movement for the defence of 'Mohajir rights' followed an entirely different route. All along, it was controlled by an authoritarian party based in Pakistan, the Mohajir Qaumi Movement (Mohajir National Movement, MQM), whose leaders managed to retain their control over the party's activists worldwide after they went into exile in London in 1992. This transnational control is remarkable and offers a striking example of a 'centralized', or 'unicentric', form of 'long-distance nationalism', which remains focused on the homeland, under the control of a hegemonic organization. The Mohajirs are not an isolated case, here: other minorities have been articulating a similar blend of long-distance nationalism, such as the Kurds around the PKK (Grojean, 2005) and the Tamils around the LTTE (Fuglerud, 1999).

This paper, which looks at Sikh and Mohajir long-distance nationalisms from a comparative perspective, is divided into two parts. The first one relates to Sikh and Mohajir 'ethnic diplomacies', i.e. to the transnational lobbying networks of Sikh and Mohajir long-distance nationalists, oriented towards national public opinions, state authorities and international organizations. Notwithstanding their analogies, these two private diplomacies offer striking differences, which reveal the various shapes that ethnic protest can take in the international arena.

The second part of my discussion will be more theoretical, since it would like to contribute to ongoing debates, among political scientists, over new processes of identity and State formation. At this point, I will concentrate on the ideological and strategic dilemmas faced by present-day nationalists, who promote the 'local' in an increasingly globalized way.

SIKH AND MOHAJIR ETHNIC DIPLOMACIES: ACTORS, TARGETS AND STRATEGIES

As Francois Constantin shows, the privatization of diplomacy involves two distinct dynamics: (1) individual actions with an international outcome, inducing an answer from states; (2) private relations supported by governments, in order to implement a public or personal policy (Constantin, 1999). Although Indian and Pakistani state authorities have secretly supported Mohajir and Khalistani militants,[3] I will concentrate here on the first dimension of private diplomacy, as it is less obscure and hence more propitious to sociological analysis.

The active lobbying animated by Sikhs of the diaspora and MQM international workers (during the last two decades in the first case and since the beginning of the 1990s in the second) has been targeted at public opinion and at politicians of their host states (at the parliamentarian or governmental level), to global human rights NGOs and, finally, to international and supranational organizations. This advertising process therefore followed logics of accumulation rather than selection, ethnic diplomats avoiding to 'put all of one's eggs in one basket', as the dean of the Khalistan movement in the US, Ganga Singh Dhillon, once suggested to me. This strategic eclecticism goes hand in hand with a flexible rhetoric, ethnic diplomats adapting their discourse to their audience, focussing on geopolitical issues with state representatives and on human rights and cultural issues with NGOs and international bureaucracies.

Among the Sikhs, the main protagonists of this international lobbying are six organizations based in the diaspora: the Khalistan Council (founded in 1980 in the Punjab but until recently led from London by Jagjit Singh Chauhan[4]); the Dal Khalsa (founded in the Punjab in 1978 but divided between an Indian faction and a British one); the Babbar Khalsa (also founded in the Punjab in 1978 and divided between a national and an international branch with little intercommunication); the International Sikh Youth Federation (ISYF), founded in 1984 in Britain and now active in the UK,[5] Canada, the US and Pakistan); the World Sikh Organization (WSO), founded in New York in 1984 and soon operating from the US, Canada and, to a lesser extent, the UK and, finally, the Council of Khalistan, founded in 1987 in the US by Gurmit Singh Aulakh. These organizations competed for the monopoly of representation of the *Sikh qaum* on the international scene and in the countries of residence of Sikh minorities settled abroad. But if these organizations had a global agenda, as their names often suggest, none of them has been able to monopolize the support of the Sikh diaspora and the attention of the international community. The movement for Khalistan, whether in the Punjab or in the diaspora, has been suffering from its pre-organizational character. In its early developments, the movement was led by a charismatic religious leader without any political affiliation (Sant Jarnail Singh Bhindranwale). His closest aide, Amrik Singh, was more politicized and could have contributed to the political organization of the movement, but he preferred to attain martyrdom with his friend and mentor during Operation Blue Star. The movement for Khalistan was beheaded while it was still in its infancy and it never recovered from the disappearance of these charismatic leaders. In the following years, the insurgents reproduced the factional politics which has been the main characteristic of Punjabi and particularly Jat politics since Independence (Pettigrew, 1985). Khalistani guerrillas never swore allegiance to their 'commander'. They remained loosely associated with him until they felt assured enough to set-up their own guerrilla group. Those who did not fall prey to such power politics often chose to obey their ardent and deeply individualistic death wish rather than follow the advice of their commanders, who tried to contain this desire for martyrdom as it dilapidated their groups human resources. In the diaspora, the movement for Khalistan suffered from the same fissiparous tendencies, even if its 'leaders' did not have to tame the suicidal tendencies of their followers. The two major organizations advocating the cause of Khalistan abroad, the ISYF and the WSO, have been undergoing several rifts and purges, with their dissidents setting up rival factions, contesting the legitimacy, the morality and the sincerity of their adversaries. Each of these leaders has been using ethnic diplomacy as a source of personal legitimization and, thus, as a symbolic rather than as a strategic device, searching for prestige rather for the enforcement of the Khalistani agenda in the Punjab. Low-ranking militants, for their part, committed to the movement on a highly subjective and often temporary basis, out of personal convictions or emotions rather than in a sign of devotion to the cause of Sikh sovereignty or in allegiance to a particular leader. A Khalistani activist that I met in New York suggested this vividly by presenting his engagement as a highly individualistic commitment to dissidence, reminiscent of the 'permanent provocation of power', talked of by Michel Foucault (Foucault, 1982).

> I'm generally very anti-government and the reason I'm a Khalistani now is that the government has not been formed yet. When it will be formed, I will be the first one to criticize the government because if there are no people criticizing the government, then corruption will dominate and the level of accountability will decrease, so you must have distance, that's fundamental for every democracy.[6]

Mohajir private diplomacy was different, in that a single group monopolized it: the MQM, led from London since the exile of its leader, Altaf Hussain, in 1992. Although the MQM imploded at the beginning of the 1990s with the creation of the MQM (Haqiqi), which received the support of Pakistan's intelligence agencies, most of the party workers remained loyal to Altaf Hussain and the Haqiqis never promoted themselves on the international scene. Hence, I propose to categorize Sikh ethnic diplomacy as a *diffuse* blend of transnational identity politics, whereas the MQM's transnationalization followed a more *centralized* pattern. Among the Sikhs, international lobbying was essentially conducted by the diaspora, and it was as ostensible as fragmented. On the contrary, among MQM overseas activists, visibility was less of a preoccupation than efficiency and unity. In the first years of the 1990s, the situation in Karachi triggered the interest of some Urdu-speaking Pakistanis settled in the UK, Canada and the US. These individuals enjoyed citizenship in their country of residence and they had built strong political and economic networks there over the years. Hence, they could have helped the MQM to receive more attention from Western powers. This is precisely what they tried to do by setting up party units abroad without any formal assignment from the headquarters of the party in Azizabad (Karachi). This was very unusual for an organization known for its discipline and hierarchism. However, the party leaders in Karachi did not bother about the advent of such overseas units until the exile of Altaf Hussain to London in 1992. At that time, the situation changed drastically. The headquarters of the party was relocated in a suburb of Middlesex (Edgeware) and the West became a sanctuary for its top militants. Globalization was imposed on the MQM with the exile of its top leadership, and internationalizing its activities became a matter of life or death for the party. It is in this context that it struck its iron hand on the first wave of Mohajir overseas militants. During this episode, party workers from Karachi took control of the party's overseas units, after having evicted local sympathizers, whose advocacy for a more decentralized pattern of organization infuriated the MQM's top brass. I will discuss later the socio-political implications of such a purge. Let me only emphasize, at this point, the differences between Mohajir and Sikh ethnic lobbying, both in terms of actors and strategy. The MQM leadership formed in Karachi, unlike the Khalistani leaders based in the Punjab, was able to retain control over the transnational networks advocating its cause. More significantly, MQM overseas militants generally kept a low-profile, so as to ensure the safety of their sanctuaries outside Pakistan. To a large extent, the party actually functions as a secret society sharing some affinities with Sufi orders. Altaf Hussain was for a long time referred to as *pir* and the party workers then saw themselves as *murids*. Although Altaf tried to secularize this relationship by asking his followers to refer to him as *bhai* (brother),[7] the devotion remains. This cult of the leader, inspired by totalitarian ideologies and by the Sufi relationship between the Master and his disciples, turned out to be the main asset of the MQM in its globalization. It ensured the ideological unity of the party and the centrality of its decisions, lying in the mind and the body of its charismatic leader.

The *pir–murid* relationship recycled by the MQM facilitated the exile of its centre of command, which was already de-territorialized, embodied in the *Quaid-e-Tehrik*. Yet, the IT revolution offered an invaluable contribution to the MQM in its process of transnationalization. Indeed, if Sufi masters always travelled and yet remained in touch with their followers, fax machines and modems now help them to retain stronger ties with their audience, compensating their physical absence by electronic guidance. Altaf Hussain could hence recently claim: 'Indeed, the telephone and the IT has [*sic*] never ever [been] used the way I have used them.'[8] Undoubtedly, Altaf has set up an ingenious transnational system of communication through networks of mobile phones plugged to amplifiers and thus spreading the word of the *quaid* to several places at the same time, bestowing ubiquity upon him. One should not overestimate the reliability of such communication networks, though. I attended one of these performances[9] in Toronto, during which Altaf Hussain was supposed to address all his militants of North America at the same time. To the great disappointment of his party workers, the attempt failed miserably and Altaf could not make his way through the air waves that night.

Communication politics is not immune to the patterns of organization of its protagonists. Thus, if the MQM has been strengthened by its frequent and diversified uses of IT, the Khalistanis are as divided in cyberspace as they are offline (Gunawardena, 2000). The Sikh presence in cyberspace is plethoric, anarchic and egoistic: it uses several idioms (that of 'religion,' 'nation' or 'diaspora'), it lacks hegemonic institutions and it is centred on prestige—thirty personalities who have used the internet to serve their own quest for recognition rather than to promote the more abstract cause of 'Khalistan.'

THE IDEOLOGICAL AND STRATEGIC DILEMMAS OF SIKH AND MOHAJIR NATIONALISTS, IN THE CONTEXT OF GLOBALIZATION

The second part of this paper looks at the intermingling of local and external factors at work in 'new ethnicities' (Hall, 1992), and particularly in diasporic ones. My point, here, will be to shed light on what I identify as the two major dilemmas faced by nationalists in the present phase of globalization: (1) their ideological positioning beneath or beyond the State; (2) their strategic orientation, which derives from their political positioning, within or outside their homeland. My hypothesis is that one should not expect nationalists to adopt clear-cut positions on these issues, as no post-national mode of governance seems powerful enough to replace the national framework yet, while the transnationalization of their activities has become a command for present-day ethnic-entrepreneurs. Nationalism will then survive *par defaut* as long as no alternative will be found to the national paradigm. However, this does not mean that state power and identity politics are not changing: nationalism and transnationality are now walking hand in hand and new paradigms of identification and governance may well arise from such an improbable alliance.

At first sight, it may seem that Khalistanis and, to a lesser extent, certain Mohajir activists are simply another blend of separatists, in continuity with the 'freedom fighters' of the past. Thus, their fantasies for an independent Punjab or a sovereign city of Karachi would simply express the resilience of the State in world politics. Dreamt of by cohorts of deprived nations, State structures would still be the hegemonic mode of governance and the last abstraction for which men and women seem to be ready to lay down their lives or to brutally put an end to that of the other. However, if looked at more thoroughly, the reference to the State in Sikh and Mohajir nationalism is far from being clear. None of the 150 people I interviewed in the course of my doctoral research could present me with a clear reflection on State-building and political sovereignty, their emphasis being put on the 'Mohajir Qaum' or the 'Khalsa Nation' rather than on Urdudesh or Khalistan. In the case of the Khalistanis, this was also noticed by Ram Narayan Kumar who, after extensive fieldwork, concluded that 'Khalistan is not a serious concept even with those who engage in terrorism in its name. Although the resolve to fight is undaunted, the goal is not necessarily Khalistan' (Kumar, 1997). My hypothesis is that these 'Troyan nationalisms' (Appadurai, 1996) actually hide out non-national aspirations, which vary according to the localization of the nationalists, to their personal exposition to violence and discrimination, and to their place in the hierarchy of the nationalist movement. Such motivations can be economic (the appropriation of private or public donations or the integration to the world-economy), emotional (fear and suffering inspiring the individuals, inside or outside the homeland) and political (recognition and patronage by the home or the host state). The magical formula of nationalism differentiates, unites, and represents. However popular it remains, one should not stop here though, as it is only the package, and certainly not the gift itself.

If the resilience of state-centric references among long-distance nationalists seems to wither away under close examination, one has to acknowledge the resistance of state sovereignty to ethnic diplomacy. Indeed, whatever success they may claim in the course of their international lobbying, Sikh and Mohajir ethnic entrepreneurs have constantly been under the pressure of state authorities, whether in their home or host states. In the case of the Khalistanis, the movement suffered a serious blow due to the pressure exerted by New Delhi on its Western counterparts. In 1993, the British and Indian governments signed jointly the Suppression of Terrorism Act, which enables extradition of 'terrorists' operating from Britain against Indian interests. In February 2001, this was extended by the adoption of the Terrorism Act 2000 in Britain, under which two Khalistani organizations have been outlawed: the Babbar Khalsa International and the International Sikh Youth Federation. In Canada, after the explosion of an Air India Boeing above the Sea of Ireland in 1985, the government, suspecting Canadian Sikhs to be implicated in the bombing, started considering the whole community as a threat to its national security and a supporter of international terrorism. An extradition treaty was subsequently signed between India and Canada on 6 February 1987 and the Canadian authorities have not been receptive to the Sikhs' call for Khalistan ever since. However, state and federal officers have been lobbied more successfully in favour of the protection of Sikh religious rights on Canadian soil, which is becoming the main activity of most Khalistani organizations operating in Canada and the UK (Gayer, 2001). At the same time, it seems that the Indian government has used private infiltrators in the ranks of overseas Sikh separatists and an MQM party worker with whom I met was approached by Indian agencies for help in Montreal. US authorities, for their part, offered discrete support and political training to a handful of MQM and Khalistani activists.[10]

Beyond their ambivalent relationship with the world of state-centric actors and norms, Sikh and Mohajir ethnic entrepreneurs have been facing another challenge by transnationalizing their movements: the coordination of home-based and long-distance nationalists operating from abroad. Against all odds, the globalization of an ethnic movement does not obviously lead to its success. As Mark Granovetter suggests, the strength of social networks lies in the weakness of their ties (Granovetter, 1973), but this lack of institutionalization may become lethal when such networks extend transnationally. This is a core issue for the sociological understanding of globalization at the micro-social level but I do not have the ambition to address it directly here. I would only like to emphasize that the decentralized, horizontal and informal patterns of organization characteristic of social networks are often detrimental to social movements when they extend beyond borders. This is particularly true for nationalist movements, whose obsession for unity and discipline is proportional to their innate inclination to fragment. Containing fissiparous tendencies inside these movements becomes a delicate task, when the diversity of interests and political cultures of the activists increase. I have already mentioned the purge operated by the MQM leadership in its overseas units at the beginning of the 1990s. This clearly exemplifies the threats of implosion with which every globalized nationalist movement is confronted. In the Sikh case, I also mentioned that the Khalistan movement partly lost its popularity in East Punjab due to its confiscation by the diaspora. To avoid any misunderstanding, let me emphasize that the primary causes for this decline should be searched in the Punjab rather than in the diaspora. The strategic shift of the insurgents from guerrilla to terrorism, under the influence of Pakistani intelligence agencies, alienated many former sympathizers of the secessionist movement. At the same moment, in the beginning of the 1990s, Indian federal authorities took the decision to restore political normalcy in the Punjab, thus bringing the Sikhs back into the national fold. For this reason, the vocal commitment of a minority of overseas Sikhs to Khalistan can only be a secondary explanation for the decline of the secessionist movement in the Punjab but it is still worth mentioning. For many Sikhs residing in the Punjab who gave their support to the Khalistanis at the height of the insurgency, in the late 1980s, long-distance nationalists have hijacked a cause which was first articulated in Punjab and, by doing so they intended to anchor their identity in an imaginary homelad rather than to craft an actual nation state (Shani, 2000: 199). Indeed, diasporic Sikhs who have endorsed the demand for Khalistan in their country of residence have often done so to serve their personal quest for recognition, oriented towards their 'community' but also towards the authorities of their countries of residence, particularly when the multicultural ideology and institutions of these states encouraged local ethnic entrepreneurs to root their identity in a state of their own, however, imaginary it may have been (Dusenbery, 1995; Gayer, 2000). This conflict between Sikh home-based and long-distance nationalists exemplifies the internal tensions faced by nationalist movements on their way to globalization: politics of the homeland articulated in a diasporic context does not involve the same kind of actors, nor does it carry the same motives as homeland politics. Yet, with the IT and the transport revolutions, long-distance nationalists are bound to be increasingly involved in their homeland politics, even if it is for very different reasons and in very different ways from home-based nationalists.

CONCLUSION

So far, the MQM has been able to tackle the strategic and ideological dilemmas induced by its transnationalization process through an astute cocktail of discipline, charisma and information technologies. Khalistanis, on the contrary, were not able to adopt a transnational platform coordinating homeland politics and diasporic politics of the homeland. Rather than the history and morphology of each ethnic group, it is the 'grammars of authority and consent' (Cefaï, 2001: 102-3) and the patterns of organization of their nationalist organizations which explain this discrepancy. Whereas the MQM is a well-organized authoritarian party which present several analogies with the Kurdish PKK and the Tamil LTTE, the movement for Khalistan has always retained a pre-organizational form, as it was loosely coordinated by competing 'leaders' lacking an institutional support.

The discrepancy between Sikh and Mohajir long-distance nationalisms is not limited to their patterns of transnational (dis)organization. The transnational trajectories of these nationalist movements have had very contrasting effects. Whereas the MQM has retained the support of the majority of Mohajirs in Pakistan after the exile of its leaders, *par defaut* if not out of devotion for Altaf Hussain, Sikh long-distance nationalists have alienated potential sympathizers of the nationalist cause when they started using the demand for a separate state in their homeland in order to attain greater recognition from their local 'community' or from the authorities of their country of residence. This gap between Sikh homeland politics and

Khalistani politics of the homeland exemplifies the ambiguities of today's processes of identity formation. The transport and IT revolutions have facilitated transnational movements and communication but they have also reinforced the pluralism of ethnic groups around the globe. Identity formation processes are becoming increasingly transnational but at the same time, they are also becoming more localized. For this reason, the notion of 'translocality' proposed by anthropologists (Appadurai, 1996) and refined by International Relations scholars (Mandaville, 1999) seems to be the most heuristic device to analyse present-day processes of identity formation, which involve ethnic entrepreneurs and audiences spread out in several localities, who interact without necessarily converging.

NOTES

1. This song by the British Punjabi band DCS can be found on their *Panjabi Dance Nation* album, which was released by Kamlee Records (Birmingham) in 1998.
2. For an opposite perspective on the colonial 'New World Origins of Nationalism', see Anderson, 1983.
3. The Pakistani ISI has provided shelter and training to hundreds of Khalistani guerrillas in Western Punjab. This process started right after Operation Blue Star, when the first wave of Sikh militants gathered in Faisalabad jail (this information is based on interviews with Khalistani militants formerly active in Pakistan). On the Mohajir side, Indian diplomats have offered support to MQM overseas workers and a reporter at *Newsline* (Karachi) even told me that he had met several MQM activists who had received military training in India. Beyond this covert support to the enemy's enemies, both 'governments' (or, rather, certain factions among the federal and provincial authorities) have initially lent support to the nationalists who would soon turn against them. General Zia is thus suspected to have supported the creation of the MQM to alienate the Mohajirs from the Jamaat-e Islami and the Pakistan People's Party (PPP), while Indira Gandhi used Sant Jarnail Singh Bhindranwale against the more moderate Akalis.
4. Chauhan went back to East Punjab in June 2001, after having spent years negotiating his return with Indian authorities in London.

5. At least until February 2001. Its activities are unknown ever since, as the group has been outlawed under the Terrorism Act 2000, along with the Babbar Khalsa International.
6. Interview, New York City, 12 April 2000.
7. The MQM is committed to the separation of politics and religion, breaking away from the fundamentalist past of the Mohajirs, who supported the Jamaat-e Islami before shifting their loyalty to the MQM. The party cannot be described as perfectly 'secular', though, as it enjoys playing with religious symbols and feelings when it suits the interests of its leaders.
8. Transcription of Altaf Hussain's online chat with *Indiatimes*, 5 July 2001, available at http://www.indiatimes.com/chatevents/altaf.htm
9. The term is to be taken literally here, as the whole event is *mis en scene* by MQM activists. A stage is set and adorned with huge portraits of Altaf Hussain standing on the floor or clung to the wall behind the scene. Orators then address the crowd before the intervention of the Quaid-e-Tehrik himself, whose physical absence is to be compensated by his omnipresent image.
10. I personally met one activist of the MQM who was invited to the US and enrolled in a political training programme organized by the State Department for several months, through a private foundation. A Sikh Human Rights activist, well-known for his advocacy of Khalistan, was also invited to the US through Freedom House, an NGO linked with the Democratic Party which has no real presence in India. This individual was surprised to discover that: 'There were some other Asian people [in the corridors of the State Department]: Pakistanis, Bangladeshis, Bhutanese Hindus, someone from the Maldives, others from Sri Lanka. . . . Then I realized that what they were trying to do was to identify potential opinion makers and leaders and cultivate them and have personal relationships with them' ; interview, Chandigarh, 23 March 2001.

REFERENCES

Anderson, B., *Imagined Communities: Reflections on the Origin and Spread of Nationalism*, London: Verso, 1983.

———, 'Ice Empire and Ice Hockey: Two fin de siècle Dreams', *New Left Review*, no. 214, November-December 1995.

——, *The Spectre of Comparisons: Nationalism, Southeast Asia and the World*, London: Verso, 1998.

Appadurai, A., *Modernity at Large: Cultural Dimensions of Globalization*, Minneapolis: Minnesota University Press, 1996.

Cefaï, D., 'Expérience, culture et politique', in Daniel Cefaï (ed.), *Cultures Politiques*, Paris, PUF, 2001.

Constantin, F., 'La privatisation de la politique étrangère: à partir de la scène africaine', *Pouvoirs*, 88, 1999.

Dieckhoff, A., *La nations dans tous ses états: les identilés nationales en mouvement*, Paris: Flammarion, 2000.

Dusenbery, V., 'A Sikh Diaspora? Contested Identities and Constructed Realities', in Peter van der Veer (ed.), *Nation and Migration*, Philadelphia: University of Pensylvania Press, 1995.

Foucault, M., 'Afterword: The Subject and Power', in Hubert L. Dreyfus and Paul Rabinow (eds.), *Michel Foucault: Beyond Structuralism and Hermeneutics*, London: Harvester Wheatsheaf, 1982.

Fuglerud, O., *Life on the Outside: The Tamil Diaspora and Long-Distance Nationalism*, London: Pluto Press, 1999.

Gayer, L., 'The Globalization of Identity Politics: The Sikh Experience', *International Journal of Punjab Studies*, vol. 7, no. 2, July-December 2000.

——, 'Un turban pour les Mounties: multiculturalisme canadien et politiques du corps sikhes', *Raisons politiques* [1st formula], no. 4, March 2001.

Granovetter, M., 'The Strength of Weak Ties', *American Journal of Sociology*, vol. 78, no. 6, May 1973.

Grojean, O., 'Les répertoires du conflit kurde', in Gilles Dorronsoro (dir.), *La Turquie conteste: Mobilisations sociales et régime sécuritaire*, Paris: Editions du CNRS, 2005.

Gunawardena, S., 'Constructing Cyber-nationalism: Sikh solidarity via the Internet', *International Journal of Punjab Studies*, vol. 7, no. 2, July-December 2000.

Hall, S., 'The New Ethnicities', in James Donald and Ali Ratansi (eds.), *Race, Culture and Difference*, London: Sage, 1992.

Jasper, J.M. and J.D. Poulsen, 'Recruiting Strangers and Friends: Moral Shocks and Social Networks in Animal Rights and Anti-nuclear Protests', *Social Problems*, vol. 42, no. 4, 1995.

Jeganathan, P., 'Eelam.com: Place, Nation, and Imagination in Cyberspace', *Public Culture*, vol. 10, no. 3, 1998.

Kumar, R.N., *The Sikh Unrest and the Indian State: Politics, Personalities and Historical Retrospective*, Delhi: Ajanta, 1997, pp. 391-2.

Levitt, P., *The Transnational Villagers*, Berkeley: University of California Press, 2001.

Mandaville, P., 'Territory and Translocality: Discrepant Idioms of Political Identity', *Millenium*, vol. 28, no. 3, 1999.

Pettigrew, J., *Robber Noblemen: A Study of the Political System of the Sikh Jats*, London: Kegan Paul, 1985.

Shani, G., 'The Politics of Recognition: Sikh Diasporic Nationalism and the International Order', *International Journal of Punjab Studies*, vol. 7, no. 2, July-December 2000.

11

Diaspora and Homeland Politics

Comparative Experiences of Mobilization for Hindutva and Khalistan

MARIE CARINE LALL AND SHINDER S. THANDI

INTRODUCTION: GROWING INTEREST IN DIASPORAS AND DIASPORA POLITICS

Diasporas have long been a feature of the world stage, but the acceleration of migration in the last 30 years, both for economic betterment and to escape conflict and persecution—in short, to assure economic and human security—has greatly expanded their reach and significance in world affairs. Within any one diaspora community and in any one location, such as for instance the 15-20 million Indians dispersed in 70 odd countries, there is great variety and differentiation both in terms of period of settlement and reasons for migration. Diaspora communities have emerged due to a mixture of economic, social, and political forces operating in different historical periods and contexts.

Aide by rapid and massive leaps forward in communications technologies compressing time and space, diasporas now have the capacity to exert far greater influence and leverage on their homelands than ever before. Diasporas have emerged as the most prominent actors that link international and domestic spheres of politics and have become aptly suited to manipulate international images of their community. But the influence of these 'old' as well as 'new' diasporas on their homelands depends on the resources they can mobilize, and this in turn depends on where they are located. In addition to links with their homelands, diasporas also maintain multi-layered intra-diaspora connections leading to continuous circulation of people, money, resources, ideas, and values amongst them.

Given that diaspora-homeland relations have strengthened during the current phase of globalization it is becoming increasingly recognized that a country's diaspora can have a significant political and economic impact on the region of origin. This impact can be positive and/or negative, for example positive in the economic domain but negative in the political domain. Since both effects are simultaneous, at certain times the negative effects may appear to dominate the positive ones. However, the diaspora's potential to influence its home country is a function of both its own characteristics and those of the country or region of origin. The potential for a diaspora to act as an agent or at least a catalyst for change depends on a number of factors: its size, its education, its skills, length of migration, etc., and the political and economic profile of this diaspora, e.g. its socio-economic make-up and the extent of its economic and political activities in the host country. Given the close relationship between the level of education, level of income and size, we would expect to see a very positive contribution by diasporas. Acknowledging the growing importance of diasporas in the global economy, the World Bank (2000: 39) stated:

> Diasporas serve as information channels for the flow of information, market intelligence, capital and skills. They may supplement formal channels that rely on market institutions, providing a way for migrants to conduct transactions in an atmosphere of trust. In this way they act to offset information asymmetries and other market failures. Modern diasporas . . . expedite business transactions by resolving monitoring problems, reducing opportunism, and building reputation and ethnic trust based on networking. As migration continues, diasporas will expand, tying together regions and continents. Even if governments attempt to slow down the process, communications, technology and human relationships will maintain this trend.[1]

Not surprisingly therefore many governments throughout the world have begun to see their diasporas as a 'strategic asset' which needs to be nurtured and mobilized for the socio-economic development of the mother country. However, in many cases their potential contribution lags behind actual contribution due to a variety of reasons but most crucially it is dependent on the prevailing economic and political environment of the host and home country. For example, the nature and level of engagement with the diaspora, prevailing regulatory environment and priorities in economic policies all have an influence on their actual contribution to economic development. The intensity of attachment of the diaspora community is also crucial and this can vary depending on length of settlement abroad, reasons for relocating in the first place and the political environment especially in framing policies towards diaspora communities. The Indian State has only belatedly woken up to this changed understanding regarding the opportunities offered by diasporas.

It is also becoming acknowledged that even in the political sphere diasporas can play a constructive or a destructive role. Although diasporas are known to contribute significantly to the political process in their home countries by promoting international ties, acting as bridges or peace mediators, it is their negative actions that get more academic attention. So, for instance, there is a vast and growing literature on how diaspora groups can fund sub-nationalist or ethno-nationalist movements which pose either a threat to national security or challenge the territorial integrity of the nation state since diasporas are increasingly perceived to represent the 'paradigmatic Other of the nation-state.' In terms of South Asia for instance there already exists literature which examines the causes and effects of long-distance nationalism amongst the Sikhs, Tamils, Kashmiris, Sindhis, Mohajirs, etc. This paper intends to contribute to that literature and offer a comparative perspective on diasporic influences of two relatively wealthy communities sited in two relatively wealthy locations—Hindus and Sikhs in the USA and the UK—in order to better understand the specific contexts which give rise to political mobilization amongst these groups.

The comparative framework will enable us to move on from the more mainstream discourses on diasporic nationalism which often tend to focus exclusively on religious identity as an instrumental tool for mobilizing for a separate nation state.

COMPARING TWO DIASPORIC COMMUNITIES

Hindus and Sikhs are the chosen communities because they do have some stark differences. Hindus form the majority of the population in India whereas the Sikhs are merely 2 per cent of India's population but are historically overrepresented in the overseas Indian population in the two chosen diaspora sites. In the UK for instance, of the total number (around 900,000) who identified themselves as Hindus and Sikh, the latter constitute around 30 per cent. This is also the case for both the USA and Canada. This poses an interesting challenge for the Indian State as it is forced to engage with a highly globalized Sikh community at home or abroad. The mobilization and support for Hindutva (Hindu nationalism), although a much later phenomenon than the Sikh diaspora's support for Khalistan, also does not fit into the neat diasporic models where diasporas are usually conceptualized as dispersed and powerless 'diasporas in exile'. In fact, the two cases complement each other because the Sikh case, arguably falls into the classic category of 'long-distance nationalism' whereas the Hindu case is one of reverse—where a part of the religious majority community courts the Hindu diaspora by instilling patriotic and cultural nationalism abroad. In his article entitled 'Nationalism by proxy', Bidisha Biswas also compares these two diaspora communities and concludes that despite similar external opportunities, their nationalist movements developed different mobilizing structures, due to 'varying mechanisms used by the leadership' (Biswas, 2004).

Our paper goes beyond the structural analysis offered by Biswas and uses the two case studies to challenge the current conceptual frameworks around diasporas to analyse the linkages between disapora and homeland politics. In doing so it will also demonstrate the variations in diaspora nationalisms. For instance, whereas Sikh diaspora nationalism (support for Khalistan) can arguably be characterized as resulting from the Sikh imaginings of being a 'victim' diaspora,[2] mobilization of support for Hindutva can be characterized as developing an overarching homogenizing diasporic consciousness amongst a heterogeneous Hindu people through emphasizing their ancestral roots to India.

In both our chosen cases the use of the term 'diaspora' is problematic as it does not capture the variety of cultural interconnections, networks and trans-border circular movements in trade, technology, labour and tourism. Although romanticized diaspora sentiments may linger with a small minority of people, the vast majority now engage in multi-layered transnational practices and the term 'transnationalism' may offer more analytical value. A further issue that this paper attempts to deal with is whether we should differentiate between disporas as a set of differentiated phenomena (i.e. the notion that India has many diasporas) and diasporas as political rhetoric where discourses of diaspora are part of a political project which aims to weave together diverse populations who can be ethnicized into a single 'global Indian family'. The most clear (and perhaps also extreme) case of these discourses is the increasing use of information technologies (to foster 'cyberpublics') by various Hindu and Sikh organizations to essentialize and unify identities which do not fit the diversity within diaspora populations and their experiences.[3]

Finally there are some fundamental differences between the Hindu and Sikh diasporic engagement with homeland politics. As a result of exclusive and secular Nehruvian policies, political and religious fundamentalism in India has had a certain level of diasporic support. Benedict Anderson's analysis of 'long-distance nationalism' explains in part why communities abroad tend to support nationalist parties and policies despite not 'benefiting' directly from the policies they support (Anderson, 1991). The case with India is, however, more complex. The Hindu diasporic community has for the best part of half a century not had a stake in Indian politics. Nehruvian policies effectively 'orphaned' them and relegated them to their host country. As will be detailed below, organizations linked to the Sangh Parivar were the only 'official' and 'public' means by which they were able to take part in India's development. The BJP policies finally drew them back into the family fold, which many interpreted as restoring their rightful place in India's political arena.

There is a significant contrast here in the case of the Sikh diaspora which has historically maintained a variety of socio-economic ties with families and friends in villages back home and had long shown an interest in homeland politics.[4] It was inevitable that some sections of the Sikh diaspora community who had a homeland politics leaning would engage with the Khalistan movement at an early stage. Even before this movement began, a section of the overseas Sikhs had begun to portray the Sikh community (*qaum*) as a 'nation without a state' (a legacy of Partition of India and Punjab perhaps) and had emerged as potentially important new political actors in international relations. As Guibernau argues such new political actors have the potential to 'capture, and promote new political sentiments of loyalty, solidarity and community among individuals who seem to have developed a growing need for identity'.[5]

However, despite the differences, it is primarily the changing nature of homeland politics that have shaped and dictated political activism amongst the diaspora in the host country.

EVOLVING DIASPORA-HOMELAND LINKS: FROM INDIFFERENCE TO ENGAGEMENT

Before Independence the Indian National Congress (INC) had expressed a certain amount of responsibility and solidarity towards those who had left India. Colonial policies had sent them abroad as indentured workers. They were therefore seen as victims of the Empire's rule and Congress raised the issue of their conditions of labour with the British. During the independence movement the unity and solidarity of the Indian people at home and abroad was important to the INC. Funds from the diaspora also supported the movement, demonstrating that the solidarity was mutual (Lall, 2001).

However, after Independence Nehru clearly announced that the ethnic Indians who chose to remain abroad would not be able to take up Indian citizenship and adopt the nationality of their host country. The diaspora Indians were not expected to take part in India's political or economic development. This was a complete refutation of ethnic ties, which, however, was politically expedient. A strong line on the fate of Indian minorities in other countries would have been counterproductive for Indian relations with these countries (Heimsath and Mansingh, 1971: 302).

It has been argued that the turning point for state–diaspora relations in India was the post-1991 economic reforms. However, despite special concessions to try and encourage NRI investments, the diaspora involvement remained painfully low (Lall, 2001). Further, as part of ongoing reforms the Indian government tried to share out the economic pain by devolving the responsibility for raising FDI to state governments (Jenkins, 1999). Many of the southern states, but also some in the north such as the Punjab, decided to elicit funds from NRIs originating from their States (Lall, 2001b). Such campaigns have been moderately successful, with NRI investments rising particularly in many southern states.

Aside from the newly defined economic role the diaspora was supposed to play, issues pertaining to dual nationality started to make it onto the political agenda. This was partly related to the 'ethnic' conception of the Indian nation that the BJP espoused, but also had an economic dimension (Adeney and Lall, 2005). At first only a Person of Indian Origin (PIO) card was offered. In 2002, after the Singhvi Committee report on the Indian diaspora,[6] the BJP government announced that Indians abroad would also be granted dual citizenship (*India Today*, 2002). This was reiterated again in January 2003 at the first Pravasi Bharatiya

Divas (PBD), held in New Delhi. However, dual nationality was restricted to certain countries and on certain conditions.[7]

Although the changes *vis-à-vis* the diaspora has been facilitated by the policy of economic liberalization since 1991 it was no coincidence that the BJP rather than the 'secular' Congress Prime Minister Rao introduced them. One explanation is that the BJP is part of a movement that articulates a cultural-religious basis to Indian national identity. Beyond the cultural-religious explanation, the policy turn by the BJP has to be seen from two very different angles. First and foremost the BJP, unlike Congress, tends to command financial and moral support from Indians settled abroad. '. . . [T]he Hindu revivalist message of the BJP was sharpened and strengthened through its overseas connections' (Abraham, 2003). This is another example of 'long-distance nationalism', but used in reverse to strengthen party appeal and policies back home. The only way to maintain such ties is to recognize the ethnic ties of the Indian diaspora. The second, no less important aspect of this policy change was linked to the low level of NRI investments in India after 1991 which the BJP wanted to increase. Dual nationality would in part solve this problem. The changing global market meant that international economic realities were more important than in Nehru's time, although the ethnic dimension to the change in policy was still important.

The current government, though Congress led, has endorsed the policies that were put in place by the BJP-led NDA government. At the last PBD in January 2005 dual nationality was promised for all PIOs and the children of those who had left after 26 January 1950.[8] On the face of it this seems to be a more inclusive policy than what had been offered by the BJP, however, the cut-off date means that in practice there will be not much difference. The PBD 2006 did not bring any dramatic news. It seems that the Congress led government has decided to build on the state–diaspora ties initiated by the previous government and that it has resulted in the complete refutation of the Nehruvian policies which governed government-diaspora relations in India for half a century.

MIGRANT TRANSNATIONAL POLITICAL PRACTICES: MODES OF MOBILIZATION

Mobilization Amongst the Sikhs

The history of Sikh overseas migration starts in the final quarter of the twentieth century and is intrinsically linked with the expansion of the British Empire in large parts of the world. Thus by the beginning of the twentieth century there is a sizeable settlement in Australasia and on the west coast of north America especially in California and British Columbia. In the first two decades of the twentieth century there is a further movement of Sikhs overseas to East African countries.[9] With the global spread of Sikhs there emerged cultural and political associations which catered for their needs and encouraging transnational links and practices. In these earlier transnational links leading Sikh intellectuals and members of the Chief Khalsa Diwan as representative of the Singh Sabha movement in Punjab, travelled around different diaspora locations encouraging the establishment of Sikh gurdwaras and cultural societies. Thus by the first two decades of the twentieth century we witness the construction of Sikh gurdwaras in Hong Kong, Kenya, England, Canada and the USA. The well-documented *Komagata Maru* affair also demonstrates the already heightened degree of politicization amongst overseas Punjabi, mainly Sikhs, to the predicaments of colonial India.[10] Thus among the Sikhs, political and cultural organizational transnational links have a long history—in fact, over 100 years and overseas activities of Chief Khalsa Diwan and *Ghadrites* represent two good examples.[11]

In the post-1960s period, when immigration laws became more relaxed, especially for North America, a trend in replication of most Punjab or India-based political parties in the USA and the UK can be identified. Overseas branches of Congress, Akali and Communist parties begin to mushroom and towards the end of 1970s, and 1980s, the establishment of religious organizations also begins to be evident, e.g. Akhand Kirtni Jatha and Damdami Taksal had also set-up overseas branches. The role of visiting religious leaders or *sants* to these locations also begin to have an influence on the diaspora communities and many of them actively encouraged the development of separate organizations and gurdwaras, creating further differentiation within the community. Thus, by the time of Operation Blue Star in June 2004, well-established networks among political and religious organizations are already in place. These networks are fully mobilized after Operation Blue Star and then again after the November 1984 anti-Sikh violence in Delhi.

In the post-1984, period, main militant groups and their factions were also replicated in the diaspora. Figures 11.1 and 11.2 clearly illustrate this phenomenon at the height of the militancy period in the case of both UK and USA. As we can see, the Sikh political movement is clearly split amongst those following Akali Dal or Congress or Communist Party politics, with the later two comprising the main anti-Khalistan bloc. The charts also demonstrate that the factionalism amongst pro- and anti-Khalistan groups was clearly based around personalities rather than ideology.

In the post-1984 period three major sites for mobilization emerge—the gurdwara, vernacular press, and the internet.

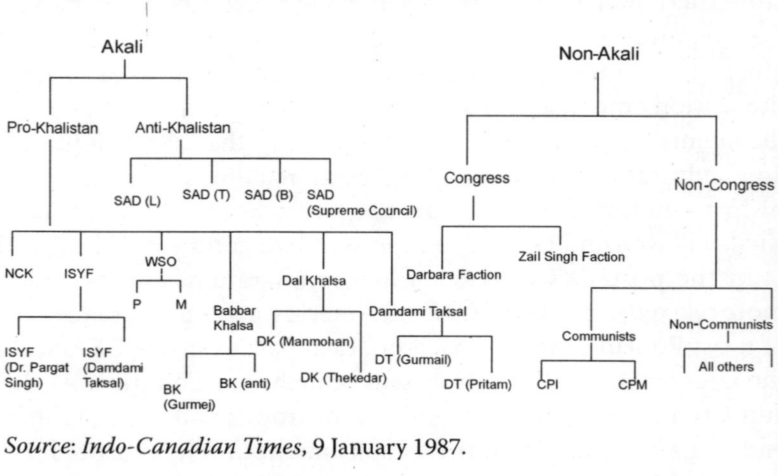

Source: *Indo-Canadian Times*, 9 January 1987.

FIG. 11.1: SIKH POLITICAL ORGANIZATIONS, UK, 1987

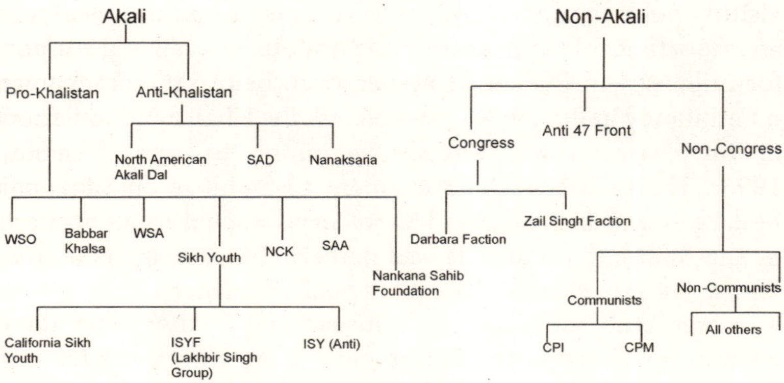

Source: *Indo-Canadian Times*, 9 January 1987.

FIG. 11.2: SIKH POLITICAL ORGANIZATIONS, USA, 1987

Gurdwaras emerge as the premier site and control of gurdwara committees (hence access to gurdwara finances) becomes a crucial issue. Most of the appeals for funding by militant groups occur through gurdwaras or through organizations that control them. As a consequence there are many battles and tensions amongst diaspora-based communities over their control leading to polarization amongst different types of diaspora Sikhs (Thandi, 1996; Tatla, 1999). This tension sometimes leads to overt violence and it is worth noting that two newspaper editors—Tara Singh Hayer, editor of the influential *Indo-Canadian Times* and Tersem Singh Purewal, editor of the pioneering Punjabi vernacular paper based in the UK, *Desh Pardesh*, were both murdered, allegedly linked to factional fighting amongst anti- and pro-Khalistani groups. The Canadian community's angry response to the long running but recently concluded Air India bombing trial also demonstrated the extent of community polarization.[12]

The major period of the Khalistani movement overseas runs from 1984 to the early 1990s although there are still some die-hard groups which continue to operate today but under the cover of cultural organizations. During the movement's period, visiting politicians, *ragis, sants* to various diaspora sites played an important role in nurturing the faithful and rallying support for militancy in Punjab. However, even before the crackdown on militancy in Punjab was completed, the Khalistan movement in the diaspora was already beginning to wane (Thandi, 1996). The failure of the movement to mobilize all Sikhs can be largely attributed to its lack of mass appeal to all sections of the Sikh community. It was perceived primarily as a *rural* and a Jat movement. As a sectional movement it began to lose credibility amongst Sikhs abroad and further discredited when it became associated more and more with extortion and criminal activity in Punjab. To fully understand the inability of the pro-Khalistanis to sustain their mobilization, it is important to disaggregate the mobilized members into three categories: the *core* members (i.e. the organizing elites who are intensively active in diasporic affairs and in position to appeal for mobilization of the larger diaspora), the *passive* members (who avail themselves for mobilization when the *active* leaders call upon them) and the *silent* members who are the larger pool of people who are generally not involved in diasporic affairs but who may be mobilized in times of crisis).[13] Operation Blue Star of June 1984 outraged the whole diaspora but the core and active members were never able to translate that into sustained support for Khalistan amongst the passive and silent members. The vast majority—the silent category—are mostly part of Benedict's 'imagined community' often existing only in the minds of diasporic political activists or in the minds of home as well as host governments.

The pattern of mobilization and mobilization strategies in the USA are no different from the UK except for the different set of political actors and the fact that the Sikh community is smaller, less concentrated and more polarized into different socio-economic classes. The major followers of the Khalistan movement tended to be recent migrants, those who migrated for political reasons, or those who were self-employed in one capacity or another.[14]

Mobilization strategies change after the end of militancy in both the USA and the UK and this period also gives rise to different forms of lobbying host governments. In both locations the emphasis begins to shift from promoting Khalistan to promoting anti-India propaganda especially through hijacking of the Human Rights and Minority Rights agenda. There is also an attempt to forge alliances with other anti-India groups, e.g. challenging the India Caucus on Capitol Hill in alliance with other South Asian dissident groups.

There is yet a further change in strategy in the post-9/11 period after political groups such as Babbar Khalsa and International Sikh Youth Federation are banned by the UK, Canada and US governments for their alleged terrorist and money-laundering activities. Many of these groups re-orient their activities and develop alliances with cultural organizations based in Sikh gurdwaras in Pakistan and Punjab. In the UK for instance attempts have been made to forge an alliance of disparate Sikh organizations such as in the floating of the Sikh Secretariat and the Sikh Federation (UK), the latter also claiming to be the first Sikh political party.[15] Also significant is the floating of the All Party Parliamentary Group in the British Parliament under the chairmanship of John McDonnell, MP for Hayes & Harlington. This parliamentary grouping has attempted to widen the agenda, for example to include, human rights, health, education and environmental issues but Sikh representatives in this group remain dominated by previous Khalistani youth leaders. These organizations have also attempted to mobilize support for Sikh issues by identifying constituencies with large Sikh electorates to sway support for self-determination for Sikhs amongst British MPs. Some other recent activities include initiating Early Day Motions in Parliament and holding regular Lobby Days on specific issues such as for Sikhs to be recognized as a separate ethnic group in ethnic monitoring policies and in the next Census.[16]

Mobilization Amongst Hindus

The interaction between homeland political associations and political actors in the host country is particularly interesting with regard to the Hindutva movement. The overseas Sangh

Parivar has set up a wide net and various funding streams across the world and all of them connect back to the mother-organization back in India. This is exemplified in Figure 11.3.

One of the central aims of the Sangh Parivar's overseas branch is political mobilization. This, however, does not tend to happen on a political platform. The Sangh uses principally cultural and religious activities for these ends. In fact, it generally does not admit that its activities are in any way political, propagating that its main aim is to link the Hindu diaspora culturally and religiously to the motherland. Since the political side of the organization remains covert, a large number of Indians abroad are not explicitly aware that they are supporting a political agenda. This also means that the Sangh appeals to many more people who would otherwise shun political activities. Educating the children within the diaspora in matters pertaining to the

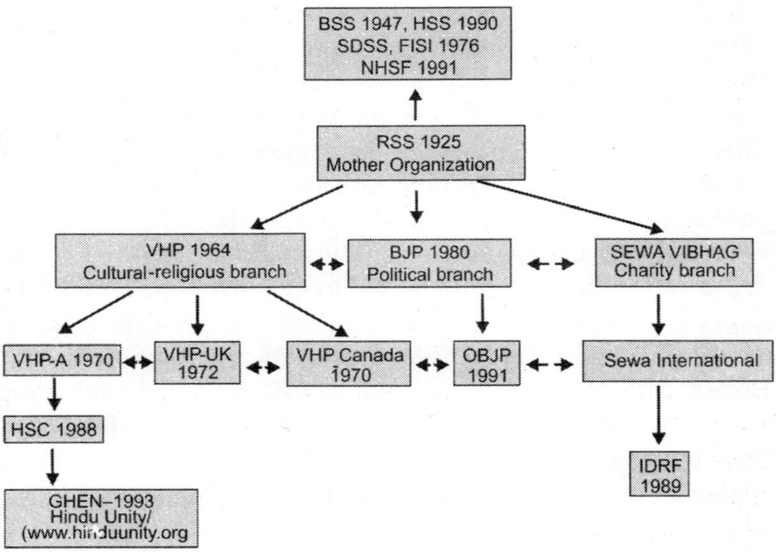

Source: Ingrid Therwath, '"Far and Wide": The Sangh Parivar's Global network', in Christophe Jaffrelot (ed.), *The Sangh Parivar: A Reader*, New Delhi: Oxford University Press, 2005, pp. 411-28.

FIG. 11.3: THE OVERSEAS SANGH PARIVAR NETWORK

Hindu religion and culture is a central pillar of the strategy as is the concept of '*seva*' or service by which volunteers aim to help their brethren back in India as well within the diasporic community. Other ways of mobilization such as the internet are used to distort Indian history and especially active in this arena is the Global Hindu Electronic Network (GHEN) (Lall, 2003).

Differences between the Diasporic Mobilization in the US and the UK

In part the difference between the diasporic mobilization in the US and the UK is also based on the political and cultural context of those host countries. The US advocates the idea of 'multiculturalism', which encourages people to engage with their cultural identity while at the same time granting them status as 'Americans'. This has been extremely important in relation to the Indian context, because while Indians are encouraged to discover their roots, it has to be done in a way that really oversimplifies and essentializes their culture both in the eyes of the Indian community as well as of other Americans. India is known as a country with an ancient civilization and a place that is inherently spiritual. Other aspects generally 'known' about India are that it is a poor developing country. According to Vijay Prashad:

> The well meaning multiculturalist hails the first generation migrants as representatives of an 'Indian culture' that is itself not homogeneous. Multiculturalism draws on its own ideas of India from US orientalism and sees it as fundamentally spiritual (represented by certain icons); this India resonates in the classroom and on celluloid. Thus there is an expectation that desis must be spiritual and so spirituality is authorized for them, as in the presence of temples and mosques. Desi culture in imperial eyes, is to be fundamentally a sort of religious culture, since religion is seen as the subcontinents' cultural essence. (Prashad, 2003: 51)

Given this American understanding of Indian culture, it is not entirely surprising that the Indian community has been actively involved in developing religious organizations. Many first generation Indians take pride in the fact that they have a superior culture with traditional morals and values, which they feel are lacking in the West. They try to hold on to their Indian identity and seek to preserve the India they left behind, which has led the Indian community on the whole to be very conservative, sometimes even more so than the Indians in India who have moved on with time (Tharoor, 1997). They are often depicted as a model minority, who with no clear interest in domestic politics are no trouble, yet contribute to the American economy.[17] However, as a result of the low level of interest in American politics, and an identity link with India, the diaspora community has been a fertile ground for the expansion of Hindu nationalist organizations.

VHP/HSC in the USA

The VHP America was established in 1974 in New York and has always referred to itself as a 'cultural' organization that promotes 'Hindu Dharma' and represents Hindus in America. A large part of the organization is centred on *seva* or service. On the website and in its literature, it always claims to promote harmony between different religions, races, creeds, etc. Despite pretending to be a cultural organization it was denied recognition as such by the UN in 1999. In the US today the VHPA is registered as an independent charity. Its literature emphasizes its global vision and mission.

The VHP has appealed to Indian Americans along two lines: patriotism and guilt in order to gain financial contributions. Nostalgia and long distance patriotism is exactly what the VHP has exploited and used to further its own goals. There are four main ways of mobilizing the diaspora:

- Sending brochures to Indian families presenting a very upper caste, Brahmanic Vedic type of Hinduism;
- Organizing conferences and youth camps (*Bal Vihars*);
- Publishing literature (Rajagopal, 2001);
- Organizing cultural events in American university campuses.

The VHPA aims to be a solution to the Hindu migrant's social anxieties—to channel their political energies into 'liberation of a homeland' which they are guilty to have abandoned as well as ease anxieties of Hindu parents who are afraid that their children are becoming Americanized and will not understand or care for anything to do with their 'own' culture.

There is an interesting parallel that can be drawn between the education provided by the VHP and its allied organizations for the children of the diaspora on Hinduism and Hindu culture, and the social science textbooks which the BJP government issued in India during their term in power.[18] In both cases religious nationalist values, some might even argue fundamentalist values, were thrust on ignorant children in order to create an exclusivist Hindu identity. Expatriate nostalgia of the home land might go a long way to explain why Hindu families in the West allow their children to be taught historical distortions on India and Hinduism. The fact that these classes also emphasize respect for elders and traditional family values could also explain why parents who face a crisis of parental authority are happy with their children being educated under the VHP banner (Rajagopal, 2001).

There seems to be more recently a certain level of tension arising from the fact that aside from the VHP, other, not necessarily Hindu organizations have emerged to represent the Indian in America politically and economically. The VHP see those rival organizations as competing for the same NRI funds. Some of the new organizations which have emerged, such as GOPIO (concerned with promotion of NRI business and global business networking) and the Hindu leaders forum might emerge out of or have loose links with the Sangh Parivar, however, as the American Indian lobby diversifies, the VHP feels that its representation of the Hindus in America is being hijacked by organizations whose principal aims might not be in line with those of the Sangh Parivar or the BJP back in India.

Sangh Parivar in the UK

Things have emerged slightly differently in the UK especially as the Indian diaspora is more diverse because a large part of it migrated from East Africa in the 1970s. The Sangh Parivar in the UK is made up of a number of organizations. Amongst others there are the Hindu Swayamsevak Sangh (UK), which is the RSS's representative in the UK. It has several affiliated organizations active across the UK. The HSS has existed in the UK since the mid-1960s, and was registered as a charity in April 1974. In 2002 it had about 70 branches (*shakhas*) nationally. It is the core organization to which the other organizations discussed below are affiliated to. Its central office is based in Leicester. The VHP UK was formed in the UK in 1971 and registered as a charity in August 1972. It is affiliated to the Vishwa Hindu Parishad International and maintains strong links with the Indian VHP. SEWA International UK (SI) is the HSS's fundraising wing. Since it is not a registered charity it uses the charity number of the HSS UK for its fundraising campaigns. It is, however, a limited company (company number 04482628) incorporated in July 2002 and sharing the same address as the HSS.[19] There is also the National Hindu Students Forum (NHSF), which is the largest body of Hindu students in the UK. The NHSF was created with HSS support and its UK offices shared the same address as the HSS. It is very active around all British university campuses.

These organizations in many ways mirror those in the US and again education is the crux of their activities. The HSS runs around 70 training cells in the UK. Through the NHSF they are heavily represented on British university campuses. But education issues even reach the British mainstream where the publication in 1996 of *Explaining Hindu Dharma: A Guide for Teachers* lays claim to a unitary Hindu identity, represented by the HSS. A further book entitled *Hinduism for Schools* by Seeta Lakhani depicts Sewa International as an independent charity, and the linkages to the Sangh Parivar are kept hidden.

Despite its wide network, Sangh activities in the UK have been more covert. The report *In Bad Faith* investigated how the £2 million raised for the Gujarat earthquake by SEWA International had been utilized. Awaaz, a research organization uncovered that most of it was sent to Sewa Bharati to expand

Hindutva networks in India. It also showed that many who donated had not been aware of either Sewa's Sangh linkages or the purpose for which money was used once it reached India: 'Many in the Indo–British community donated funds in good faith on Sewa International's Gujarat earthquake appeals, would not have done so had they known that the organization was linked to the RSS.'[20]

The organizations investigated have vociferously claimed that they are non-sectarian and non-discriminatory. Despite this, however, Sewa Int., the HSS and the VHP did not launch a humanitarian appeal after the Gujarat violence in 2002. According to Harsh Kabra:

> SIUK, now a private limited company sharing its address with the HSS-UK's Leicester office, is not a registered charity and has been using HSS' registration number to raise money, often without mentioning the parent organisation. These connections were unknown even to SIUK patrons like Adam Patel, a British Muslim and a member of the House of Lords, who eventually resigned on learning about it. (Kabra, 2004)

Similarly in the US, the concept of a Hindu vote has recently emerged. Hindus can make a serious difference in 30 constituencies in Britain if mobilized to vote as a bloc. The Hindu Forum, established to encourage more Hindus to vote has been trying to get its own candidates into the House of Commons.[21] Whilst the organization itself is not based on Hindutva, the questionnaire circulated amongst potential voters did list problems such as 'attacks by other communities on the Hindu way of life and religious traditions . . .'.

POLITICAL LOBBYING IN THE DIASPORA: HOW REPRESENTATIVE AND ACCOUNTABLE ARE THESE ORGANIZATIONS?

Whilst politics divided along the lines of ethnicity is nothing new, the Indian community in the USA and the UK can be observed for the first time to be fragmenting along religious lines. For example, in the UK Hindu organizations are becoming more aware of the concept of a 'Hindu vote' whilst for Sikhs a new political party aiming to push for better Sikh representation in key British institutions has been floated and a case for more state funded Sikh schools is also being promoted within the community (Alibhai-Brown, 2003).

Many different factors shape politics of the diaspora, simply because of its diversity. Amongst other things the state or region they are from as well as their socio-economic or caste background will influence how far homeland politics play a role in their everyday life. Not all are supportive of religious nationalist movements at home or of the satellite organizations which have sprouted abroad. However, the focus of research and the press is invariably on those who are most visible. This in turn throws up the question posed at the start of the paper: Does India have one or many diasporas and if there are many, how are the various groups to be differentiated from each other? This again ties in with state- and religion-based politics in India, a phenomenon which would be difficult to understand in the political realm of the UK and the US where ethnic minority groups are essentialized as homogeneous.

More recently, as a reaction to religious nationalism, other secular groups have also sprung up within the Indian diaspora. In the US a web-based monthly letter is sent out by a group which rejects the Sangh's politics. The 'Saffon Dollar' is a direct response to the report *The Foreign Exchange of Hate: IDRF and the American Funding of Hindutva*, which had uncovered the destination of the funds collected by the affiliated Sangh organizations parading as independent charities.[22] The group aims to remind the Indian diaspora that the Sangh's allegedly cultural organizations have political aims in India and that its message of unifying the Indian community abroad is one which is deeply divisive at home.

But Hindutva's aim to unify the diverse community abroad has made it politically strong. Increasingly the HSS and VHP are seen as representing the Indian community (Mukta, 2000), as their front organizations are recognized by the British and American political scene and are seen as an independent lobby group representing Indians. So it is the voice of these groups that is heard on the lobbying floors of the host governments. It is at this stage also interesting to note that whilst support for the Khalistan movement has been on the wane, support for Hindutva has increased considerably amongst the Indian diaspora during the 1990s.

Diasporic lobbying is of course not always about a religious nationalistic cause. For example, the Indian lobby in Washington during the Kargil war managed to get the US government to pressure Pakistan to back down as an extensive war would have damaged India's economic status in the world. Increasingly the Indian lobby in the US is employing multi-pronged strategies, lobbying international organizations, such as the UN as well as home governments, sometimes associating with other lobbies, such as the Jewish lobby in Washington (Hathaway, 2004).

Most diaspora-based organizations also lobby for and promote their case through internet sites and discussion forums and Hindus and Sikhs are no exception. The internet enables new kinds of borderless ethnic identifications and forms of opinion making. By appealing to a variety of co-ethnic groups under an electronic umbrella, diaspora groups attempt to construct broad ethnic coalitions that cut across national spaces and play a strategic role in shaping and ethnicizing cultural discourses for audiences which are scattered throughout the world. For example, if one examines the content of Sikh internet discussion groups, the role of memory and trauma remain popular and important topics for discussion and for developing an anti-India discourse.[23] An important question for us is to identify who owns and participates in such sites and discussion groups that promote ethnic absolutism. The forms of representation and accountability of political organizations, websites and discussion forums is a hotly debated issue within Hindu and Sikh diaspora communities and in the case of Sikhs was a major reason for lack of popular support for Khalistan. For example, during the heyday of the Khalistan movement an important role was played by the now defunct www.burningpunjab.com. Currently http://www.panthkhalsa.org/index.asp and http://

www.khalistan.com/, two pro-Khalistani websites seek to act as disembedded and placeless watchdogs on behalf of the Sikh nation (*qaum*). These cyber nationalists who base their case on nation and religion, are able to evade state oppression, expose injustices and turn a global gaze on their homeland state's shameful behaviour and put pressure on their home governments to be accountable to their own citizens as well as to the global community. Hindutva websites are similar to their Sikh counterparts and appeal to the Indian diaspora through an allegedly cultural discourse.

But whom do they represent and who are they accountable to? Research on diaspora internet sites reveals that many such sites are usually controlled by newly migrated professionals who are direct beneficiaries of economic globalization. These may be managers, entrepreneurs, engineers and programmers and since they are recent migrants they are more likely to maintain family, economic and professional links with their homelands.[24] However, although they have an economic clout, this is undercut by their invisibility in the host country's cultural and political life, creating a social vacuum and conditions for promoting ethnic absolutism.

There is a need for more research on the role of cyber forums and their effect on diasporic support for homeland politics. The exact implications of their influence on diaspora communities, home and host governments are at this stage not clear. What is certain, however, is that a large part of the debate has shifted to the web-based world, where it is more difficult to follow the linkages created and measure the effects of these linkages.

CONCLUSION AND POLICY IMPLICATIONS FOR HOST AND HOMELAND GOVERNMENTS

This paper has highlighted the nature of transnational political practices of two Indian diaspora groups, Hindus and Sikhs, their orientation towards homeland politics and towards their satellite political organization in the UK and the US. This triangle highlights how many Indians, whether Hindu or Sikh, although living outside of India over long periods, do nevertheless live their homeland politics in their adopted countries. However, the long-distance support which emerged in the case of both the Hindutva and the Khalistan movements does show an important variation in diaspora nationalism. The Hindutva case is a form of reverse long-distance nationalism, as the religious nationalist movement based in India specifically targets and courts the diaspora. The aim is to bind Hindus abroad into their movement in India, and their satellite organizations feel threatened by any host country political involvement the diaspora might have. As a consequence the VHP in particular has lobbied hard to be seen as the sole representative of a unified, homogeneous Indian (Hindu?) diaspora in the US and the UK. In the Sikh case, there is a long history of involvement in homeland politics, going back even to the colonial period and the recent phase in the form of the Khalistan movement is simply a continuum along those lines. The overseas Khalistan movement was heavily based around dissident factions of the Sikh dominated Akali party and on individual ideologues who appeared to have an axe to grind against India for the perceived injustice India may have perpetrated against them personally or the Sikh community generally. Individuals such as Ganga Singh Dhillon and G.S. Aulakh in the US and Jagjit Singh Chauhan in the UK started their political careers in Punjab and after recognizing that they were getting nowhere in meeting their personal aspirations, chose to migrate and start mobilization for the cause of Khalistan, an idea whose seeds had been sown during the Partition of India in 1947 when the Sikh community felt let down as the only religious community of Punjab not to have their own homeland. Since the Sikhs built their case around the concept of victimhood or as a 'diaspora in exile', their case tilts more towards the commonly understood category of long-distance nationalism.

Whilst the movements described in this paper do have many variations such as different aims, different forms of mobilization and consequently different results on the ground, they nevertheless operate in a similar ideological way. As noted by van der Veer, they link issues of history, territory and identity (van der Veer, 2000). They also end up having both a destabilizing and often violent impact on home country politics. It is for this reason we hope the paper contributes towards a better understanding and perhaps an attempt at deconstruction of the amorphous concept of the 'Indian diaspora'. The paper also raises important issues for homeland and host states, especially the requirement for them to understand, acknowledge and incorporate diaspora sensitivities into their foreign policies. Finally we hope the paper provides important lessons for the Indian government towards fostering policies which nurture and strengthen the positive and constructive aspects of diaspora and homeland relations.

NOTES

1. World Bank, *World Development Report 1999/2000: Entering the 21st Century*, Washington: World Bank, 2000, p. 39.
2. For an elaboration of this characterization of the Sikh diaspora see D.S. Tatla, *The Sikh Diaspora: The Search for Statehood*, London: UCL Press, 1999, pp. 5-8.
3. There is now growing literature which examines the development and influence of Internet-based sites and discussion groups on diaspora-homeland relations and on homogenizing religious or ethnic identities. For a discussion of these relating to the Sikh diaspora community see the special issue on Globalization, Identity Politics and the Sikh Diaspora in the *International Journal of Punjab Studies*, vol. 7. no. 2, July-December 2000.
4. For further information about the Ghadar movement, see Darshan S. Tatla, *Ghadar Movement: A Guide to Sources*, Amritsar: Guru Nanak Dev University, 2003; for the important role of home-land politics among Indian Worker's Association see John Dewitt, *Indian Workers Associations in Britain*, London: Oxford University Press, 1969.
5. For further discussion see Montserrat Guibernau, *Nations without States: Political Communities in a Global Age*, Cambridge: Polity Press, 1999, p. 16.
6. The Singhvi Committee (also known as the High Level Committee on the Indian Diaspora) was set-up by the BJP government to

discuss issues relevant to Indians abroad and to explore how NRI funding could be mobilized. The committee submitted its report in 2002 and is available from the website of the new Ministry of Overseas Indian Affairs at http://moia.gov.in/

7. 'The USA, the UK, Canada, Australia, New Zealand, a large part of Europe and Singapore.' Ironically it did not include all the countries within the EU. The ties of these 'old Diaspora' communities have not been political. They are rather based on cultural and family realities and not on economics. Most importantly, they are still not perceived as dollar rich communities that might in any way contribute to India's contemporary development. See also *The Tribune*, 'PM: Issue of Dual Citizenship Resolved,' 9 January 2002. www.tribuneindia.com
8. For more details on the differentiation between PIOs and NRIs and the dual nationality debate see M. Lall, *India's Missed Opportunity* and K. Adeney and M. Lall, 'Institutional Attempts to Build a "National" Identity in India: Internal and External Dimensions,' *India Review* (2005), vol. 4, no. 3.
9. For an early study on the emergence of the Sikh diaspora see N. Gerald Barrier and Verne A. Dusenbery, *The Sikh Diaspora: Migration and the Experience beyond Punjab*, Delhi: Chanakya Publications, 1989.
10. *Komagata Maru* is the name of the famous ship that started its journey from Hong Kong in April 1914 and arrived in Vancouver harbour in May with 376, mostly Punjabi, passengers on board. The Canadian authorities did not allow the passengers to disembark, except for 27 people who had been to Canada before. After a few days of demonstrations by locally settled Sikhs, an armed Canadian navy ship escorted the ship out of the harbour. For further details of the episode, see Hugh Johnston, *The Voyage of the Komagata Maru: The Sikh Challenge to Canada's Colour Bar*, Vancouver: University of British Columbia Press, 1989.
11. For an interesting attempt to illustrate early examples of transnational practices and their continuities amongst Punjabis in California, see Margaret-Walton Roberts (2005), 'Transnational Educational Fundraising in Punjab: Old Practices, New Readings,' *International Journal of Punjab Studies*, vol. 12, no. 1, pp. 129-52.
12. For details of events preceding the trial and the trial itself see Kim Bolan, *Loss of Faith: How Air India Bombers Got Away with Murder*, Toronto: McClelland & Stewart, 2005.

13. For further discussion of these categories see Yossi Shain and Aharon Barth, 'Diasporas and International Relations Theory', *International Organization*, 57, Summer , 2003, pp. 449-79.
14. For details see Cynthia Kepply Mahmood, *Fighting for Faith and Nation: Dialogues with Sikh Militants*, University of Pennsylvania Press, 1997.
15. For details of the first national convention held by the Sikh Federation (UK) see Sanjay Suri, 'Blast from the Past' *Outlook*, 7 January 2002.
16. Further details on activities of these groups are available on the Sikh Federation website at www.sikhfederation.co.uk.
17. The financial status of Indians in America reveals them to be one of the richest groups in the USA: Indian Americans account for only 0.68 per cent of the population and yet have the highest median household income which is $61,322 compared with the general population which has a median income of $41,994. http://www.hinduonnet.com/fline/fl2106/stories/20040326005212700.htm (accessed January 2006).
18. For more on the BJP textbook controversy see M. Lall, 'Globalisation and the Fundamentalisation of Curricula: Lessons from India', in M. Lall and E. Vickers (eds.), *Education as a Political Tool in Asia*, London: Routledge, 2009, pp. 157-78. The Congress government which was elected in 2004 has been trying to remove the textbooks with historical distortions but has not been successful in all states.
19. The other organizations are: the Kalyan Ashram Trust (KAT), is another fundraising organization for the RSS projects among *adivasi* populations to inculcate them into the ideology of Hindutva. It is a registered charity and shares the same address as the HSS; The Overseas Friends of the BJP organizes lobbying and support for the Hindu nationalist BJP political party; The Hindu Sahitya Kendra (HSK) is a Hindutva literature dissemination centre.
20. Suresh Grover, one of Awaaz's directors quoted in Ashish Kumar Sen, UK charities scam linked to Sangh Parivar, *The Tribune*, 25 February 2004. http://www.tribuneindia.com/2004/20040226/world.htm#1
21. The idea behind this political mobilization was based on Operation Black Vote, which helped seven Asian and black people get into Parliament.

22. The full report published by Sabrang Communications Pvt. Ltd. is available online at http://www.stopfundinghate.org/.
23. For an elaborate discussion on internet dialogues among Sikh diaspora groups see N. Gerald Barrier, 'Trauma and Memory within Sikh Diaspora: Internet Dialogue', unpublished paper presented at a workshop conference on 'Remembering and Forgetting: Memory and Trauma in Contemporary Sikh Experience', Hofstra University, 8/9 May 2004.
24. There is now a growing literature which assesses the impact of the Internet in developing diaspora consciousness and mobilization strategies. For an interesting study that looks at the Chinese diaspora see, Loong Wong, 'Belonging and Diaspora: The Chinese and the Internet', *First Monday*, online magazine at http://www.firstmonday.org/issues/issue8_4/wong/#w1. (accesssed on 26/01/2006)

REFERENCES

'Dual Citizenship to Indian Diaspora', *India Today*, 21 January 2002.

Abraham, I., 'Dual Citizenship: Of What and for Whom', *Himal*, http://www.himalmag.com/read.php?id=3642. (accessed 2003).

Adeney, K. and M.C. Lall, 'Institutional Attempts to Build a "National" Identity in India: Internal and External Dimensions', *India Review*, vol. 4, no. 3, 2005.

Alibhai-Brown, Y., 'Sikh Separatism Is a Problem, Not a Solution', *Independent*, 15 September 2003.

Anderson, B.R.O.G., *Imagined Communities: Reflections on the Origin and Spread of Nationalism*, London: Verso, 1983.

Barrier, N.G., 'Trauma and Memory within Sikh Diaspora: Internet Dialogue', in *Remembering and Foregetting: Memory and Trauma in Contemporary Sikh Experience*, Hofstra University, 2004.

Barrier, N.G. and V.A. Dusenbery, *The Sikh Diaspora: Migration and the Experience Beyond Punjab*, Delhi: Chanakya Publications, 1989.

Biswas, B., 'Nationalism by Proxy: A Comparison of Social Movements among Diaspora Sikhs and Hindus', *Nationalism and Ethnic Politics*, no. 10, 2004, pp. 269-95.

Bolan, K., *Loss of Faith: How the Air India Bombers Got Away with Murder*, Toronto: McClelland & Stewart, 2005.

DeWitt, J., *Indian Workers' Associations in Britain*, London: Published for the Institute of Race Relations by Oxford University Press, 1969.

Guibernau I Berdún, M.M., *Nations without States: Political Communities in a Global Age*, Malden, Mass.: Blackwell Publishers, 1999.

Hathaway, R., 'Washington's Strategic Partnership', *Seminar*, no. 538, 2004.

Heimsath, C.H. and S. Mansingh, *A Diplomatic History of Modern India*, Bombay: Allied Publishers, 1971.

Jenkins, R., *Democratic Politics and Economic Reform in India, Contemporary South Asia*, New York: Cambridge University Press, 1999.

Johnston, H.J.M., *The Voyage of the Komagata Maru: The Sikh Challenge to Canada's Colour Bar*, 2nd edn., Vancouver: University of British Columbia Press, 1989.

Kabra, H., 'Alms for the Killer', *Outlook*, 8 March 2004.

Lal, V., 'Domain Name Hindutva', *Indian Express*, 8 August 2003.

Lall, M.C., *India's Missed Opportunity*, London: Ashgate, 2001.

———, 'Centre-Periphery Tensions in a Globalizing World: The Case of India and the Punjab', *International Journal of Punjab Studies*, vol. 8, no. 2, 2001b, pp. 225-38.

Lall, M.C. and E. Vickers, *Education as a Political Tool in Asia, Routledge Contemporary Asia Series*, New York: Routledge, 2008.

Mahmood, C.K., *Fighting for Faith and Nation: Dialogues with Sikh Militants, Series in Contemporary Ethnography*, Philadelphia: University of Pennsylvania Press, 1997.

Mukta, P., 'The Public Face of Hindu Nationalism', *Ethnic and Racial Studies*, vol. 23, no. 3, 2000.

Prashad, V., 'Bruce Lee and the Anti-Imperialism of Kung Fu: A Polycultural Adventure', *Positions: East Asia Cultures Critique*, vol. 11, no. 1, 2003, pp. 51-90.

Rajagopal, A., *Politics after Television: Religious Nationalism and the Reshaping of the Indian Public*, Cambridge, UK; New York: Cambridge University Press, 2001.

Roberts, M.W., 'Transnational Educational Fundraising in Punjab: Old Practices, New Readings', *International Journal of Punjab Studies*, vol. 12, no. 1, 2005, pp. 129-52.

Sen, A.K., 'UK Charities Scam Linked to Sangh Parivar', *The Tribune*, 25 February 2004.

Shain, Y. and A. Barth, 'Diasporas and International Relations Theory', *International Organization*, no. 57, 2003, pp. 449-79.

Suri, S., 'Blast from the Past', *Outlook*, 7 January 2002.

Suri, S., 'Vote's the Good News', *Outlook*, 3 November 2003.

Tatla, D. S., *The Sikh Diaspora: Search for Statehood, Global Diasporas*, Seattle, Wa: University of Washington Press, 1999.

———, *A Guide to Sources: Ghadar Movement*, Amritsar: Guru Nanak Dev University, 2003.

Thandi, S.S., 'Punjabi Diaspora in the UK and the Punjab Crisis', in *The Transmission of Sikh Heritage in the Diaspora*, ed. Pashaura Singh and N.G. Barrier, New Delhi: Manohar, 1996.

———, 'Counterinsurgency and Political Violence in Punjab', in *Punjabi Identity: Continuity and Change*, ed. G. Singh and I. Talbot, New Delhi: Manohar, 1996.

Tharoor, S., *India, from Midnight to the Millennium*, New Delhi/New York: Viking, 1997.

Veer, P. v.d., 'Religious Nationalism in India and Global Fundamentalism', in *Globalizations and Social Movements: Culture, Power, and the Transnational Public Sphere*, ed. J.A. Guidry, M.D. Kennedy and M.N. Zald, Ann Arbor: University of Michigan Press, 2000, pp. 315-36.

Wong, L., 'Belonging and Diaspora: The Chinese and the Internet', *First Monday*, 2006.

World Development Report 1999/2000: Entering the 21st Century, Washington: World Bank, 2000.

Contributors

JULIE BAUJARD holds a PhD in Social Anthropology from the University of Provence, Aix-Marseille I, France. She is currently member of the Research Institute on Southeast Asia (IRSEA, Marseille) and Assistant Professor at the University of Provence. She has worked on refugees living in Delhi since 2001. She started researching as an intern at the UNHCR in New Delhi and carried on with further research trips among the refugee communities in the capital city. In 2004 and 2005, she was affiliated to the Centre de Sciences Humaines, New Delhi. Her post-doctoral research topic deals with international migrations in India with a focus on refugees in urban settings.

MARK-ANTHONY FALZON, holds a doctorate in social anthropology from the University of Cambridge. He is the Head of Department of Sociology at the University of Malta and a Life Member of Clare Hall, Cambridge. He is the author of *Cosmopolitan Connections* (2005) and *Multisited Ethnography* (2009). He has done fieldwork in London, Mumbai, Malta, and the Pelagic Islands (off Sicily). His research interests and publications include cosmopolitanism, diaspora, gated communities, Mediterranean hunting practices, and soundscapes.

LAURENT GAYER is a CNRS research fellow, presently posted at the Centre de Sciences Humaines (CSH), New Delhi. He received his PhD in 2004 from Sciences Po Paris. His doctoral thesis consisted of a comparative study of the dynamics of internationalisation of Sikh and Mohajir nationalisms. He recently published (with Christophe Jaffrelot) the edited volume *Armed*

Militias of South Asia: Fundamentalists, Maoists and Separatists (2009).

RAVINDRA K. JAIN is the Elected Chairman of the Indian National Confederation and Academy of Anthropologists (2008-11). He was recently Visiting Professor, Universiti Kebangsaan Malaysia Bangi, Selangor, Malaysia and the University of KwaZulu Natal, Durban, South Africa. He taught social anthropology and sociology at Oxford (1966-74) and Jawaharlal Nehru University, New Delhi (1975-2002). He was Emeritus Fellow, University Grants Commission (2005-7) and National Fellow, Indian Council of Social Science Research (2007-09). An international authority on Indian Diaspora, Ravindra K. Jain is on the editorial board of two journals, namely *Global Networks* and *South Asian Diaspora*. He is the author of *South Indians on the Plantation Frontier in Malaya* (1970), *Indian Communities Abroad: Themes and Literature* (1993), *The Universe as Audience: Metaphor and Community among the Jains of North India* (1999), and the editor of *Text and Context: The Social Anthropology of Tradition* (1977). His more recent publications include *Between History and Legend: Status and Power in Bundelkhand* (2002) and *Indian Transmigrants: Malaysian and Comparative Essays* (2009). His book has been selected for the Professor G.S. Ghurye Book Award as the best publication by an Indian author in Sociology and Anthropology for the year 2009. His latest publication is *Nation, Diaspora, Trans-Nation: Reflections from India Routledge* (2010). In February 2011 Professor Jain has been awarded the prestigious Tagore National Fellowship for Cultural Research by the Ministry of Culture, Govt. of India.

PRALAY KANUNGO is Professor at the Centre for Political Studies, Jawaharlal Nehru University, New Delhi. He has taught at the University of Delhi and was a Fellow at Nehru Memorial Museum & Library. He teaches a course on the Indian diaspora at the Master's level and his publications include *RSS's Tryst with Politics: From Hedgewar to Sudarshan* (2002).

BINOD KHADRIA is a Professor of Economics and Education at Jawaharlal Nehru University (JNU), New Delhi and Director of the International Migration and Diaspora Studies (IMDS) Project, co-sponsored by Government of India. His publications include *The Migration of Knowledge Workers: Second-generation Effects of India's Brain Drain* (1999) and several research papers published by the ILO, OECD, GCIM, IRD (France), IDE-JETRO (Japan), *Harvard International Review, 2010 World Social Science Report,* etc. He is Deputy Chair (South Asia) and Regional Coordinator (India) at Asia Pacific Migration Research Network (APMRN), and sits on the Boards of International Network of Migration and Development (INMD), Zacatecas (Mexico); International Geographical Union (IGU); the Metropolis Project (Canada), IOM's *World Migration Report 2010; Encyclopedia of Global Human Migration; Asian and Pacific Migration Journal; Journal of South Asian Diaspora; Journal of International Migration and Integration; Oxford Review of Migration,* and *International Journal of Organizational Studies.*

MARIE CARINE LALL, PhD, FRSA, is a South Asia specialist with 17 years of field experience in India. She is Senior Lecturer at the Institute of Education (IoE), University of London. She is also an associate Fellow of the Asia Programme at Chatham House, UK. Her area of research is the politics of South Asia, specifically India, Pakistan as well as Myanmar. She has written widely on issues of political economy, energy security, foreign policy formulation including pipeline diplomacy and diaspora politics. She also works on the education policy in India and Pakistan and the formation of National Identity in South Asia. She is the author of *India's Missed Opportunity* (2001) and a large number of articles and chapters on the region. She regularly appears on BBC World and is widely cited in the international press.

ERIC LECLERC is Associate Professor of Geography at the University of Rouen (France). He started his research in south India on developmental issues, both in rural areas as well as in small towns. After completing his PhD in 1993, he was engaged with the Research Laboratory for Arid and Semi-arid Region (LEDRA) in two collective projects of atlases in Mauritania and Mali. This decade in Africa was an opportunity to question the validity of mapping and GIS tools for development activities. Coming back to India from 2004, he was for two years the head of the Regional Dynamics in South Asia and International Relations team at the Centre de Sciences Humaines (New Delhi). His research analyses the impact of the Indian diaspora on the globalization of the Indian society through the example of the circulation of IT professionals.

CHRISTINE MOLINER (CEIAS-EHESS) is doing her doctoral research on the issue of multiple identities in the Sikh Diaspora, in Great Britain and continental Europe. She is also working on East and West Punjab's budding relations and the Punjabis' involvement in the Indo–Pak reconciliation process and the impact on the diaspora.

P.V. RAO is the Director of the Centre for Indian Ocean Studies, Osmania University, Hyderabad and the editor of *Indian Ocean Survey* (a biannual journal published by Indian Ocean Research Group). He has edited *India and Indian Ocean: In the Twilight of the Millennium* (2002), and *India and Australia: New Horizons* (2003).

SHINDER S. THANDI is currently Head of the Department of Economics, Finance and Accounting at Coventry University and has teaching interests in the areas of development economics, international business in the Asia-Pacific region and the global political economy. He has published widely on Indian and Punjabi migration and settlement in the UK and on different dimensions of Indian and Punjabi diaspora–homeland relations. He is founder editor of the *Journal of Punjab Studies* and has co-edited two books: *Punjabi Identity in a Global Context* (with Pritam Singh, 1999) and *People on the Move: Punjabi Colonial and Post Colonial Migration* (with Ian Talbot, 2004). He is also co-author (with Michael Fisher and Shompa Lahiri) of *A South Asian History of Britain: Four Centuries of Peoples from the Indian Sub-Continent* (2007). He is currently working on a book 'The Sikh Diaspora: From Struggles to Celebration' to be published in 2012.

INGRID THERWATH is now heading the International Relations section at the Centre de Sciences Humaines in New Delhi. She completed her PhD on 'The Indian State and the Diaspora Factor' under the supervision of Prof. Christophe Jaffrelot at the Institut d'Etudes Politiques – Centre d'Etudes et de Recherches Internationales, Paris. Her research focuses on public policies, diasporas, nationalism and the Sangh Parivar.

Index